FRIENDLY REMAINDERS

Friendly Remainders

Essays in Musical Criticism after Adorno

MURRAY DINEEN

McGill-Queen's University Press
Montreal & Kingston • London • Ithaca

© McGill-Queen's University Press 2011

ISBN 978-0-7735-3884-9 (cloth)
ISBN 978-0-7735-3919-8 (paper)

Legal deposit third quarter 2011
Bibliothèque nationale du Québec

Printed in Canada on acid-free paper that is 100% ancient forest free
(100% post-consumer recycled), processed chlorine free

This book has been published with the help of a grant from the
Canadian Federation for the Humanities and Social Sciences, through
the Aid to Scholarly Publications Program, using funds provided by
the Social Sciences and Humanities Research Council of Canada.

McGill-Queen's University Press acknowledges the support of the
Canada Council for the Arts for our publishing program. We also
acknowledge the financial support of the Government of Canada
through the Canada Book Fund for our publishing activities.

Library and Archives Canada Cataloguing in Publication

Dineen, Murray, 1953–

    Friendly remainders : essays in musical criticism after Adorno /
Murray Dineen.

ISBN 978-0-7735-3884-9. – ISBN 978-0-7735-3919-8

    1. Adorno, Theodor W., 1903–1969 – Criticism and interpretation.
2. Adorno, Theodor W., 1903–1969. Negative Dialektik – Criticism
and interpretation. 3. Musical criticism. 4. Music – Philosophy and
aesthetics. I. Title.

ML3880.D583 2011   781.1'7   C2011-902259-1

Typeset by Jay Tee Graphics Ltd. in 10.5/13 Sabon

Contents

Preface

In the title *Friendly Remainders: Essays in Musical Criticism after Adorno*, I use *after* to mean that this volume of essays comes after Adorno (who died almost half a century ago) in a strictly temporal sense, one that implies both foreclosure (the full scope of his thought in its time is beyond us now) and supplementation (in addition to his *Nachlass* of published writings, his work's subsequent reception must be considered). But *after* has a curious double sense about it, both *to pursue* – I'm *after* Adorno's meaning – and *to follow* – my work is modelled *after* Adorno's, in the sense of adapting Adorno to my needs. Both senses apply to these essays: on the one hand, I am exploring Adorno's thoughts about music in pursuit of useful perspectives; on the other, I am applying the fruit of these explorations to new pursuits as if they were models.[1] This double sense of *after* necessarily has its limitations for a student of Adorno's work: the explorations undertaken here are not meant to be exhaustive, not meant to reveal comprehensively Adorno's thought on any given subject, nor are they necessarily the full exposition of my thoughts on any given subject. The book is avowedly selective; focusing on particular thoughts – Adorno's and mine – expressed in particular writings, it tries all the while to avoid doing extensive damage when excising them from the fabric into which they have been woven.[2]

I use *essay* in the title to mean a literary foray in a geographical sense, a path followed through the territory of Adorno's thought and undertaken with the company of other Adorno *amateurs*, be they scholars or laypersons.[3] However, a geographical essay of this sort is necessarily limited in scope and non-linear: part of Adorno's territory is impassable and the part that allows essay is strewn with obstacles to be avoided rather than tackled head on. Each chapter is thus meant as a separate essay on that territory, but the effect of the whole is intended as cumulative (chapters 5, 6, and 7 in particular), a mapping out of musical criticism. Postcards, miniature reports from the field, are set off at the end of chapters, as mini-essays along the lines of Adorno's *Minima Moralia* (but without the skill at the micro-logical so evident in Adorno's tales).

Last, I use *music criticism* to mean the observation of music from an objective critical perspective, the term *objective* qualified by my reservations (after Adorno) about musical observation. Given its lack of substance, its ephemeral physical qualities, music poses severe problems for critical objectivity, problems recognized in their modern form since the days of Kant, these allied with the notion of purposefulness without purpose (or *Zweckmässigkeit ohne Zweck*). In other musicological endeavours, such problems are salved by the choice of a critical framework. In much critical musicology after Adorno's death, the framework of choice was positivistic, after Arthur Mendel's "Evidence and Explanation" of 1961, where critical purposefulness has a real purpose – the dating of a manuscript, for example.[4] So too, a critical framework comes to Adorno's aid in music criticism, but his framework is in certain regards the very converse of positivism (and draws on the notion of purposeless purpose, albeit in its own manner).[5] The essays in this book borrow elements of their critical framework from what Adorno called *negative dialectics*, a vehicle of criticism that he brought to music (among other subjects), a vehicle with which to say critical things about music that seem objective, even if their purpose is not always clear.

My adaptation of negative dialectics is a blend of at least five elements proper to Adorno's thought and life. I have drawn on Adorno's writings on the subject, principally the book *Negative Dialectics* but also the recently published lectures, as well as Adorno's other published work where relevant. Added to this are elements of Marxist thought drawn selectively from the Marxist and pre-Marxist writings of Georg Lukács and Walter Benjamin, and elements of the philosophies of Kant and Hegel (and these with circumspection, given the contentious nature of their relevance to Adorno).[6] I have tried to take into account something of Adorno's life – the Central-European traditions of criticism to which he fell heir, the Holocaust and the war that surrounded it, and his exile in America and subsequent return to Europe. Last, my principal expertise is as a music scholar, in particular a scholar of Schoenberg's music and thought. Thus, I have taken into account Adorno's close engagement with music of all kinds but especially modern Viennese music, with Schoenberg's work as a locus. Drawing on the aforementioned elements (and others not touched on here), I observe that Adorno created his own form of critical objectivity. This book tries to emulate something of his critical faculty. It does not aim at dethroning the many uncritical subjectivities that govern music scholarship in our day (although it will address the assertion of an absolute beauty so perennial in scholarly criticism of music). But it does seek to illuminate a few.

Negative dialectics as I have derived it here from Adorno produces what I call concrete observations about music. While, as a framework, negative dialectics does not renounce musical subjectivity – the subjectivities of amateur and scholar alike – it transforms subjectivity into what I shall call an unexpected *remainder*, a residue of thought, something concrete left over after an incomplete synthesis of concepts. In my title, I call this remainder *friendly*, in the sense of helpful: after Adorno, this remainder helps music criticism gain both a procedure and an object.

The concept of negative remainder will be explained in the first chapter with recourse to a particularly fortunate, albeit free, translation of a passage from Adorno's *Negative Dialectics* by E.B. Ashton. The musical object of these essays is the negative development produced at Adorno's hands by bringing together two seemingly congruent musical ideas so as to show a discrepancy between them.[7] I refer to this remainder as an object since it compares with the customary objects of musicology, be they the musical score, a sonorous object such as a performance, or a cultural object through which music takes place. It is assumed here that the negative remainder is the objective equal of the objects produced regularly by a positivist musicology, albeit in different manner and degree, given the purposes of musical criticism after Adorno.

The second chapter, "Just for Nice," assesses this critical tool derived from Adorno's negative framework in light of limitations to musicological objectivity, the musicology of popular music studies in particular. In the third chapter, "The Work of Music," the term *musical work*, which in its common sense means an actual work of music, is given another interpretation as musical labour.[8] The fourth chapter, "Technique," observes certain regularities in Schoenberg's compositional technique and in Adorno's prose, and reviews their consequences for Adorno's Schoenberg appreciation. Chapters 5, 6, and 7, on Wagner, Zappa, and Marilyn Manson respectively, take up the threads of what Adorno called *social character* and *physiognomy*, starting with the social psychosis Adorno discerned in Wagner and his music and ending with my examination of Manson's work as it expresses a broad social malaise for which he remains largely blameless. Chapters 5 to 7 are loosely progressive in thought and should be read in sequence. The last chapter, "*Moses und Adorno*," applies the notion of negative remainder to Adorno himself by sketching traces of autobiography found in Adorno's essay on Schoenberg's opera *Moses und Aron*.

As a set of essays, then, this book is neither a textbook nor a survey of Adorno's work on music. Many such books exist, of course, and I have relied on them extensively. In particular, Max Paddison's *Adorno's Aesthetics of Music* is indispensable, although to call it a textbook or a survey is to give it much less than its due. As the product of a massive research enterprise, Paddison's book set the English-language study of Adorno's musical criticism on its feet. I have addressed only a small fraction of the issues raised therein and my debt to the work is both general and profound (and reflected only in very small part in the notes accompanying this book). I have relied constantly on Richard Leppert's recent edition of Adorno's work not merely for its translations but also for the insights conveyed by the author in his introductions to various essays. By combining the bibliographies of recently published works such as those of Paddison and Leppert, a research tool quite formidable in scope can be produced. Accordingly, deferring to these two scholars and other readily available Adorno bibliographies, my bibliography is selective, concerned principally with the works cited here. The work of Rose Rosengard Subotnik, especially as collected in *Developing Variations*, is truly comprehensive; many thoughts expressed in this book are simply threads taken up from her prose. Although dated in terms of recent critical literature on Adorno, Susan Buck-Morss's *The Origin of Negative Dialectics: Theodor W. Adorno, Walter Benjamin, and the Frankfurt Institute* and Gillian Rose's *The Melancholy Science: An Introduction to the Thought of Theodor W. Adorno*, which are both now over thirty years old, have served as touchstones. The translations and essays of Robert Hullot-Kentor, which seem to increase daily, have proven a boon and a corrective to sometimes intemperate thoughts about Adorno. Numerous authors familiar to students of Adorno – Jay, Bernstein, Goehr, Müller-Doohm, Tiedemann among others – will simply be acknowledged with a general debt, in hopes that their influence on this book is sufficiently documented in the scholarly apparatus.

While I had heard of Adorno at an early age in my scholarly upbringing, I am indebted to Clovis Lark, a student colleague at Columbia University, whose irrepressible enthusiasm for Adorno kindled my first true interest in the man. An Adorno reading group, held at Carleton University in the early 1990s, with (among others) Jocelyn Guilbault, Will Straw, Paul Theberge, Geraldine Finn, Rob Shields, Steven Purvis, Don Wallace, Jenny Giles, and Jody Berland, helped solidify the roots of this book, as did conversations with the composer Martin Arnold in Toronto and Ottawa. With the aid of a subvention from the Social Sciences and Humanities Research Council of Canada, versions of chapter 1 were read at the University of Alberta, the University of British Columbia, the University of Victoria, and at a meeting of the St. Lawrence Chapter of the American Musicological Society in the spring of 2003. The chapter has benefited immeasurably from the comments received in those forums. A Standard Research Grant from SSHRC enabled much of the research leading to this book, and a grant from the Aid to Scholarly Publications Programme of the Canadian Federation for the Humanities and Social Sciences has supported its publication. Friends too numerous to mention have given advice and encouragement on the book as a whole. Kate Merriman has caught more than her fair share of editorial details left by an author too preoccupied with Adorno to have noted them; my heartfelt thanks to her. As is a professor's wont, I subjected several seminar classes at the University of Ottawa to my developing thoughts. I hope this book is in some small way recompense for their endless patience with my stumbling attempts at articulation. Students are one's worst and best critics. Last, the book is dedicated to my family – my wife and daughters, and my parents before them – who have seen me through the worst and the best of this enterprise.

FRIENDLY REMAINDERS

No, it is not easy, really, to speak of it, that I will say – in truth one can't speak of it at all, since the actual is not possible to express by words. Oh, one can adopt and adapt many terms, but in sum total they are nothing but symbols, standing for names which don't denote, are incapable of claiming the right to indicate what can nevermore be indicated and denounced in words. That is the secret pleasure and the security of hell, incapable of denunciation, protected from speech, that it just is, but can't be announced in the newspapers, can't become public, brought to a critical awareness through any word.

Thomas Mann, *Doktor Faustus*

I

Ashton's *Remainder*

There is a gap between words and the thing they conjure. Hence, the residue of arbitrariness and relativity in the choice of words as well as in the presentation as a whole.

Adorno, *Negative Dialectics*

In the 1980s gay men in Vancouver took up an advertising phrase coined by the British Columbia Ferry Corporation: "B.C. Ferries: Cruising the Straits." In one sense, it means British Columbia ferry boats plying the Georgia Strait between Vancouver and Vancouver Island. Obviously a "straight" person – unenlightened heterosexual – would have no interpretive problem with the phrase: a strait is a body of water between two land masses, while ferries are boats that transport passengers over stretches of water. Closed loop.

Gay Vancouverites, however, saw the slogan quite differently, in accordance with what we shall call a synthetic *negating* appreciation. By their duality, *double entendres* negate the simple one-dimensional straight sense of the phrase: straits are stretches of water, but straights are also heterosexuals; ferries are boats, but fairies are also homosexuals. And to cruise means not only to go sailing but also to solicit sex. On the gay account, there are two kinds of speakers involved in this phrase: unenlightened straights who unwittingly produced this phrase, and enlightened gays who with but a moment's reflection see a double meaning quite opposed to the single dimension of the advertising slogan. I call the straight understanding a *synthetic positive* in the sense of a single fact – B.C. ferries cruise the Georgia Strait. The singularity of that understanding is *negated* by a synthesis, the twofold nature of the gay reinterpretation – ferries and fairies. The negation is necessarily synthetic, fused of two particles. Whereas the straight understanding can get along without the gay, the reverse is not true: the gay understanding requires the straight, to which it is a response, indeed a subversive response. (So it was understood with melancholy[1] hilarity by my Vancouver friends.) I call the difference between the two understandings a *negative difference* which is produced synthetically by *negative dialectics*.[2]

Theodor Adorno might have enjoyed the opportunities afforded by this case.[3] He might have seen that the gay interpretation is both the opposite of and a supplement to the heterosexual. In the tense sexual politics of Vancouver during that era, straight and gay were seen as two poles of a binary opposition. And given that a straight government culture – the corporation called B.C. Ferries – produced the slogan without conceiving of its consequences, the gay interpretation follows the straight assertion like an afterthought – ferries *and* fairies.[4] Between the two – single and double – lies a synthetic negative discrepancy, Kafkaesque in nature, a remainder left over after one subtracts the hetero interpretation from the gay: advertising slogans are not as they seem, but instead often devolve to encompass something contrary.

This little *minimum moral* is a synthetic negation with the useful purpose of a diagnostic. To attain the status of a dialectic – after Hegel and Adorno – synthetic negation needs to assume fully this role of diagnostic, the discernment of some deeper unity to which the contradiction is an index.[5] After Hegel and Adorno, extreme opposites – in discrepant form here – coincide like the fissures in plate techtonics.

Returning to our example, in a modern context of multiple sexual orientations, to ignore the *double entendre* implicit in the word *ferries* in association with *cruising* and *straits* is to take an extreme position; naïveté is political. As an extreme it must, in Hegelian fashion, give rise to a contrary extreme – the wisdom of *fairies*, *cruising*, and *straights*. Both Hegel and Adorno sought to discover a deeper unity in this contradiction, an affirmative unity in Hegel's case,[6] the negation of unity in Adorno's.[7] As Adorno put it in the introduction to *Negative Dialectics*, in which he qualifies dialectics ("dialectics is the consistent sense of non-identity"[8]) with constant reference to Hegel and to Kant, "No object is wholly known; knowledge is not supposed to prepare the phantasm of the whole. Thus the goal of a philosophical interpretation of works of art cannot be their identification with the concept, their absorption in the concept; yet it is through such interpretation that the truth of the work unfolds ... The un-naive thinker knows how far he remains from the object of this thinking, and yet he must always talk as if he had it entirely."[9] Here, Adorno states the necessity of a complete synthesis in knowing something and at the same time opposes it as impossible, this in the riddle-like fashion so characteristic of his prose style.

The discrepancy between *ferry* and *fairy* (the synthesis that would not allow itself to be spoken in good company in the 1980s) is negative not only in the sense of negating opposites – straight versus gay – but also in a pejorative sense: an unenlightened heterosexual, a one-dimensional-thinking straight, would have been incapable of seeing it, and a gay person would have held that fact as a critique of straight consciousness. This critique, ultimately a critique of straight society, transforms negation into a negative dialectic. To understand the double entendre critically is to understand gender relations in Canada (and in like measure, the Western world): the supposed liberal nature of Canadian thought is inexplicably contradicted in the unwitting actions of an agency whose employees (as advertising specialists) were trained surely to head off just such a *double entendre*. Since the advertisement was aimed at a single, narrow understanding of transportation across Georgia Strait as a commodity, this dialectic must open up in part on the world of capitalism. For the Vancouver affluent, *cruising* meant luxury exclusive to the well-healed traveller. Such a world, that of the merely rich, denied the multiplicity of subjectivities implicit in *ferry* and *fairy*. To cruise the straights in a yacht, you need only be rich; on this capitalist account, sexual orientation – gay orientation in particular – is irrelevant and thus remaindered.

Negative dialectics offer the possibility of critical thought not only about sexual orientation but also about music. As we shall see, negation puts the musically subjective – our personal appreciation of music, for example – into perspective through discrepancy. It then gives that discrepancy a material form as a remainder or difference, an object by which we might diagnose a larger societal discrepancy.

Since the dialectics of a discrepancy carried out at a societal level are a tall order, *synthesis* will often be used instead of *dialectic*. *Negative synthesis*, then, means the dialectic working out of contraries restricted in scope to a local level. This is not to limit the nature of discrepancies such as *ferry* and *fairy* but merely to restrict them to concrete particulars in the case of music.

With negative synthesis as a tool, we can account for enigmas such as Adorno's constant critical attraction to popular music, even while he was immersed in what is sometimes taken as its polar opposite, the music of Schoenberg and his students, and of Stravinsky. (As Susan Buck-Morss put it, "Far from belittling mass culture, Adorno took it extremely seriously, applying to its phenomena the same sophisticated analytical method, the same intellectual spleen, that he used in interpreting Husserl, Kierkegaard, and Stravinsky."[10]) After Adorno, I will be interested critically in music in which two discrepant appreciations apply.[11] In the material fact of popular music, for example, discrepancy is writ large (in much the same way as it is written across the face of classical music). Popular music, for Adorno, pits the listener for whom hits are ever fresh against the recording executive for whom a series of hits is characterized by the minimum differences necessary to avoid charges of copyright infringement. (A comparable discrepancy is true in classical music: the culture consumer holds the value of the ticket and program to a Toscanini concert to be much greater than that of the actual concert, and in this sense the putatively elevated status of the classical music concert is reduced to the equivalent of any other mass commodity – "Beethoven" and "bikinis," as Adorno put it.)[12]

After Adorno, I will be interested as well in music in which these interpretations can be associated with some material aspect, for example, the standardization of form and chord progression or the kind of labour required of an audience at a concert of Schoenberg's music. Adorno's principal critique of popular music is based on the notion of "standardization," that the music is subject to a set of standard practices that vary minimally from song to song (a notion which, deservedly, has come under considerable criticism when applied across the board to popular music). The listener is attracted aesthetically to the superficial alterations of the standardized form and harmony, whose subtle details suggest novelty in the face of genre stereotypes. In this regard, the popular music listener becomes sophisticated, picking out subtle alterations that a non-expert listener might miss. Recording executives are equally skilful – capable, from the perspective of craft, of effecting minimal but highly calculated alterations to the stereotypical formula. Both listener and executive are, in this regard, experts in their own right, albeit from different, discrepant perspectives – consumer and capitalist, respectively. Standardization offers us, then, a concrete point of reference by which to articulate the discrepancy between those who, oblivious to their labour, consume music, and those who commodify music and in doing so exploit labour. A comparable discrepancy will be shown to be at work in Schoenberg's oeuvre.

Furthermore, like Adorno, I will be interested in music in which these critical interpretations and distinctions can be associated with some material aspect of life. Take for example the life of a common worker who spends the minimal residue left over (after expenses are deducted from earnings) on a recording of a latest hit, versus the life of a record executive whose income is derived from many such residues; or the life of a famous conductor who flits from one world capital to another, flying in and out in a weekend, versus the life of the average musician in one of the orchestras the conductor visits. In both instances, one person derives considerable profit from the forgotten or ignored labour of others. Labour in this and other instances is a material fact around which negative synthetic interpretations can be made (and negative dialectics is then writ large).

Given music with such discrepant attributes, Adorno rose to the critical occasion. His critiques are bitter in tone, frequently indicting not only the music but all participants in its production, dissemination, and consumption. In this sense, Adorno paid a compliment to popular music in particular, since it would seem to bear the brunt of his attentions. For Adorno, popular music was a most interesting genre in critical terms, a veritable font of material for critical reflections, and this is about as high a compliment as one might reasonably expect from Adorno. Adorno's critics have missed the fact that, although he sometimes says nasty things about popular music,[13] criticism is the pillar upon which he places, indeed exalts, the repertoire.[14] While it seems like faint praise, if popular music lacked this critical attraction, he would not have devoted such a large amount of his time to it.[15] After Adorno, I take a similar approach, elevating popular music (even above classical music) for the critical insight it might foster (and thus not for its inherent beauty or pleasures).

Negative synthetics help us understand a quotation from Adorno's essay "Perennial Fashion – Jazz," taken from the collection entitled *Prisms*: "While the leaders in the European dictatorships of both shades raged [*eiferten*] against the decadence of jazz, the youth of the other countries has long since allowed itself to be electrified, as with marches, by the syncopated dance-steps, with bands which do not by accident stem from military music."[16] In the first

phrase Adorno establishes one term in a synthesis (ultimately a dialectic): as was their wont, the European dictatorships raged unthinkingly against some target, in this instance jazz. In the second phrase
Adorno sets up another term in the synthesis, the complement to
dictatorship: as was their wont, the youth of other countries raged,
allowed themselves to be electrified – swept away unthinkingly – by
syncopation. Jazz, it would seem, is all the rage.

Adorno appears to set up a positive unity here: jazz elicits rage
from dictator and youth alike. But malevolent dictators and innocent youth surely do not go together (unless one looks upon dictators more benevolently or re-examines radically one's conception of
youth). The initial synthetic whole – dictators equal raging youths
– carries within it the seeds of discrepancy, and therein negation. In
other words, the product of negative synthesis lies here in the difference between, on the one hand, our naive opposition of dictator and
youth and, on the other, their mutual agreement in the cause of rage.

In truth, Adorno's object was not jazz music in and of itself. Nor
was it youth, nor even European dictators. Adorno's object was the
kind of present-day reality that encourages a rage for music, as it
might be equated in kind with dictatorial rage, the two producing
dialectically a vision of oppressive arousal in our society in general.
(That capitalism is deeply implicated in this dialect is a subject I
shall turn to in later chapters.) Objects of this discrepant nature will
become the subject of criticism.

To reiterate, Adorno was attracted to jazz. Jazz was not something
to be stamped out or exalted in its own right; he neither advocated
repression nor showed enthusiasm to the point of electrification.
Instead, jazz was a symptom, a mirror or reflection, a glass – highly
prized – through which to see dark things darkly. Like the jitterbugging youths, Adorno was attracted to jazz, but he did not surrender
himself to the music; indeed, he rarely surrendered to any music
in his critical prose. Instead, listening to jazz was, for Adorno, an
activating mechanism for a kind of dispassionate criticism, a kind
of heightened critical experience. Jazz seems to have set all Adorno's
finely honed critical tools into action.

Wounded by Adorno's critique, jazz and popular music scholars
have overlooked the fact that he makes similar observations about
much classical music[17] and some of Schoenberg's music (and about
Schoenberg himself, as I shall demonstrate in a later chapter).[18]
In the essay on Schoenberg in *Prisms*, the same synthetic frame-

work is at work. Not far into the essay, Adorno sets forth a series of negative-synthetic propositions wherein he says the following
about Mahler's music: "If one does not understand something, it is
customary to behave with the sublime understanding of Mahler's
jackass [*Esel*], and project one's own inadequacy [*Unzulänglichkeit*]
on to the object, declaring it to be incomprehensible [*unverständ-
lich*]."[19] In the jackass, sublime understanding is mated brilliantly
with inadequacy and incomprehension to produce the kind of negative remainder so characteristic of Adorno's jazz reception.

Mahler's jackass believed two aspects of an apparent unity: first,
he believed that he understood Mahler's music, and second, he
believed that Mahler's music was incomprehensible. In other words,
he understood that Mahler's music was incomprehensible. And this
is true: in understanding Mahler's music as incomprehensible, the
jackass unwittingly (and thus sublimely) recognizes a negative truth,
that when it comes to understanding Mahler's music, he is perfectly
capable of finding it incomprehensible. He is perfectly capable and
indeed eminently suited to understanding it as incomprehensible.
The result is the kind of backhand revelation so characteristic of
Adorno's critiques. Mahler's music points to a sublime that, in its
full comprehension, lies well beyond adequacy on the part of any
listener. This is a marvellous fact that, ironically, even a jackass can
attest to.

Further along in the essay, Adorno characterizes Schoenberg's
listener in synthetic terms reminiscent of the jackass: "The more
[Schoenberg's music] gives its listeners, the less it offers them. It
requires the listener spontaneously to compose its inner movement
and demands of him not mere contemplation but praxis."[20] The
synthetic pattern should by now be familiar: first Adorno says one
thing, then states (or in this case leaves unstated) a counter-propos-
ition, the two united in a positive synthesis. The positive synthesis,
so customary to present-day music appreciation, says that "the more
[a composer's music] gives his listeners," the more it offers them, the
more satisfied they should be. In other words, the longer and more
complex the work, the more satisfaction it should afford the listener.
The converse holds true as well (as the "light-classical" or pops concert paradigm): the less a musical work offers the listener, the less
satisfied they should be.[21]

The two parallel positive clauses – more it gives, more it offers
– should merge into a unity. But with Schoenberg's music they fall

apart instead into an image of incongruity.[22] Schoenberg's music gives much more to its listeners, but in a paradoxical fashion "offers them less." By its unfamiliarity and unpredictability it requires them to work, to supply meaning.[23] Schoenberg's music negates any easy synthesis of a work and its intrinsic value. The result is a negative synthesis, a discrepancy between the customary reception of a musical work and the kind of reception Schoenberg's music demands.[24]

Note that Adorno has not offered us an aesthetic judgment on Schoenberg's music in and of itself. He has not called it sternly dissonant, or heroically resistant to easy appreciation. He has not commented on its particular qualities or the pleasure one might derive from it, for those are properly individual assertions that have only minimal relevance to his critical perspective. He addresses the music solely as the vehicle of a synthesis leading ultimately to a negation that spawns a revelation. After Adorno, I shall apply a similar kind of synthesis to music – the bringing together of two apparently concordant elements that produce, however, a discordant third element, called shortly a *remainder*, as the basis for criticism.

Adorno's judgment is forthright and direct when it comes to Schoenberg himself. Some of Adorno's critics will be surprised to learn that he called the composer naive: "The truth is that Schoenberg was a naive artist, above all in the often hapless intellectualizations with which he sought to justify his work. If anyone was ever guided by the tide of involuntary musical intuition it was he ... [His music] combines aesthetic avant-gardism with a conservative mentality [*konservative Gesinnung*]. While inflicting the most deadly blows on authority through his work, he seeks to defend the work as though before a hidden authority and ultimately to make it itself the authority."[25] Schoenberg's biography is cast thus in negative terms: for Adorno, Schoenberg was not completely responsible for his accomplishment. Barely conscious of the true importance of his work, a naive Schoenberg was guided by a tide of involuntary intuition which rendered his music capable of inflicting deadly blows.[26] Despite the best of intentions, his music succeeded heroically. In Schoenberg's mind, however, a positive synthesis works miraculously to explain his music as the inheritance of Brahms blended with Wagner, the explanation rendered in complex terms of motives and technical detail and in light of modern developments: "The music I composed ... mirrored the influence of both these masters."[27] He can say with positive certainty that his work assures the supremacy of German music: "Nobody has yet appreciated that my music, produced on German soil, without foreign influences, is a living example of an art able most effectively to oppose Latin and Slav hopes of hegemony and derived through and through from the traditions of German music."[28] Schoenberg on his account is a reluctant revolutionary, at heart a conservative, and yet destiny has offered a revolutionary's role to him, which he has taken up at great personal sacrifice.

This is a little too miraculous for Adorno. The facade comes apart when Schoenberg "seeks to defend the work as though before a hidden authority and ultimately to make [the work] itself the authority."[29] This phrase is one of the harshest in all Adorno's critiques of music. It asserts that Schoenberg shirked recognition of his individual responsibility as an artist (as a vehicle for revealing bourgeois musical culture in Late Capitalism) and hid instead behind an absolute belief in the God-given rectitude of his musical vision. As Schoenberg himself put it, "What I believe, in fact, is that if one has done his duty with the utmost sincerity and has worked out everything as near to perfection as he is capable of doing, then the Almighty presents him with a gift, with additional features of beauty such as he never could have produced by his talents alone."[30] For Adorno, this kind of appeal to mythic authority keeps Schoenberg from discerning the broader truth of his situation and thus (like the jackass) he is sublime in a sense far beyond his comprehension: inadvertently, by appeal to an "Almighty" (whom he calls elsewhere the "Supreme Commander") Schoenberg recognizes that the value of his music far exceeds his ability to grasp it. Schoenberg is a combination of Caspar Hauser and Good Soldier Schweick; thrust upon the world stage by forces far beyond his control and imagination, he succeeds despite his considerable effort to fail.

Schoenberg's music, like jazz, is a dialectic synthesis that leaves a negative remainder. The exercise, however, does not diminish Schoenberg's work in the slightest in Adorno's esteem (nor should it in ours). As an artifact, an object for the purposes of social critique, nothing is compromised by its composer's naïveté. This is true, even if the critical consciousness of the composer suffers considerably in Adorno's estimation.

After Adorno's dialectic critique, I apply a synthetic negation to John Coltrane's late music (and in doing so, hope to redeem Adorno ever so slightly in the jazz afficionado's eyes). I begin by linking the commonly held conception of timeless immortality and mysticism often attributed to Coltrane's late work with Ulrich Schönherr's suggestion that "Coltrane's version of 'My Favorite Things'... strips from the piece ... its commodity character."[31] On this positive account "My Favorite Things" achieves a mystical immortality at Coltrane's hands, and this immortality transcends any commodity exchange value that might have originally accrued to the popular song by its recorded distribution.

Seen from a negative perspective, however, it is the material poverty of the song, not transcendence, which is made evident by Coltrane. As a commodity, the song has little substance, just a skeletal melody and simple harmonies, perfect material for commodity exchange – for performance and distribution by a host of artists in a host of circumstances quite unrelated to the song's original conception and the original labour of its composer. Instead of stripping commodity character from the song, however, Coltrane makes its commodity nature abundantly clear by cataloguing this poverty in every musical dimension possible. As his improvisations become richer and deeper, the song itself diminishes in value until its ghost-like skeletal form is revealed perfectly. Like Schoenberg, the more Coltrane provides, now by improvisation, the more he strips away from the original, leaving a music of intense negativity. Thus in "My Favorite Things" the commodity character of the popular song is revealed with the greatest negative clarity. Coltrane's audience must work to appreciate this insight; any appeal to transcendence merely serves to obscure this fact.

In terms of negative difference, then, the elemental material quality of Coltrane's work far exceeds any transcendent quasi-mysticism attributed to it. Adorno might have said that the quasi-mysticism, the invocations of Eastern spirituality, and even the perceived avant-garde qualities swathe the elemental nature of the musical material in mirrors and smoke, the latter issuing from fires stoked diligently by Coltrane's devotees.[32] Hailing its putative sublime transcendent quality, his supporters, like Mahler's jackass, sublimely confirm Coltrane's materialism. Coltrane becomes a kind of pathetic and naive figure, penetrating to the material essence of music only to find himself wrapped tighter and tighter by a winding cloth of irrelevant absolutes. Such is the plight of visible minorities, even or perhaps especially in liberal societies. Had Adorno pursued such a negative dialectics in Coltrane's jazz, he might have found easy corroboration in the persons of Booker Little, Herbie Nichols, Billie Holiday, and even Charlie Parker, for the list of its sublimely dead is as fresh as jazz is perennial.

Translating *Negative Dialectics*, E.P. Ashton, like most translators, amends the German original from time to time so as to add some expressive term, and thus arrives at a felicitous insertion, like the phrase "without leaving a remainder" in the following passage. Ashton's translation is followed here by its German original: "The name of dialectics says no more, to begin with, than that objects do not go into their concepts without leaving a remainder, that they come to contradict the traditional norm of adequacy. [Ihr Name sagt zunächst nichts wieder, als daß die Gegenstände in ihrem Begriff nicht aufgehen, daß diese in Widerspruch geraten mit der hergebrachten Norm der adaequatio.]"[33] A more literal translation might read as follows: "Its name says to begin with no more than that objects do not go into their concept, that these get into (go into, produce a) contradiction with the traditional norm of adequacy." In this literal version, the result is merely a contradiction [*Widerspruch*]. Ashton, however, gives negation the full-fledged status of a "remainder," more substantial than a simple contradiction. The translation is fortuitous, for it seems that Adorno is always on the lookout for such remainders, those aspects of things that don't fit into their concepts.[34]

After Ashton, I shall adopt this notion of *remainder* as central to my critical approach (and in doing so reconcile myself to its origin as a mistranslation, since it seems to express with fidelity one aspect of Adorno's negative dialectics).[35]

A remainder will often arise from a discrepancy, then, as the residue left over when two things are otherwise identical: "the coming apart of whatever appears to be historically attained synthesis."[36] So in the instance of Coltrane's music, the absolute poverty of "My Favorite Things" is remaindered – along with the song's commodity character – when Coltrane's devotees liken the song to mystical transcendence: the commodity character of the song will simply not go peaceably into the union of *Coltrane* and *mystical transcendence*.

The following two passages rely on the concepts of *identity* and *non-identity*, which are defined at greater length later in *Negative Dialectics*.[37] Let it suffice for the present to say that when something conceived equates exactly with some concept, their relationship is one of identity.[38] Negation and negative dialectics critique identity and identity thinking. Negation "indicates the untruth of identity, the fact that the concept does not exhaust the thing conceived. [Er ist Index der Unwahrheit von Identität, des Aufgehens des Begriffenen im Begriff.]"[39] Again, the translation is felicitous, putting the emphasis on *untruth*, as a substantial thing, rather than the abstract *index*. A literal translation might read "It is the index of the untruth of identity, of the resolution of the conceived into the concept"; in identity, the conceived equates exactly with, and thus disappears into, the concept. But for Ashton's Adorno, negation points to an untruth, "indicates the untruth," the fact that nothing disappears into its concept entirely, without leaving a remainder. The other operant term in Ashton's translation is the substantive *fact*: when concept fails to exhaust the thing conceived, a fact is left over to attest. This "fact," then, is a truth indicated by the negative dialectic in the face of untruth.[40]

The Kantian and Hegelian roots of Adorno's notion of non-identity are well beyond comprehensive treatment here, but let it suffice to point out what Adorno called a "Copernican revolution" applied to the Kantian relationship of subject to object.[41] Under the auspices of capitalism, the exchange relation "constitutes people" in the form of the "standard social structure" based on exchange value; thus it leaves to one side "what they are for themselves, what they seem to be to themselves." Identity thinking sees people only in terms of this standard structure of exchange, whereas non-identity thinking understands what is left to one side by that exclusive vision. So too the Kantian doctrine of the transcendental subject is based on "abstractly rational [relations], detached from ... human individuals and their relationships."[42] The negative dialectic postulates the reversal – the "Copernican" reversal – of Kantian and identity thinking: things do not go quietly into their objects without dragging subjectivity along with them. *Subject* is constituted, then, as a remainder, a non-identity in relation to its object expressed as identity.

The notion of a substantive product in negative dialectics – that which I am calling *remainder* after Ashton – is set forth by Simon Jarvis with his customary clarity: "For Adorno, to think is always to think something. Even the most formal of formal logics would be unthinkable without the 'something' to which it refers, and therefore an absolute separation of logic from ontology is impossible." Jarvis goes on to postulate negation: "Thinking necessarily contains within it a reference to something that is not thinking – something, that is, which is therefore transcendent with respect to thinking. In that respect, a 'metaphysical' impulse – a drive to a knowledge *of objects that would break the circle of logical immanence* – is already implicit in thinking itself."[43] The emphasis in the last sentence is mine, added to draw attention to the notion of object. Seen from this ontological perspective, that which Jarvis calls the "circle of logical immanence" – equated here with identity thinking – carries with it (as a haunting spectre) a thought object it cannot shed: objects of non-identity, that which is left over after identity thought has attained synthesis.

Identifying is bound up tightly with thinking, so tightly that the identification of truth – the action of identifying "this is true" – is inextricable from the truth of the thought itself:[44] "To think is to identify. Conceptual order is content to screen what thinking seeks to comprehend. The semblance and the truth of thought entwine. [Denken heißt indentifizieren. Befriedigt schiebt begriffliche Ordnung sich vor das, was Denken begreifen will. Sein Schein und seine Wahrheit verschränken sich.]"[45] Concepts are all too willing to supply thought's need to identify, to slake its thirst for identity, and that makes them culpable. Concepts, instead, ought to resist easy synthesis. So in calling Mahler's critics jackasses, we might be content to say they are merely stupid. But Adorno's point is that the mere alliance of jackass and stupidity ought to be resisted in this case, for a third term is missing here – *sublime* – as in *sublimely stupid*. It takes a leap of thought – conceptual work on the part of Adorno's readers – to resist an easy assimilation of *jackass* and *stupid*, and to see the jackass in Adorno's charitably uncharitable light.

Adorno held the exact identification of object with subject in suspicion and sought to represent this suspicion in the terms of his own form of the dialectic.[46] In the following passage, Ashton goes beyond Adorno's text to capture again the essence of the passage, its central importance to Adorno's project. The dialectic critic – Ashton's "I" – must break through the appearance of total identity. The vehicle for doing so is contradiction – the object contradicts the concept applied to it by not fitting exactly therein. What appears as heterogeneous will ultimately contradict heterogeneity:

Aware that the conceptual totality is mere appearance, I have no way but to break immanently, in its own measure, through

the appearance of total identity. Since that totality is structured
to accord with logic, however, whose core is the principle of the
excluded middle,[47] whatever will not fit this principle, whatever
differs in quality, comes to be designated as a contradiction. Contradiction is nonidentity under the aspect of identity; the dialectical primary of the principle of contradiction makes the thought
of unity the measure of heterogeneity. As the heterogeneous
collides with its limit it exceeds itself. Dialectics is the consistent
sense of nonidentity. [Dem Bewußtsein der Scheinhaftigkeit der
begrifflichen Totalität ist nichts offen, als den Schein totaler Identität immanent zu durchbrechen: nach ihrem eigenen Maß. Da
aber jene Totalität sich gemäß der Logik aufbaut, deren Kern der
Satz vom augeschlossenen Dritten bildet, so nimmt alles, was ihm
nicht sich einfügt, alles qualitativ Verschiedene, die Signatur des
Widerspruchs an. Der Widerspruch ist das Nichtidentische unter ·
dem Aspekt der Identität; der Primat des Widerspruchsprinzips
in der Dialektik mißt das Heterogene am Einheitsdenken. Indem
es auf seine Grenze aufprallt, übersteigt es sich. Dialektik ist das
konsequente Bewußtsein von Nichtidentität.][48]

(Ashton is to be forgiven for translating freely here, for the German
is ambiguous both grammatically and in meaning.[49]) Dialectic totalities are structured logically in such a way as to exclude anything
but two opposing terms. A third term (*sublime* in the case of Mahler's jackass), however, contradicts the dialectic; in doing so the contradiction will exceed the dialectic (and move immanently – in the
dialectic's own terms – beyond it). This is the *contradiction principle*
[*Widerspruchsprinzips*]: thought will always exceed and thus contradict a seamless dialectical synthesis. It is clothed here as immanence: within the binary form of the dialectic lie the seeds of its own
contradiction – the middle term, the possibility of an excluded term.

In the passage below, Adorno emphasizes the importance of this
middle-term principle: an excluded or remaindered possibility will
always plague any attempt on the part of consciousness to strive for
the unity of subject and object. In effect, any attempt to differentiate elements in a unified whole will go on differentiating (through
the introduction of third or middle terms) and thus turn unity into
negative disunity: "What we differentiate will appear divergent,
dissonant, negative for just as long as the structure of our consciousness obliges it to strive for unity. [Das Differenzierte erscheint so

lange divergent, dissonant, negativ, wie das Bewußtsein der eigenen Formation nach auf Einheit drängen muß.]"[50] In other words, any attempt at the unity of identity will always be frustrated, negated by a supplementary divergent, dissonant element, which will take on the substance, after Ashton, of a negative or negating remainder. In the case of Coltrane, the commodity aspect of "My Favorite Things" will always frustrate any attempt at uniting the work with mystical transcendence.

In the dialectics of aesthetic positivism, musical object and musical appreciation synthesize completely. The listener identifies with – is as one with – the music; appreciation is complete fusion, where music and conception coincide exactly. There is a moment – Vienna circa 1805 – when, perhaps, dialectics effects synthesis and unity, producing Beethoven's middle symphonies, quartets, sonatas, and *Fidelio*, among other works, and resolving music to its conceptual image like a fairytale glass slipper on a diminutive foot.

In the vision of negative dialectics following Adorno, however, the conception as listener includes awareness of the limitations of the positive. Where initially we strove for unity through identity, now we recognize divergence and dissonance, these as indexes pointing toward divergence and dissonance in broader society, not just music. This insight is perhaps the principal negative remainder left by dialectics.[51]

The negative dialectic is an active vehicle by which to represent reality, to set it forth for our appreciation, no matter how fractured: "A contradiction in reality is a contradiction against reality."[52] But (in a sense contrary to Ashton's translation as a substantive *remainder*) Adorno refers to it also as an active "sense [Bewußtsein]": "Dialectics is the consistent sense of nonidentity."[53] It is an "appearance," the product of differentiation: "What we differentiate will appear divergent, dissonant, negative for just as long as the structure of our consciousness obliges it to strive for unity."[54] I shall concentrate, however, on the substantive form of the concept: "Dialectics unfolds [*entfaltet*] the difference between the particular and the universal ... serves the end of reconcilement [*der Versöhnung dient*]."[55] The dialectic is like a knife, slicing open, revealing – representing in the sense of *Darstellung* – and thus reconciling the falsehoods that cover the splits and antagonisms of reality.[56]

Negative dialectics follow in part from Adorno's reading of the literary theorist Georg Lukács. In his early work, certainly the books

History and Class Consciousness and *The Theory of the Novel*, Lukács shows reality as contradictory in a way that anticipates Adorno's thought. As Buck-Morss puts it, Lukács offered the premise and Adorno responded: "Given the premise of an essentially antagonistic, contradictory reality, it is clear why Adorno felt that knowledge of the present demanded the juxtaposition of contradictory concepts whose mutually negating tension could not be dissolved."[57] To return to the parable of the gay Vancouverites with which this chapter began, this reality was essentially antagonistic and contradictory, a fact made crystal clear to them by the phrase *B.C. Ferries cruising the Straits*. The attempted unity of *ferries*, *cruising*, and *straits* made objective what every gay Vancouverite knew, that their very being had been remaindered negatively (quite unconsciously presumably) when the government advertising firm went to work. The slogan merely advertised that fact all over the province, and with a biting irony. (In terms of the consciousness produced in gay British Columbians, however, this slogan went well beyond mere irony.)

Identity thinking is inflexible and rigid (taking on the aspects of "second nature," after Lukács); non-identity thinking and contradiction are kept fluid in dialectics, and under its auspices, certain truths are attained – revealed as dialectic remainders, to return to Ashton's term: "It was precisely his intent to frustrate the categorizing, defining mentality which by the twentieth century had itself become 'second nature.' Only if thought remained fluid and avoided dogma could it be the ally of history as it ought to unfold. In Adorno's essays, dialectically opposed pairs of concepts, each of which in itself had two opposed levels of meaning, were juxtaposed to reveal the truth of a contradictory social reality."[58] Opposition – "opposed pairs of concepts," "opposed levels of meaning" – reveals the truth of a generalized contradictory reality. Or, as Buck-Morss puts it, "By juxtaposing antithetical concepts ... and by exposing the irreconcilability of concepts with the reality which they were supposed to describe ... Adorno was engaged in a double task of seeing through the mere appearances of bourgeois reality and the alleged adequacy of bourgeois concepts used to define it. As with Hegel, contradiction, with negation as its logical principle, gave this thinking its dynamic structure and provided the motor force for critical reflection."[59] Although all other forms of criticism, it follows, assume an adequacy of reality mated with concept, such forms will ultimately prove defective for criticism applied after Adorno.

An excellent example of reality juxtaposed against concept is the passage cited above from Adorno's *Prisms* essay on Schoenberg: "The more [Schoenberg's music] gives its listeners, the less it offers them. It requires the listener spontaneously to compose its inner movement and demands of him not mere contemplation but praxis."[60] Suppose that I go to concerts for the sake of leisure, and thus I go to a Schoenberg concert. In going to a concert, in other words, one is confronted with an identity concept: concerts are a form of leisure. As Adorno understands it, however, concerts of Schoenberg's music are not for leisure, nor are Schoenbergian concerts leisurely; one has to "work" for one's leisure when listening to Schoenberg. Schoenberg's concerts negate the positive synthesis of leisure and concert. The revised consciousness this produces (the self-conscious awareness that things are not as they seem) becomes that which we called after Ashton the *remainder*, a substantial thing floating above the identity of *concert* with *leisure* at any concert of Schoenberg's music, where listeners occupy themselves furiously with their impatience.

Non-identity thinking goes also under the rubric of *unintentional truth*, a substantive that takes us back to the substantial, material nature of Adorno's negative dialectics – Ashton's remainder. The truth of the synthetic negation is unintentional, certainly not intended by the positive, which it contradicts. The truth of Schoenberg's music – one must work for one's leisure – is an unintended truth produced as a remainder after the intended truths are exhausted.

Unintended truth takes on a life of its own in particulars. Adorno calls the revelation of this life "interpretation." (In the sphere of music, I shall call it *analysis*.) Interpretation is "materialist knowledge," as Adorno calls it: "Interpretation of the unintentional through a juxtaposition of the analytically isolated elements, and illumination of the real by the power of such interpretation: that is the program of every authentically materialist knowledge."[61] As Buck-Morss puts it, truth lies in logical breaks: "The truth content of bourgeois thought lay ... in the 'breaks' [*Brüche*] in its logic, the gaps of its systematic unity." And these have a palpable quality (again reminiscent of Ashton's *remainder*), the expressive equivalent in feeling: "Indeed, because truth revealed itself in the non-identity between psychological intent and its concrete objectification, the bourgeois thinker was most likely to express truth when he felt himself farthest away."[62]

To reveal the truth, the task of the critic is to isolate contradictions and tensions between the thinking subject and the objects of thought, between the word and the thing denoted. And as noted above, this revelation should take a concrete form, substantive enough to be pointed at. I belabour this point here: for analysis to be effective – to produce a useful understanding – it ought to have an objective referent. I say that the gay understanding of the advertising slogan is remaindered, and by this I mean it was first distinguished in contrast to the seamless synthesis of *ferries* and *straits*, then confirmed and made objective, and thus rendered useful in praxis (helping in small part to oppose discrimination according to sexual orientation).

While Marxist thought will not explain completely the notion of remainder, consider a particularly cogent passage on alienation in Marx's *Grundrisse*, where all the various aspects of alienated labour are brought together in the objective personification of the capitalist.[63] It is as if, in the eyes of the bourgeois who purchases a commodity, the synthesis of labour and exchange value is complete – a synthetic identity. Workers, however, see matters differently, knowing that a portion of their labour value has been taken from them in the conversion to capital. This abstract fact – the workers' alienation from their labour – is made objective, Marx says, in the form of the capitalist, through the confrontation of "living labour" with "personified" capital, a "personification" with its own inherent vitality, its "will and interest," a personification to rival the person of the worker. In the confrontation between the worker and capital, the capitalist is an abstraction made objective, capitalism personified – "independent and indifferent towards living labor capacity ... exchange value which confronts [living labor's] mere use value."[64] The capitalist – top hatted, waistcoated, spat-shoed, cigar smoking (or one of his modern progeny) – is the remainder produced when a worker's labour is brought together with the exchange value abstracted from it, this in a synthetic unity produced by capitalism. The capitalist is thus capitalism made objective, and in the gaps around him a useful understanding congeals – a revolutionary consciousness congealed in the mind of the worker.

Remainders of this sort will be described throughout this book. So, for example, in our gay Vancouverite example a consciousness is remaindered, and in the instance of Coltrane's music, an aspect of a commodity – the commodity nature of "My Favorite Things" – is produced as a remainder (produced by an alienating consciousness that identifies Coltrane with mysticism). While the example of the capitalist as capitalism remaindered is perhaps extreme in its reductive nature, let it serve as a referent for *remainder*: ultimately the synthetic and dialectic remainders that concern us here will take a cogent form (sometimes symbolic, often allegoric) around which to shape an understanding not tied to a one-to-one correspondence of object and thought.

Adapting Walter Benjamin's notion of "constellation," I will say that when contradictory subjects and objects are juxtaposed with themselves and with their negative remainder, a constellate shape or form is produced. (We shall return to this in the chapter on Frank Zappa, below.) Negation as a practice, then, constructs its arguments in the fashion of a "constellation."

Buck-Morss calls this "differentiation": constellate space places words and concepts in juxtaposition, as if the space were divided by an axis of "differentiation" around which terms moved (for example, *leisure* and *concert*, with *Schoenberg's music* as the axis). She describes a tripartite poetics according to which differentiation is drawn in Adorno's thought: by reversing the meaning of a word, by juxtaposing unrelated words or the "elements" they signify, or by juxtaposing opposites so as to reveal unintended possibilities of relations: "A variation of this principle of differentiation was turning a word or concept against the phenomenon it was intended to signify ... ('life does not live'; gratification is the enemy of gratification) where they function to set the constellation and critical thinking in motion ... A second was the reverse of this principle: to juxtapose seemingly unrelated, unidentical elements, revealing the configuration in which they congealed or converged."[65] And third, "'Juxtaposing extremes' meant discovering not only the similarity of opposites but also the connecting links (the 'inner logic') between seemingly unrelated elements of a phenomenon."[66] This poetics transforms a positive critique into a negative philosophy, the self-enclosed into the dialectical, historical, and materialist. And so with Coltrane's "My Favorite Things," commodity (against Schönherr's interpretation) is juxtaposed with mysticism and transcendence.

Unintentionally (in the sense of an unintentional or accidental truth), capitalism renders a great service to the student of society through what Lukács called the capacity of a person's "own labor" to become "something objective and independent of him, something that controls him by virtue of an autonomy alien to man."[67] Here is the classic Marxist contradiction between a reified conception based on "the fantastic form of a relation between things" and a true understanding of labour as a social relation between labourers, not commodities. As Gillian Rose puts it, "Reified concepts describe social phenomena, the appearance of society, as if it has the properties to which the concepts refer."[68] Reified concepts are fictions, and fictions are susceptible to analysis by means of negative dialectics.[69] Commodities are fictions and thus susceptible to analysis. Thus Adorno allies with Marx: reification is identity thinking; capitalism is reified thought:

> Identity thinking is reified thinking – not only our paradigmatic mode of thinking, but also the mode of thinking of non-dialectical sciences. Identity thinking makes unlike things alike. To believe that a concept really covers its object, when it does not, is to believe falsely that the object is the equal of its concept ... Adorno construes the process of commodity exchange as involving an analogous mechanism: "The exchange principle, the reduction of human labour to its abstract universal concept of average labour-time, has the same origin as the principles of identification. It has its social model in exchange and exchange would be nothing without identification."[70]

I link Ashton's *remainder* with Rose's thought: Adorno was, after Marx, interested in the way a relation between men (in a capitalist society) appears in the form of a natural *property* of a thing,[71] the way in which class relations, once reified, would appear to take on a "natural" quality, when in truth they are highly contrived. Class relationships get reified, then, as the property of a thing, the appearance of a natural property.[72] In terms of Ashton's substantive *remainder*, the fictive natural property is the thing left over – the thing that doesn't fit – when class relations are seen in light of commodities and capitalism. A commodity – a recording of Coltrane's "My Favorite Things," for example – transforms itself objectively into a negative remainder when the listener grasps fully both the nature of the original labour (Coltrane's labour) and its reified reconstitution as a putatively "mystically transcendent" commodity.

Lest we think again of the object of a negative dialectic as merely a thing reified – *res facta* – Rose says that the process of reification is not inanimate. It is a form of thought, of active thinking.[73] For

Adorno, the task of negative-dialectical criticism is to recognize and reveal the "cognition of non-identity": "To confront it, present society, with what 'it is', that is, to ... *see* the non-identity in the relation between the concept and the object."[74]

This notion restores a ray of optimism to an otherwise bleak picture. In purely psychological terms, if society is completely reified, there can be no awareness – no capacity for non-identity thinking.[75] But non-identity will be constantly rekindled by the contradictions of dialectics built into commodities, which produce negative remainders afresh: "[Adorno] reaffirms that there must always be a possibility of non-identity or critical thought,"[76] and therein resides hope.

Indeed, despite Adorno's bitter style, there is abundant cause for optimism. Non-identity, and thus the possibility for criticism, is to be found in the very substance of commodities. Hope is all around us.

This I understand to be the purpose of Schoenberg's music and indeed of popular music for Adorno, or of Coltrane's music for criticism after Adorno. By their contradictions, these repertoires exist not merely to express ironies – listeners working for leisure, the mystically transcendent nature of a commodity. Their ultimate purpose, certainly to criticism after Adorno, is the goal of all good critique – to reveal the nature of things otherwise obscured, so that one might orient oneself to these same things if not in an absolutely correct manner then at least with an objective regard to one's fallibility.

If a work of music is to be a truly critical success, it should embody contradiction. (This explains Adorno's attraction to popular music, a thought I return to later.) As Richard Leppert succinctly puts it: "contradiction lies at the heart of any art which has any claim to truth. 'A successful work,' [Adorno] pointed out, 'is not one which resolves objective contradictions in a spurious harmony, but one which expresses the idea of harmony negatively by embodying the contradictions, pure and uncompromised, in its innermost structure.'"[77]

Contradiction is revealed in substance – the substance of "suppressed detail," "leftovers," and "particulars." Music criticism should reveal details. Leppert again: "Dialectics, for Adorno, was a language-act by means of which suppressed details were made visible, palimpsests read, and otherness articulated instead of subsumed. Dialectics retrieved leftovers – particulars – from the universalizing tendencies of concepts that conventionally determine philosophical practice."[78] Normally the thinking subject conceives

of musical objects as if they could be grasped entirely, as a unit –
details resolved in wholes. But musical objects are not fully grasped
by subjective thought; the musical object is not fully compatible
with the musical subject. Completeness stands only as the difference
between subject and object.

This notion of completeness is a form of recognition. In Adorno's
thought, completion is a locus around which subject and object are
reconciled only as *necessarily contradicted*. To grasp this necessity is
a first step toward a negative synthesis. As O'Connor puts it (using
a term we attributed to Ashton), "The object – nature, the object
world external to the self – ultimately stands outside the totality of
the subject's conceptual grasp, as it were, as a *remainder*. To recognize this ungraspable leftover, and indeed to think the self in the
context of the object, marks the first step toward a possible reconciliation of subject and object, the subject and its other. Adorno's
concern was to retain in thought the object's fundamental particularity against its universal analogue captured in concepts."[79]

Some critics have argued, after Adorno, that the situation of music
has polarized to the extent of forbidding dialectical synthesis.[80] Serious music and popular music are not the extreme ends of some synthetic whole; they do not constitute the two poles – north and south
– of an aesthetic magnet. The aesthetic of wholes has shattered and
left only shards. The critic's task is to approach the broken whole
through these shards (and be content never to succeed in reconsti-
tuting the whole).

To test the mettle of such skepticism, Jürgen Ritsert reintroduces
the notion of a middle term which might have mediated between
extremes and thus preserved something of wholeness, the properly
Hegelian excluded middle turned to positive synthesis.[81] But he sets
aside such optimism; for him a positive mediation is no longer possible. The idea is now that of a "fractured whole," a whole which
can only be approached via the fragmented parts – the remainders
of wholes – rather than through the harmonist notion of the reconciliation of opposites.[82] At one time, serious and popular music
(for example) were complementary parts of a unitary whole. A com-
petent listener could distinguish the two as the polar extremes of
one unified listening experience (with its defining polarities – high
music and low music). Now that adequate listening and its unitary
wholes are no longer possible, the possibility of distinguishing such
complementary parts is made likewise impossible. For Ritsert, any

differences between serious and popular music are elided. Both are now merely shards, indistinguishable fragments rather than complementary parts. If this sounds like extreme pessimism, so be it; as we shall see in a moment, pessimism will yield a practical purpose despite its extreme nature.

Adorno's practical pessimism does not accord with customary scholarly practice in music studies or in sociology. Negative dialectics departs from "mainstream sociology," a certain "philosophical utopianism," as Stephen Bronner calls it (noting the differences, sometimes bitter, to be observed between Adorno and his sociologist colleagues).[83] Mainstream sociology aims at a homogenization of method based on social fact; it elides the difference between subject and object, individual and society, and relies instead on "facts" discerned empirically or through positivist experiment. But empiricism and positivism fail to account critically for the condition of the individual in Late Capitalism because social individuality in Late Capitalism will not allow itself to be expressed as a set of mere social facts.

Much the same criticism might be aimed at "mainstream" musicology (as I shall take aim in a later chapter). Empiricism and positivism fail to account fully for the condition of the musical work of art in Late Capitalism. The individual identity of the musical artwork cannot be expressed merely as a set of facts such as the date of its composition or the nature of its harmonies.

Mainstream sociology reifies class relations. It does nothing overtly to illuminate them, all the while embodying them with a clarity that direct address can only seek to emulate. In similar ways, mainstream musicology reifies a consciousness: it treats music as an object defined primarily by the notion of a musical work, all the while ignoring the labour that produces and then sustains such a notion – the conferences, subsequent monographs and articles, course syllabi, theses and dissertations. The mainstream notion of musical work attributes to musical objects the mystical qualities of commodities, and in doing so reifies a particular kind of musical consciousness in these objects. As Bronner puts it with regard to sociology, "Remaining stuck within the realm of 'social facts' necessarily produces a form of thinking in which the subject or individual is collapsed into the object or society. Mainstream sociology, by stripping the social outcome from the value-laden conditions of its constitution, thus contributes to the reification of the very subject it seeks to study."[84] Mainstream sociology and by extension mainstream musicology, in other words, cannot countenance the fundamental gap between individual subjectivity and the so-called "objective" society.

Like the positive scholars who became the objects of his critiques, Adorno recognized the priority of the object, so often a musical object. But his object exists solely as that which will not make a complete dialectical synthesis with the subject.[85] In musical criticism after Adorno, that fact – the failure of complete synthesis – becomes more objective than any other putative object, such as a score or performance.

The musical object is particular. Being particular and thus proper to itself, it is not capable of complete unity with a subject, no matter how deep the attraction, or the repulsion, exerted by such a subjectivity. In the case of "My Favorite Things," the mystical veneer applied by Coltrane's devotees comes off as an attempt to encompass and thus tame conceptually a power that aims at liberation. No doubt Coltrane had a mystical conception of his music (which his wife attempted to sustain after his death). But that conception seems rooted in incommensurable differences – Black and White, material poverty in a time of inordinate riches – and the history of such differences, their social history, cannot be covered over by a patina of mysticism.

Being particularities, critical objects such as Coltrane's music (or Schoenberg's) will not give way to identity, to "identical moments" as Brian O'Connor calls them, with regard to philosophy:

> Adorno sees the retrieval of particularity as involving, in effect,
> no less than a reversal of the priority of subject to object that has
> characterized the subjectivist tendency of modern philosophy.
> This means constructing a philosophy built around what Adorno
> polemically calls "the priority of the object." The thesis of the
> priority of the object holds that objects are irreducible to con-
> cepts, that they cannot be made identical with concepts. So what
> is required, to put it within these terms, is an account of the sub-
> ject-object relation – of experience, in effect – that can establish
> the nonidentity of concept and object. For Adorno, this entails
> that experience has a nonidentical moment in which the irredu-
> cible particularity of the object (and not just our concept of it) is
> a significant or meaningful element of the experience.[86]

From this regard, Adorno's sociology does not seem quite so pessimistic, despite its negative modus operandi.[87] At the heart of negative dialectics lies an optimism: dialectical criticism of musical objects might transcend the limits of identity thinking (the "covering concept," as Bernstein calls it): "What negative dialectic *offers* ... is the conceptual possibility of there being actual possibility. If there is 'more' to an item than what its covering concept determines, then there must be more possibilities for the object to be than what the system dictates."[88]

The musical criticism undertaken in these essays takes objects, not subjectivities, as the constitutive force in meaning. As wayward and implacable protagonists in the negotiation of meaning, Adorno's musical objects resist all attempts at smooth and untroubled synthesis into dialectical wholes. Musical objects – musical commodities in particular – simply will not go into their concepts without remainder. Refusing a simple synthesis, they become the operant force in creating music meaning. Our critical task is to find and describe such objects, and do so with a style appropriate to its object.

In the normal style of scholarly prose, the writer's subjectivity takes control over the object described, and thus the perspective is largely one-sided, that of the writer. The subject matter does not talk back, claim its due; Coltrane does not rise up from the grave and cry a halt to this debilitating mysticism: "J'accuse!" Instead the object lies largely in the mind of the writer and succumbs to the whiles of that mind. From this pattern arises the accusation levelled often at musical analysis: the work is anaesthetized if not dead on the dissecting table. This situation of inequality is made all the more pronounced by a mind given to identity thinking – that the writer might exhaust his subject, take it entirely within the compass of his prose.

For Adorno, such an overt presentation of content (along the lines of "standard expository form" as Rose puts it) marks an essential failure in the "thought process itself" on the part of the writer. Thus Frederic Jameson describes the matter of prose style as follows: "outright presentations of sheer *content* are stylistically wrong, this stylistic failure being itself a mark and a reflection of some essential failure in the thought process itself ... The overt presentation of content in its own right, whether in sociological or in philosophical writing, stands condemned as a fall back into that positivistic and empirical illusion which dialectical thinking was designed to overcome."[89] On these lines, the notion of a self-sufficient content is a myth. A truly critical conception of content – musical content in our instance – is produced by non-identity thinking. Such content is produced in the form of a remainder (to return one final time to Ashton's formulation).

Adorno in this sense is an optimist (and we shall mimic his optimism by designating our remainders as "friendly"). Negative dialectics, negated syntheses, and non-identity thinking do not mark necessarily a failure in music. The "formal contradictions" of social reality displayed by music are diagnostic, pointing to a state of affairs. And as diagnostics, they are substantial, the concrete basis for a subsequent praxis. Dialectic contradiction, then, constitutes a signpost (a *Wegweiser*, perhaps in the sense of Schubert's *Winterreise*) inclined toward concrete reality. Jameson refers to "precious indications": "So it is, for instance, that in a classic essay on society Adorno shows not only how every possible idea we form about society is necessarily partial and imperfect, inadequate and contradictory, but also that those very *formal* contradictions are themselves the most precious indications as to how we stand with respect to the concrete reality of social life itself at the present moment of time."[90] On this account, society can be known only in the guise of formal contradictions seen in the cold light of negative dialectics. Criticism after Adorno is obliged to observe this insight.

2

Just for Nice

People desire or decide to become musicologists, composers, or
ethnomusicologists because they have heard music that excited them.
                                    Joseph Kerman, *Contemplating Music*

The phrase "just for nice" is found in the popular culture associated
with German-speaking North American Mennonites, presumably a
transatlantic carryover from an earlier counterpart in the Central
and Eastern European homeland of the Mennonite peoples.[1] The
phrase is associated with arts and crafts, the distinct sense of pleasure
a work of craft can give as a simple aesthetic whole, devoid of intel-
lectualization. The phrase also implies a crossover between work
and leisure: "nice" is joined to the otherwise menial life experiences
of this largely agrarian cultural group. Magnus Einarsson, in *Just for
Nice: German-Canadian Folk Art*, recounts the following tale:

> A colleague was standing with a Mennonite farmer inside his
> barn near Vineland in southern Ontario. High up on one of the
> gables he noticed a design that had been cut out of the boards,
> letting in shafts of light in the pattern of a star. He asked the
> farmer whether this was a hex sign of some sort, placed there
> perhaps for protection of the animals or to ensure a good crop.
> The farmer replied in the negative, saying, "It's just for pretty."
> This phrase is a variant of a much-used Ontario (Pennsylvania)
> German saying, "Just for nice," or sometimes even "Pretty for
> nice." The casualness of the expression and its delivery, however,
> belie the significance of its underlying message; namely, that
> beauty ("pretty") is an important part of one's environment,
> even in the humdrum, workaday world, even in a place where,
> most of the time, only beasts are there to appreciate it.[2]

"Just for nice" means "not troublesome" and, by extension, a diversion from things serious. Einarsson and other contributors to the volume outline this largely decorative aesthetic and lament its passing or transmutation into contemporary popular art forms. In truth, "just for nice" crops up in many places, not merely the rural agrarian.

The status of "nice" in criticism was observed some time ago by Beardsley and Wimsatt under the rubric of the *affective fallacy*, "a confusion between a poem and its *results* (what it *is* and what it *does*)."[3] Poetry is there to make us feel nice, and thus we ought to feel nice after we read poetry.[4] They cite Eduard Hanslick in this regard, who said, "We might as well study the properties of wine by getting drunk."[5] Above the act of saying nice things about a work of music hangs a Hanslickian dark cloud, the possibility that one was too intoxicated by it to make a sound appraisal.

The musicological patriarch Guido Adler, however, recreated the tidy world of nice in his sketch of the new musicology (from 1888), where he talks about the artist, the artist's garden, and the task of the musicologist to tend the garden in order to keep it nice: "The artist builds his temple in the grove, in the grove where fragrance is newly revived, time and again, from freely growing flowers. The theoretician of art tills the earth: he educates the disciples to his life's task and accompanies the inspired creator as a lifelong companion. Should the scholar of art observe that matters are not turning out in the best interests of art, then he directs it onto the proper course ... Should [art] be stormed or brought down, then he surrounds it or withdraws it a certain distance, and saves it in this way for periods that will once again show the proper appreciation of it."[6] The task of Adler's music scholar is to guard a musical heritage by pruning and tidying. The scholar's basic orientation is toward the cleanliness of the *Denkmäler*. Only nicely arranged things will speak to a "proper appreciation."

It is not difficult to appreciate the extent to which and the means by which niceness has made inroads in musicological thought, both amateur and professional, since Adler's day. It says about Schoenberg, "His music is just not nice." In full knowledge that Wagner was a rabid anti-Semite and abused his personal power to his own selfish ends, "just for nice" will reply, "Yes, but that has nothing to do with his nice music." Should we protest that jazz has become a microcosm of the urban Black's social condition – a serious musical affirmation turned into a frivolous entertainment (recordings of John Coltrane played at cocktail parties) – then "just for nice" will reply, "Yes, but jazz helps me nicely forget my troubles. Hiccup." The bourgeois element at play here will acknowledge any insight that agrees with its own nice ends and reject as superfluous (not nice!) anything that doesn't.

My generation, born in North America in the late 1940s and the 1950s and coming to consciousness in the last decade of Adorno's life, are capable negative dialecticians of "just for nice." Born out of cynicism about civil rights and the Vietnam War, we learned first-hand the limitations of nice stuff. Our parents, who lived through the Great Depression of the 1930s, knew that chopped cabbage, lime jello, marshmallows, and mayonnaise, blended and chilled, produces a "nice" synthesis of the contradictory.[7] Their children, however, discerned in this concoction the remnants of a Depression-era economy that was irrelevant in postwar abundant luxury. They knew that "just for nice" was often brought on by their parents' guilt about material wealth, an attempt to legitimize retrospectively the hardships of the Depression (impressed indelibly on their parents' minds) in an era of suburban cottages, two cars to a household, and television. The terrifying suppertime commandment to "Eat your liver, children!" is both a *double entendre* and a negative synthesis. The children of the 1960s grew expert at discerning their parents' contradictions. For this reason among others, Adorno retains a currency with this and subsequent generations for whom the years after the Second World War remain ripe with dialectical fascination.[8]

These 1950s and 1960s syntheses are sometimes measured in the postmodern terms of a polyglot – a style of enunciation produced heterogeneously by forces unleashed (but unanticipated) by modernism. Unconstrained postmodern syntheses seem capable, however, only of reproducing themselves, constituting, as Robert Hullot-Kentor puts it, "a form of montage that never gets beyond juxtaposition."[9] Andreas Huyssens's signal mixture of a 1970s "culture of eclecticism, a largely affirmative postmodernism which had abandoned any claim to critique, transgression, or negation; and ... an alternative postmodernism in which resistance, critique, and negation of the status quo were redefined in non-modernist and non-avantgardist terms"[10] seems all too given to the reinvention of a subject that, while pretty nice, will easily dull the sharp edge of

Adorno's critique. While Cage and Duchamp (in the famous Cage-Duchamp-Wharhol axis of postmodernity) maintain by the nature of their work a critical distance from commodification, Wharhol's work – like Guevera's all too ubiquitous likeness on the Che T-shirt – is easily appropriated when the postmodern subject is set loose in the shopping malls of postmodern capitalism.

Unbridled appropriation is the case too with the American reception of the French theorists of postmodernity, as François Cusset puts it. In postmodern hands, the essential link to Marxism (which binds Adorno to French Theory) is forgotten – or pushed under the rug as not nice, an inconvenient truth. Marx's role in French Theory might become the foundation for the latter's refutation. Scared and confused, the postmodernists both east and west of the Atlantic have made Marxism a matter of "branding" and "mis-branding":

> In fact, Marx – and, more broadly, *any* social critique of capital – may be the major blind spot of French Theory's readers and commentators on both sides of the Atlantic, although for opposite reasons: Foucault, Deleuze, and even Derrida enjoyed such a success within American, but also many third-world, universities precisely because of their distance from classical Marxism, or because of what was even seen as their anti-Marxism; meanwhile, they were banned from their home country under the charges of a perverse collusion with the worst of leftist Marxism [referring here to the reception of French Theory in France after the mid-1970s]. Their texts, however, were neither pro-Marx nor anti-Marx. They were, rather, an endless confrontation with, discussion on, reinterpretation of Marxism.[11]

Adorno is not immune from similar appropriation at the hands of scholars who, grazing for quotations, excise what is convenient – the scholarly equivalent of commodity fetishism – and pay scant heed to the original labourer involved.

Albrecht Wellmer left the postmodern question hanging two decades ago: "It remains to be shown, however, what consequences [the] destruction of the *premises* of the philosophy of consciousness has for a critique of identificatory thought itself."[12] With regard to Adorno, the question remains unresolved, for the destruction Wellmer cites was more a case of abandonment of the philosophy of consciousness (as French Theory itself was abruptly abandoned in its turn). The reputed "return to Adorno" may be less a return than the taking up of slackened threads; on this account, the warp of modernism will never unravel while capitalism spreads its influence globally, although the weave will loosen from time to time under developments such as postmodernism. When Georgina Born takes up the fertile notion of "an analysis of cultural production which takes account both of structure (including psychic structures) and agency; and of aesthetic and institutional mediations,"[13] Wellmer's question is not resolved but simply left begging; despite the refinements she proposes, and the corrections to be applied to Adorno, the direction of Born's critique remains in essence set by Adorno.

The subject matter I call "just for nice" might lend itself easily to a postmodern descriptoid as a synthetic *bricolage* of unresolved subjectivities. It is meant instead to take up the shards of Wellmer's destroyed philosophy of consciousness. As the heterogeneous postmodern products of "just for nice" – café latte or cappuccino? – become exported to further and further-flung corners of capital's world, postmodernism becomes less and less tenable. Nice, but less and less tenable. Capitalism is capitalism, regardless of flavour.

Adorno took a disinterested interest in such things as just for nice. Negation and dialectic allow him a disinterest, allow him to avoid the direct assertion that might otherwise be misinterpreted as self-interest. As a result, Adorno is trusted by subsequent generations. Some of this has to do with not being nice. In his prose style, for example, he makes his meaning opaque, difficult to absorb, and thus just not nice. To the naive reader, he appears incompetent; too foggy, obfuscatory, obscure to be really interesting let alone taken seriously, and the naive reader – at heart like Mahler's jackass – is sublimely right and for the same reasons. Not taken too seriously by those in search of niceties, Adorno thus succeeds with those in search of criticism.

In criticism, as elsewhere, reason operates by means of the positive assertion: through comparison – *ratio* – everything can be fused dialectically, with nothing left over. Positivism reduces all to a common denominator – a single, unitary, and absolute vision of humankind. Everything can be absorbed into a unity, and Enlightenment spreads out like rumour to encompass, absorb, and explain everything. The world exists as a product of the number 1: "The mythologizing equation of Ideas with numbers in Plato's last writings expresses the longing of all demythologization: number became the canon of Enlightenment."[14] *Ratio* is thus a fan of "just for nice." It makes things nice and tidy, in a self-satisfied bourgeois way: "Bourgeois society is ruled by equivalence. It makes the dissimilar comparable by reducing it to abstract quantities. To the Enlightenment, that which does not reduce to numbers, and ultimately to the one, becomes illusion ... Unity is the slogan from Parmenides to Russell."[15] To resist this tidy packet, I consider (after Adorno) a negative dialectic: things (being like irrational numbers) do not go into their concepts nicely – not neatly, not without a residue, not without a remainder.

My task, accordingly, is not simply to refute "just for nice," but to appropriate it as evidence for negative synthesis and dialectics. In this, I follow a procedure readily discerned in Adorno. Typically he sets up the kind of conundrum noted in the first chapter of this book: for example, by bringing together two or more "nice" terms – *concerts* and *leisure* – and then turning them dialectically on their negative heads (at Schoenberg's concerts, listeners must work for their leisure), he renders his verdict: not nice. In truth, Adorno was an *amateur* of "just for nice," a collector of the apparently unconflicted nicety, which the *Minima Moralia* catalogues in small part.[16] Again, this explains something of his North American success: exiled into a "paradise" of niceness, the United States of America at mid-century, he never lacked for objects to study.[17]

Adorno does not necessarily say nice things about the music he most cares for as a philosopher, be it Schoenberg or jazz. For many music scholars, however, liking music – avowedly or tacitly – is a precondition: if we don't like a work of music first, then we can't get inside it and thus are barred from knowing it truly. Adorno was quite capable of liking music as a private person, and this private appreciation often spills over into his work. But as a philosopher of negative dialectics, he seeks out contradictions and contraries, and thus his approach does not necessarily accord with saying nice things. Adorno had a trick for turning niceties into brickbats. He can, thereby, be put to good use as a counterfoil to a musicological culture often Bambi-like in its mind-numbing adherence to niceness.

The assumption that scholarly engagement with music requires a love for music distinguishes music scholars from colleagues in other disciplines for whom a critical distance simply cannot be compromised by close aesthetic attraction – colleagues who study diseases or hurricanes, for example. Toxicologists can say nasty things about the substances they study. Conventional wisdom says, however, that lacking sympathy for the music under study, a musicologist ought to avoid discussing it at all. For this reason, Adorno is easily dismissed by popular and classical music scholars alike. He is a curmudgeon, a snob, and a killjoy. If only he knew, for example, Coltrane's work instead of tepid swing bands from the 1940s and 1950s, he would have learned to like jazz. But this begs a critical question: if the science of musicology is built on a foundation of "like" and "dislike," then should it take itself seriously as a critical study (and should anyone else)?

Adorno, of course, was not the first critic to be suspicious of an uncritical engagement with works of music, a fear to be traced as far back at least as St. Augustine, if not Plato. The essence of Hanslick's argument in *On the Musically Beautiful* is that feelings are untrustworthy when held to the point of intoxication, which invalidates objective criticism.[18] Hanslick sought to resolve this problem by bluntly evacuating feeling and replacing it with mechanical form as an aesthetic criterion.[19]

Unlike Hanslick, however, Adorno keeps feelings as a part of his critical project, albeit from a distanced perspective that does not implicate his own feelings. Via dialectics, emotion is an object for critical diagnosis.[20] The emotional listener has as much social significance for Adorno as does Mahler, perhaps more. Adorno can appraise the emotional listener's situation from a critical remove without direct reference to his own emotion. Thus emotions are worthy of a much greater critical attention, certainly as a sociological index.

Central to Adorno's appraisal is the possibility that music elicits only bridled feeling, an all too rational emotional constraint – the need to behave, be good, be nice. In order to belong to a social group, listeners "obey musically," they do not question critically the meaning of the music they listen to but instead follow the crowd, indeed push to the head of the line: "the pressure to be permitted to obey musically, as elsewhere, is today more general than ever."[21] The need to abase oneself – and more so the need to legitimize one's self-abasement – is a principal ingredient in the toxic cocktail that Adorno calls the "fetish character" in music.

The fetishistic listener demands, for example, that the critic condone their behaviour. The actual value of the work thus becomes secondary. They demand of the critic: "We sat here nicely, without clearing our throats or coughing for an hour and a half, and surely that counts for something. But if you say the work is no good or the performance uninspired, then you make us look like chumps, and surely we have wasted our time – sitting here so nicely behaved for nothing. We might have stayed home and watched television in comfort. So say something nice about the work and performance. Don't gripe. Don't make us feel as if we have undergone this considerable trial of patience for nothing."

Here the musical work, as a commodity, takes on anthropomorphic qualities, something not only to be revered but obeyed. It demands of the listener a form of obeisance. Recognizing the elevation of the musical work – the "commodity" – to the position of a deity, Adorno says, "Before the theological caprices of commodities, the consumers become temple slaves."[22] To question the musical work is to cast aspersions on divine right.

For this reason, Adorno is seen as *manqué*. He will not acknowledge the primacy of the musical work (and its emissaries – the maestro conductor, the virtuoso soloist, the star). Instead he subjects the work to the very same criticism as he might a zoological specimen[23] or anti-Semitism.[24] Accordingly he is dismissed as a crank and a boor, dismissal being most severe in the case of his jazz criticism.

It must be said from the outset, however, that there is an element of naïveté in Adorno's jazz critique. In the essay, "Perennial Fashion – Jazz," Adorno posits a Utopian moment, a jazz Eden.[25] In its *Ur*-state, jazz was irrational, insubordinate, and anarchic. He allies this original moment with early jazz – New Orleans and Chicago – after which comes rupture. Some of the original anarchic animation is still to be discerned where "there is real improvisation, in oppositional groups which perhaps indulge in such things out of sheer pleasure."[26] Exceptions aside, there is a conformity in jazz, the product of what we shall call, after Adorno, *rationalization*. In other words, once there was an Eden, from which jazz was later expelled and to which occasional uncontrived moments will harken. We recognize similarities to the naive accounts of pre-capitalist societies given by Marx and Engels. There is a fall from a state of grace, expulsion from the garden because of the temptations of exchange.

Thereafter, however, Adorno's naïveté is set to one side in favour of dialectics. In the case of jazz, the vehicle for expulsion from Eden is not necessarily a forbidden fruit (although heroin is the fruit of the poppy), nor is it necessarily Late Capitalism, although capitalism may be a cause. The vehicle is the jazz enthusiast, if not the jazz musician himself. Expulsion is achieved through a dialectic transformation, a self-repression that takes the form of compliance: "What is common to the jazz enthusiast of all countries, however, is the moment of compliance, in parodistic exaggeration."[27]

Compliance is effected by means of commodification, which Adorno calls here "commercialization and the audience," as a response to "commercial requirements": "The wild antics of the first jazz bands from the South, New Orleans above all, and those from Chicago, have been toned down with the growth of commercialization and of the audience, and ... efforts to recover some of this original animation, whether called 'swing' or 'bop', inexorably succumb to commercial requirements and quickly lose their sting."[28]

Compliance is also brought about through rationalization. The "wild antics" gave way to basic jazz formulae (presumably the ii-V-I pattern, the AABA head and bridge form, and certain jazz clichés): "what appears as spontaneity is in fact carefully planned out in advance with machinelike precision ... so-called improvisations are actually reduced to the more or less feeble rehashing of basic formulas in which the schema shines through at every moment."[29] The compliant result is strict adherence to convention, to the formulaic, a status quo that would seem to have gone on and will continue to go on forever; hence the term *perennial fashion*, an oxymoron, given its dialectic treatment in Adorno's hands. By its very nature, fashion should change, and in doing so attain its legitimation (Adorno calls it "dignity") as a vehicle for change. Perennial fashion means no change at all, merely the repetition of the same – everything is divisible by 1. The dignity of change is sacrificed to the indignity of the predictable.[30]

Perennial fashion is produced by capital and commodification.[31] This is what Adorno means by the term *standardization*, a term that often elicits the scorn of popular music scholars: "Standardization, moreover, means the strengthening of the lasting domination of the listening public and of their conditioned reflexes. They are expected to want only that to which they have become accustomed and to become enraged whenever their expectations are disappointed and fulfillment, which they regard as the customer's inalienable right, is denied."[32] At root here is the inherent stasis of commodification. How, after all, is one to make a profit, if forced by changing fashions to constantly and radically retool one's factories? Better to keep things nice and simple.

It makes excellent commercial sense to enlist the perennial compliance of the audience, their inherent instinct as bourgeois citizens. They become self-censors, inflicting heavy fines on those who would run against perennial fashion. Held in line thus, society becomes an ever-narrowing field of phony choices: "And even if there were attempts to introduce anything really different into light music, they would be doomed from the start by virtue of economic concentration."[33]

Here is the true subject of Adorno's jazz essay, and a lesson for critics following in his stead: the self-infliction of wounds in the service of capitalism. (And the jazz audience differs not a whit from the audience at Bayreuth in this regard.) Freedom of invention is antithetical to the free access to commodities. Capitalism achieves the latter by assuring each person the right to acquire exactly the same commodities and to precisely the same extent as their neighbour. To avoid inequality (which would compromise freedom), only a perennial equal access is allowed – no more, no less.

Sensing this, audiences recoil from the original and the inventive as if it were a transgression of liberty: not nice! In what must be one of Adorno's darkest passages on jazz music, he speaks of cultural castration – where "things not wholly integrated" are surgically removed. The result is a taboo on artistic expression. Jazz is a self-castrating art; it fears its intense personal subjectivity, its individuality; it sheds its wilder parts in deference to milder forms more attractive to the great commonwealth of listeners, and to the industry that feeds them: "The castration symbolism, deeply buried in the practices of jazz and cut off from consciousness through the institutionalization of perennial sameness, is for that very reason probably all the more potent. And sociologically, jazz has the effect of strengthening and extending, down to the very physiology of the subject, the acceptance of a dreamless-realistic world in which all memories of things not wholly integrated have been purged ... The expressive impulse is exposed to the same threat of castration that is symbolized and mechanically and ritually subdued in jazz."[34]

The removal of the non-identical (in commodification as in dialectics) becomes a common cause in consumption. The more original the artist, the more he is made to seem weird, *seltsam*. His work is transformed, as we saw in the case of Coltrane, to comply with a spurious mystical transcendence demanded by the commodity relation.

Thus in the name of freedom, jazz is repressed, turned by commercialization and standardization into a vehicle for self-repression available to all. The irony is not lost on Adorno. In the eyes of a free market, freedom of invention and expression is a pariah and should be degraded. The truly inventive artist should be made to feel that he deserves abuse. Thus Schoenberg was made to feel – one moment destroyed by lack of acceptance, one moment destroyed by acceptance: "As soon as the war was over, there came another wave which procured for me a popularity unsurpassed since. My works were played everywhere and acclaimed in such a manner that I started to doubt the value of my music ... If previously my music had been difficult to understand on account of the peculiarities of my ideas and the way in which I expressed them, how could it happen that now, all of a sudden, everybody could follow my ideas and like them? Either the music or the audience was worthless."[35] This sort of repression, as noted, is best carried out by the artists themselves (such as Schoenberg), who are made to recant their crimes as if they were sins against true freedom: "The subject which expresses itself expresses precisely this: I am nothing, I am filth, no matter what they do to me, it serves me right. Potentially this subject has already become one of those Russians, accused of a crime, and who, although innocent, collaborates with the prosecutor from the beginning and is incapable of finding a punishment severe enough ... Art is permitted to survive only if it renounces the right to be different, and integrates itself into the omnipotent realm of the profane."[36] Thus jazz co-opts its participants, musicians and listeners alike, in the suppression of their freedoms.

To extrapolate, after Adorno, in terms of death, a mythological distinction is often drawn between classical composers, on the one side, and jazz musicians such as Billie Holiday and Charlie Parker, on the other. There is an unaccountable injustice to the tragedy of the deaths of Mozart and Schubert, thus absolving the departed of any complicity. The heroes of classical music are called suddenly and unaccountably to a kind of holy transcendence, as if lofted to heaven by the strains of their heavenly work. Cut down, most in the prime of life, their passing cannot be explained by earthly behaviour; milieu, life, and work give no indication of impending demise. They fall suddenly from life into a state of grace. (And thus rumours of illicit behaviour and consequent disease on the part of Schubert, for instance, are received with horror, whereas for a jazz or popular musician they would be received as *de rigeur*.)

Not so, their jazz counterparts (with the exception of Coltrane, in his *ersatz* transcendence), for their death is quotidian. In death, they are denied the dignity accorded their classical counterparts. Instead they are branded as the authors of their misfortune or as childishly insensitive to their impending demise; either way they come up culpable. The jazz musician is either made to take full responsibility – "They were drug addicts, alcoholics, dissolutes who should have restrained themselves" – or they are turned into simpletons by forces beyond their control – "She succumbed to the overwhelming temptations of booze and heroin." By a kind of cultural profiling, jazz musicians are made guilty of death by irresponsibility until proven innocent.

To all this there is a tawdry perennial sameness, like that which Adorno discerns in the genre. The jazz musician cannot rise above his station in death. Instead he must be brought down to the level of his audience and then debased by allusion to drugs and crime.

The discrepancy between death accounts – classical and jazz – is uncanny and suggests the power of the latter form. To follow Adorno's line of thought, having made the jazz musician into something abhorrent in the course of his life, society is not content to exact of him a toll when living – requiring the destruction of his creativity, the means by which he gained identity and consequent dignity (by forcing him to "sell out" to commercial interests), or sequestering him to a life of poverty (and consequently to addiction and other forms of self-abuse) for his stubborn refusal to sacrifice creativity. Society must also pursue him into the grave to deny him the dignity of a death without blame. *Requiem aeternum* and perennial.

Given his diagnosis of self-inflicted repression on the part of the jazz audience, Adorno is filled with disdain for intellectuals who, in writing about jazz, treat it as a resurgence of a pure and true nature, phoenix-like, from the ashes of museum culture: "in Europe, where jazz has not yet become an everyday phenomenon, there is the tendency, especially among those devotees who have adopted it as a *Weltanschauung*, to regard it falsely as a break-through of original, untrammeled nature, as a triumph over the musty museum-culture."[37] Above all Adorno disparages the pretension of the intellectual jazz fan, especially those who, adopting the phony distinction between high and low forms of art, play one form off against the other to the detriment of both. Either they falsely denigrate the low from the contrived position of the high, or they attempt to raise the low (and consequently lower the high) and in doing so wind up in a barbaric middle ground where legitimate distinctions are passed over in preference for illegitimate.[38] As a consequence no one cares anymore, and the result is a perennial sameness. "Who cares?" becomes a critical verdict, heard perennially like a skip on a vinyl LP.

Jazz fans and intellectuals respond, however. Among Adorno's harshest critics are scholars of popular music, who find him anti-sympathetic and irredeemably elitist.[39] Richard Middleton's extended and subtle criticism of Adorno, "'It's all over now'. Popular music and mass culture – Adorno's theory," in the 1990 *Studying Popular Music* (a book that set the nascent field of popular music studies on its feet) represents the reception accorded Adorno generally by popular music studies.[40] At the end of the chapter, Middleton proposes that one must "put Adorno's critical pessimism in its correct place."[41] Middleton means curtailing the pessimism. He is an optimist, and he faults Adorno for not being one: "He has no *logical* grounds for the theoretical closure he operates, only a self-fulfilling pessimism ... [H]e fails to follow his quest into places where he could have found what he sought, and, more damagingly, he excludes the possibility of any other mode of critique than that associated with alienated individualism."[42] There are logical grounds for Adorno's position, certainly if one treats his response to Hegel, Kant, Lukács, and Heidegger, among other European philosophers, as logical, since it is argued from their logical premises. But my crucial disagreement with Middleton pertains to the notion that Adorno could have "found what he sought" if he had merely looked elsewhere. Adorno wasn't seeking something he failed to locate. Instead he found exactly what he was looking for in popular music – a mind-numbing climate of critical niceness, the product of identity thinking run rampant.

Middleton was seeking something he would not find in Adorno, indeed something that Adorno never promised. Middleton aims to describe a formalist aesthetic experience, like that customarily accorded classical music, with something like middle Beethoven as its acme and Hanslick as its protagonist. Although Adorno might have sought this kind of aesthetic engagement privately, it was not his project professionally. This is not to say that Adorno disregarded aesthetic engagement completely (for he devoted a major treatise to the subject). It is to say simply that Adorno's critical work on popular music was sociological in a way that should not be confused with a formalist aesthetic experience.[43]

Adorno was seeking social contradictions that, when viewed from the perspective of negative dialectics, might reveal with a modicum of objectivity the state of a given society. On the one hand he went in search of firmly but obscurely held beliefs, while on the other hand he sought out material conditions that ought to correspond to these same beliefs but didn't. For example, someone notes in a song that to his detriment he was born in country XYZ. But then as a commodity the song becomes a one-line anthem of national pride largely on the strength of its title, "Born in the XYZ," the full sense of the lyric being studiously ignored. The disparity – negative – between the fact of the song and the misguided beliefs that attend it says more about the culture of the song's reception than would any sociological analysis of the lyrics or the composer themselves.

Inevitably, from Adorno's perspective, belief and fact do not match, and this disparity validates the negative method. In the negative gulf between belief and material fact – the gulf remaindered when one is compared to the other – lies a wisdom that cannot be attained except by negation. This negative wisdom – the wisdom derived in particular from examining belief in light of materialism – is precisely what Adorno was looking for in his analyses of popular music.

Middleton's perspective, however, is the opposite of negation. His approach is essentially positive, and a positive perspective on popular music studies is not necessarily to be faulted. (Taking a positive attitude – in the sense of identity thinking – to popular music was a necessity in Middleton's day, a vehicle by which to overcome the disparagement that a traditionally positivist classical musicology accorded the study of popular idioms.)

By its positive nature, however, Middleton's approach works like oil to Adorno's water: the two positions separate from each other on an almost molecular level and are incapable of mixing. Adorno's philosophy of criticism through negation, the root and foundation of his approach (which cannot be discarded for another philosophy) is necessarily critically pessimistic. For Adorno, music is an exceptionally apt test case for philosophy. If it were possible to separate music and philosophy in his thought, one might say that philosophy – negative philosophy – comes first, and music comes second as an explication and an application of that philosophy. For Middleton, however, the appreciation of music is principal and in that regard music demands a unified perspective blended of disparate and often competing philosophies (Adorno, Benjamin, Gramsci, among others). Music comes first, in other words. Herein lies an essential difference between Adorno and Middleton, which, if not accounted for at the very beginning, will surely compound itself in later misunderstanding.

Most of the errors Middleton finds in Adorno's approach can be assigned to the following three categories:

1 Insensitive. Adorno is insensitive; by seeing popular music in one and only one light, he misses its attractive shades and nuances.
2 Too materialistic. Adorno concentrates on the commodity value of musical works and thus ignores artistic value; he sacrifices aesthetics to historical materialism.
3 Too autonomous, too totalizing. Adorno grants too much autonomy to musical works, while approaching society from too grand, too totalizing a perspective.

I shall treat each category individually by examining Middleton's argument in light of Adorno's thought.

Framing the charge of insensitivity, Middleton calls Adorno's approach monolithic.[44] Adorno's view of political economies is based on one historical period – Germany in the 1930s – when economic forces operated with a quite unusual homogeneity. According to Middleton, the current state of affairs is nowhere near so monolithic and uniform. And, most importantly, in its many subtleties certain forms of resistance to homogenizing tendencies are thriving: "What we can say ... is that the picture which emerges from [the current history of modern popular music] is not of a monolithic bloc but of a constantly mutating organism made up of elements which are symbiotic and mutually contradictory *at the same time*."[45]

The principal monolith, for Middleton, is the entertainment industry, which Adorno paints as a smoothly homogenized productive force – the system. On Middleton's account, that system has broken down and is nowhere near as homogenized as in Adorno's day. The musical situation comprises "*spaces* which the system cannot close off or remove, however much it wants to, and which ensure the *possibility* of conflicts within the productive forces as a

whole."[46] Adorno's model of the music industry, then, is incompatible with present circumstances – too insensitive. The large, multi-
national labels contest with the independents for market share and
in a complementary fashion rely on the independents for innovation. Thus the industry shakes in regular convulsions, vacillating
between innovation and consolidation, resistance and appropriation. Nowhere does Adorno address this dynamic.

If this is the case, then at best Adorno's ideas are appropriate
only to a milieu in which an extreme form of industrial or political
hegemony holds sway. (Adorno's approach would be inappropriate
in our time, where, despite the amalgamation of the grand record
companies, the independent record producers hold sway over large
parts of the industry in some parts of the world, such as the United
Kingdom.) More to the point for Middleton, Adorno's ideas are
too bound up with a single, synthesizing social perspective – commodification after Marx – that slides all forms of social endeav-
our under one vision of economics to the detriment (in Middleton's
thought) of musics that are "socially specific." Middleton's accusation against Adorno, then, is much the same as Adorno's against
Lukács – a theoretical insensitivity to the individual instance (to the
"epic modern hero" whom Lukács seems to leave behind in *History and Class Consciousness*): "But an *empirical* recognition that in
some circumstances a particular productive force (say, a composer
or a performer) may not be wholly homogenized means that such a
possibility must be allowed on the level of *theory*."[47]

But what exactly is the level of theory on which Adorno effects his
homogenization? Is it musical? If Adorno's theory is located solely
in an exclusive domain of music, then Middleton is again correct:
Adorno's work is far too totalizing and insensitive to be applicable to the dynamics of musical production in our day. But neither
musical style nor for that matter sociology exhausts the subject matter of Adorno's theoretical foundation. Philosophy does.

As a theorist, Adorno is concerned with the methodology for
discerning fundamental philosophical truths, often Marxist philosophical truths like the alienation of labour implicit in any kind of
commodified production – musical or otherwise – in capitalism.
Being a philosophical proposition (and accordingly not restricted
to one style or historical period), negative dialectics must be universally applicable. In this sense, Middleton is correct. Adorno's theory
is unquestionably homogenizing because every critical observation

must submit to the rigour of dialectic examination. This is the level at which Adorno should be critiqued, and in that critique, the elements of a philosophical alternative should reside.

To put the shoe on the other foot, how are we to determine the veracity of Middleton's account of a "constantly mutating organism made up of elements which are symbiotic and mutually contradictory at the same time"?[48] What method has he used to arrive at this assertion? Is he relying on anecdote or an empirical sample of disinterested testimony? Has Middleton been able to transcend his personal orientation to class differentiation and struggle (shaped in defiance of the politics of Margaret Thatcher) in making this assessment? Or has that orientation – held nicely in abeyance for the most part, but readily discernible from time to time – coloured the investigation in an inordinate manner?

Seen in an activist context, Middleton's claims for diversity in production may ring true (and they are a positive prescription for a healthy musical economy).[49] But they do not address Adorno's principal and thus homogenizing goal – a dispassionate if pessimistic dialectic assessment of musical affairs *in toto* in capitalism. Middleton's work is firmly enshrined in a tradition of identity thinking, and for this reason alone Adorno's work will prove counterintuitive to it.

Turning to the second category, in making his claim that Adorno is too materialist, Middleton curiously espouses a kind of romanticism. Adorno, too much the historical materialist, leaves out of consideration the appeal of a formalist aesthetics. Middleton counters that his culture is not reducible ultimately to commodity relations. He cites Simon Frith: "music can never be *just* a product (an exchange value), even in its rawest commodity form; the artistic value of records has an unavoidable complicating effect on their production."[50] In other words, music, unlike widgets, is art; it carries an artistic component that will not allow for commodification as just another product. This artistic component resists the monolith and spawns diversity.

Middleton's turn toward romanticism inscribes romantic concepts in an area largely neglected as barrenly unromantic. Popular music produces its own romantic spirits, Beethovenian in their individualistic musical conception.[51] A Pantheon of classical artists arises as a phoenix out of the ashes and general detritus of vernacular culture. Middleton cites Jon Stratton, in whose view "the 'romantic' image of the creative artist is no false veneer nor confined to 'mass culture', but part of a larger tradition, within which the dialectic of 'romanticism' and commodification is basic to capitalist culture as such; thus it implicates the 'individualism' of, say, Beethoven as well as that of pop stars and composers. If these arguments are valid, they create *spaces* which the system cannot close off or remove."[52] Stratton (via Middleton) suggests that romanticism creates a niche in the system, an aesthetic pocket that the distinctions legitimate-versus-illegitimate, classical-versus-popular, cannot penetrate. Thus romanticism smooths out nicely the polarized differences between genres.

Middleton's romanticism transcends capitalism. Pop stars are just as worthy of the distinction "classic" as Beethoven and for the same reasons – they appeal to an absolute category of individualism, one that takes no account of use value and original labour. And thus Middleton creates a new monolith with which to supplant Adorno's.

Here is Middleton's oil to Adorno's water. Criticizing Adorno for a lack of romanticism is simply inappropriate, for romanticism is invalidated by Adorno's fundamental theoretical framework. Classical music, avant-garde music, popular music – all are subject to the same provisos, but in Adorno's hands these are historical materialism and negative dialectics. Adorno exalts no artist for romantic reasons. Instead Adorno exalts artists – avowedly in the case of late-style Beethoven, tacitly in the case of Schoenberg and the artists of popular music – for the critical insight their work affords.

It may have been methodologically sound for Middleton to go looking for ideal instances in popular music, especially where his task was to legitimize popular music studies in the academic and scholarly institutions where romantic conceptions still held sway. But to hold Adorno to the same legitimizing project is anachronistic; as we shall see, in some of his writings on classical music, Adorno seems more than intent on taking romanticism apart.

Middleton's criticisms converge on the third category, which holds to one important but contradictory thesis: Adorno grants too much autonomy to musical works. For Adorno, the material fact of musical works overrides the power of individual musicians and listeners to affect change in the modes of musical production. Thus Adorno's aesthetic, on Middleton's account, is too mechanistic, overriding valid distinctions between repertoires and styles, conscious distinctions that any listener might make. For Middleton, Adorno's autonomy deprives the ordinary listener of the ability to make her own decisions.

Middleton is again correct. According to Adorno, the commodification of cultural objects is carried out in most part at a level far below the critical consciousness of all but the most perceptive listener – the ideal listener. The ideological practices of alienation are far too subtle in indoctrination to be perceived consciously by the subject, and hence their products – works of art, in particular – appear as autonomous. On the level of commodification, belief and actual material circumstance rarely coincide (and thus necessitate negative dialectics).[53]

To Adorno's materialist notion of a work's autonomy, Middleton opposes his own romantically monolithic vision of an isolated, autonomous, and thus absolute musical work (along the lines of Clive Bell's notion of the isolated work of art). As I have discussed elsewhere, Middleton demonstrates the limitations of Adorno's thought by appeal to a set of immutable criteria in an analysis of Gershwin's "These Foolish Things."[54] He states: "A pity [Adorno] could not have read Alec Wilder's *American Popular Song* (1972) which, using basically the same musical criteria as Adorno – derived from European bourgeois art music – could have been designed as a riposte to his view of this repertory."[55] The kind of analytic observations this riposte produces, however, bear only the slightest resemblance to Adorno's thought. Middleton observes: "the shapely overall curve" of the melody, "the way a certain simple (innocent?) *pentatonic* inflection ... rubs against the 'romantic' harmonies," "'foreign harmonies' that seem to function as a disturbance ... [of] tonal stability ... a technique derived directly from the nineteenth-century *Lied* and piano character piece."[56] Observations of this sort, however, would be merely a starting point for Adorno. Compare the following passage, from the collection of aphorisms entitled "Motifs" in *Quasi una Fantasia*. It contains technical details (albeit of a fictive, archetypal waltz) – the identification of pitches and chords (which I indicate as section 2 in the quotation) – to which Adorno applies emotive qualifiers. But these are only the starting point for a dialectical negation that frames the whole (sections 1 and 3):

[1] There is music from the nineteenth century which is so unbearably solemn that it can only be used to introduce waltzes. If it were left as it is, people listening to it would fall into a despair beside which every other musical emotion would pale.

All the feelings of great tragedy would surely overwhelm them and they would have to veil their heads with gestures that have fallen out of use since time immemorial. This music no longer possesses a form with which to clothe its minor key. Chords are struck alternating with plangent tunes, and each stands on its own so that the listener is exposed to them in their naked immediacy. Only the excess of pain helps which springs from the certainty that things cannot go on like this. [2] The double attack of F in the violins, the dominant of B-flat minor – a pathetic remnant of sadness together with a tiny E grace note, which a moment later will drive on the waltz melody in sharp, jolly spasms, always staccato and always in the train of the E. [3] Nowadays such music thrives for the most part only in the band music played in zoos or in the small orchestras in provincial spas. Children are its greatest fans. It sounds best when heard at a fair distance.[57]

Adorno's observations, particularly in part 2, conjure attitudes and emotions comparable to those brought out in Middleton's appreciation – in Adorno's case, a tone of sadness and pathos. But the whole is delivered tongue-in-cheek, framed in such a way as to turn pathos into bathos. The analytic observations of chord and note are all negated by the two images that frame them – on the one hand, despair and an archaic, overwhelming tragedy, on the other, zoos, spas, and children. Here again discrepant images are put together to push the observation of details into more profound revelations and thus negate the tongue-in-cheek dismissive tone: the remarkable prescience of children yields insight into a musical world where archaisms bind with a deep power (Adorno called it *chthonic*), a world that must be sequestered, however, in zoos and spas (and relegated to bands) in favour of a more readily consumable musical commodity, both classical and popular. An absolute appreciation such as that which Middleton accords Gershwin neither takes nor gives any account of itself in terms of its social milieu or a social history.

Nothing could be further from Adorno's conception of autonomy. The work is autonomous not through an isolation achieved by a solely musical perfection but because under capitalism it has become the perfect symptom, *opus perfectum et optimum*, of a bourgeois milieu – the perfect bourgeois crime. In its perfection as a symptom, it is absolute; it cannot be tampered with. Social and class relationships are reified in the musical work so absolutely that it functions autonomously, without any need of conscious interest, bourgeois or otherwise. As Adorno puts it, "The reification of art is the result of a socio-economic development that transforms all goods into consumer goods, makes them abstractly exchangeable, and has therefore torn them asunder from the immediacy of use. The autonomy of art, its quality of being a law unto itself, the impossibility of arranging it at will according to the dictates of use, is ... the expression of that reification."[58]

Middleton, then, misunderstands Adorno's position on these three crucial points. First, Adorno is indeed insensitive to the shades and nuances of popular music, but his critical aim lies far afield of shade and nuance. He is after critical perspective, a broad critical perspective, methodological at heart, a perspective that will allow shades and nuances to be grounded theoretically (as participants in a thoroughgoing dialectics). Second, as Middleton suggests, Adorno is locked into a materialist perspective. But he is locked in through distrust of romantic concepts (such as the classicizing tendency discerned in modern popular music). Third, Middleton misunderstands Adorno's concept of autonomy: commodification situates the art work as an autonomous entity beyond consciousness (certainly beyond the consciousness of the bourgeois). But this autonomy lends a rigour to the critical analysis of the work in society. Middleton, like other popular music critics, mistakes Adorno's project for something it is not and, given its theoretical framework, could not be.

Adorno exempts at least two repertoires of classical music from the acidic criticism he levels at classical music in general and at popular music. If he doesn't exactly say nice things about them, at least he does not labour to discern discrepancies in them to the same degree as in popular repertoires. The first repertoire includes Late Style Beethoven, most of Mahler's work, Schoenberg's *Moses und Aron*, and a few other works that, like these, best embody the sense of being critically *outré*. They are exempt because in them negative dialectic criticism is more than immanent. These are works of a special hypercritical nature – works that illuminate the negative dialectics in other musical repertoires; or, in the case of *Moses und Aron*, that illuminate the negative dialectics of theology or another subject beyond music *per se*. The second repertoire includes works like Schoenberg's middle-period piano pieces, the three pieces of op. 11 for example. It may be that these works are simply too close to Adorno for him to be professionally objective about them, and so he skirts them, referring to them all too briefly. (It may also be that, in the case of Schoenberg for example, the works themselves are overshadowed for Adorno by the negative dialectics of their putatively "naive" composer.)

These exemptions aside, classical repertoires, producers, listeners, and performers are regularly dipped in the acid bath of Adorno's criticism, although not with the same frequency as the objects of popular music. I shall examine these critiques briefly, not only to assuage the accusations of bias levelled at Adorno but to show the continuity with his popular music critiques. I shall touch upon three by now familiar issues: fetish, commodity, and reception.

The fetish aspect of classical music's reception is described with particular clarity in two essays, "On the Fetish Character in Music" and "On the Social Situation of Music," in terms similar to those applied to popular music. The classical music listener displays the same reifying fetishistic responses as their popular counterpart: reaction to musical stimulus is automatic, accomplished spontaneously, like saliva elicited in Pavlov's famous dog. The stimulus in the experiment is administered by the "publishers, sound film magnates and rulers of radio": "The composition business which extends peacefully from Irving Berlin and Walter Donaldson ... by way of Gershwin, Sibelius and Tchaikovsky to Schubert's B Minor Symphony, labelled *The Unfinished*, is one of fetishes ... The reactions of the listeners appear to have no relation to the playing of the music. They have reference, rather, to the cumulative success which, for its part, cannot be thought of un-alienated by the past spontaneities of listeners, but instead dates back to the command of publishers, sound film magnates and rulers of radio."[59] The fetishistic response is completely out of relation to the stimulus. The response of Adorno's "entertainment listener" (be it to classical or popular music, Adorno doesn't specify) is comparable to addiction. "The structure of this sort of listening is like that of smoking. We define it more by our displeasure in turning the radio off than by the pleasure we feel, however modestly, while it is playing. No one knows the size of the group that will, as it has often been put, let itself be sprinkled with broadcast music without really listening; but that unknown size illuminates the whole domain."[60] The operant term here is *broadcast music*, which for Adorno entails Toscanini as well as Tommy

Dorsey. The fetish gives rise to a kind of psychosis whereby the addict is pressed to defend her addiction. And so the fetish gives rise to a kind of psychosis. The listener's capacity for responsible activity (political for example) is disabled, and only those activities that feed addiction remain: "The representatives of the entertainment type are resolutely passive and fiercely opposed to the effort which a work of art demands ... He is a self-conscious lowbrow who makes a virtue of his own mediocrity ... The type has no political profile. But, as in music, he will probably conform in reality to any rule that does not patently impair his consumer standard."[61]

Not only the repertoires themselves but the very vehicle of musical sound is made subject to fetish. The violin used in a performance – the Stradivarius infatuation – assumes a mythic and thus fabulous importance, since most listeners cannot detect readily the subtleties of a great violin sound. By distracting themselves with a phantom, modern listeners make crystal clear the material circumstances of the commodity exchange: "All this reaches a climax of absurdity in the cult of the master violins. One promptly goes into raptures at the well-announced sound of a Stradivarius or Amati, which only the ear of a specialist can tell from that of a good modern violin, forgetting in the process to listen to the composition and the execution, from which there is still something to be had."[62] One object of consumption – one commodity – might be substituted freely for another; Beethoven might be substituted for a "hit song" just as easily, Adorno says, as Beethoven for a bikini (or vice versa). The stimulus evokes a perennially vapid reaction on both accounts.

> If the moments of sensual pleasure in the idea, the voice, the instrument are made into fetishes and torn away from any functions which could give them meaning, they meet a response equally isolated, equally far from the meaning of the whole, and equally determined by success in the blind and irrational emotions which form the relationship to music into which those with no relationship enter. But these are the same relations as exist between the consumers of hit songs and the hit songs. Their only relation is to the completely alien, and the alien, as if cut off from the consciousness of the masses by a dense screen, is what seeks to speak for the silent. Where they react at all, it no longer makes any difference whether it is to Beethoven's Seventh Symphony or to a bikini.[63]

In this culture of musical commodities, Adorno likens the conductor to "the head of a capitalist combine," "the monopoly lord," the magnate of the entertainment industry. Indulging the audience its fantasies, the conductor embodies corporally the fetish object. The listener yearns for "vital fullness ... uninhibited verve ... animated organic quality ... direct non-reified awareness." Since capitalism and commodification will not allow these qualities to exist as use values, the conductor will supply them *ersatz* as exchange values: "The dream image of vital fullness and uninhibited verve, of animated organic quality and direct, non-reified inwardness are provided by him corporally for those to whom capitalist economy denies in reality the fulfilment of all such wishes; and it further strengthens them in their faith in their own substance, brought to the fore by those very immortal, better to say immutable, works he [the conductor] evoked."[64] The appeal of Bruckner's music (to which few conductors are immune) is revealed in this light: a mimicry of the authentic, it gives a phony vitality and verve to the dry bones on the charnel house floor. The great conductors and Bruckner are characters in an allegory after Walter Benjamin, death masks that point to a once vital past, or at least the bourgeois mythology of a vital past. In doing so, they transmute the unruly present into a fictive past so as to bring it under control:

Such a conductor stands in an alien or negating relation to contemporary production – in strict contrast to his predecessors in the nineteenth century; from time to time he offers a modern work as a horrifying example or permits new music at most the position of a transition to the restoration of the old art of the soul. Otherwise he clings to the heroic-bourgeois past – Beethoven – or to an author such as Anton Bruckner, who unites the pomp of social event with the same claim to animation and inwardness expressed by the prominent interpreter. The same type of conductor who undertakes an insatiably engrossed celebration of the adagio of Bruckner's Eighth lives a life closely akin to that of the head of a capitalist combine, uniting in his hand as many organizations, institutes and orchestras as possible; this is the exact social corollary to the individual structure of a figure whose task it is to reduce within capitalism musical trust and inwardness to the same common denominator.[65]

So, with the stroke of a baton, individualism – non-identity – is consigned to the trash bin.

The exchange value of classical music lies at the heart of the matter. Exchange value substitutes for artistic use value; the money paid for the ticket substitutes for the actual performance. It is as if, having paid to hear the latest artist at Carnegie Hall, the listener has acquitted his obligations and is freed thereby to stay home and watch the concert on television, since the difference between a live concert and its reproduction is negligible if both are commodities. Thus the modern concertgoer merely affirms what Marx had noted more than a century ago: the fetish creates exchange value out of thin air. Musical exchange values are insubstantial, and one can derive no enjoyment from such a lack of substance without converting it first into a fetish:

> All contemporary musical life is dominated by the commodity
> form: the last pre-capitalist residues have been eliminated. Music,
> with all the attributes of the ethereal and sublime which are gen-
> erously accorded it, serves in America today as an advertisement
> for commodities which one must acquire in order to be able to
> hear music. If the advertising function is carefully dimmed in
> the case of serious music, it always breaks through in the case
> of light music ...What makes its appearance, like an idol, out of
> such masses of type is the exchange-value in which the quantum
> of possible enjoyment has disappeared. Marx defines the fetish-
> character of the commodity as the veneration of the thing made
> by oneself which, as exchange-value, simultaneously alienates
> itself from producer to consumer ... The consumer is really wor-
> shipping the money that he himself has paid for the ticket to the
> Toscanini concert. He has literally "made" the success which he
> reifies and accepts as an objective criterion, without recognizing
> himself in it.[66]

The exchange value of cultural goods, however, is imbued with a special aura. Culture, in the bourgeois mind, has a kind of exchange-value-exempt status; cultural objects appear to such a mind as if handed directly from artist to audience without a "middleman" taking a cut of the action. But in a musical world filled with middlemen (the all too helpful conductor), direct and immediate engagement with artistic works is an illusion. Exchange value will not be denied, even in the presence of the maestro: "To be sure, exchange-value exerts its power in a special way in the realm of cultural goods. For in the world of commodities [the realm of art] appears to be exempted from the power of exchange, to be in an immediate relationship with the goods, and it is this appearance in turn which alone gives cultural goods their exchange-value. But they nevertheless simultaneously fall completely into the world of commodities, are produced for the market, and are aimed at the market. The appearance of immediacy is as strong as the compulsion of exchange-value is inexorable."[67]

Objects of musical enjoyment can be particularly acute representations of commodification, their extreme nature hidden by the veneer of enjoyment they elicit. In music, "The more inexorably the principle of exchange-value destroys use-values for human beings, the more deeply does exchange value disguise itself as the object of enjoyment." Anything that eludes the force of this rule (such as Beethoven's Late Style, Mahler, *Moses und Aron*) must be seen as subversive: "It has been asked what the cement is which still holds the world of commodities together. The answer is that this transfer of the use-value of consumption goods to their exchange-value contributes to a general order in which eventually every pleasure which emancipates itself from exchange-value takes on subversive features."[68]

The effect of commodification on a classical work of music is palpable and objective, as if it were passed around by grubby hands and in the process became brittle or flabby. The most telling effect is the breaking apart of what was integrity, so that all a listener can remember is a series of "irruptions" and disconnected moments. Brahms can be turned into rubble by a self-satisfied whistler: "The works which are the basis of the fetishization and become cultural goods experience constitutional changes as a result. They become vulgarized. Irrelevant consumption destroys them ... reification affects their internal structure. They are transformed into a conglomeration of irruptions which are impressed on the listeners by climax and repetition, while the organization of the whole makes no impression whatsoever ... The man who in the subway triumphantly whistles loudly the theme of the finale of Brahms's First is already primarily involved with its debris."[69]

Having thus appraised the current reception of classical music, Adorno is free to draw the necessary dialectical conclusion: as a commodity, classical music's elevated, positive image – the radio blather about transcendence and beauty, the scraping and sweeping that accompanies the famous conductor or the diva, the petty jealousies and intrigues backstage – is merely fodder for negative dialectics. The squeaky clean, noble, purified image – classical music as high art – doesn't fit its commodified reality.

The musicological intelligentsia sense this discrepancy but are of no use whatsoever. Capitalism has bludgeoned its way into classical music exactly as it did elsewhere, reifying all thought about art. This process produces a transformation in intellectual understanding, from music as high art to music as a universal art (both conceptions being patently false). Adorno sees this as a self-serving attempt to end the alienation of the intellectual. Conjuring the spectacle of the new radio programs broadcasting classical music to wide audiences, he says, "The positive aspect for which the new mass music and regressive listening are praised – vitality and technical progress, collective breadth and relation to an undefined practice, into whose concepts there has entered the supplicant self-denunciation of the intellectuals, who can thereby finally end their social alienation from the masses in order to coordinate themselves politically with the contemporary mass consciousness – this positive is negative, the irruption into music of a catastrophic phase of society. The positive lies locked up solely in its negativity."[70]

In passages of this sort, Adorno vents much the same spleen in critically exalting classical music as he does in exalting popular music. Classical music in a time of monolithic commodification merits just as much of his acerbic critical attention. As he says, the distinction between the reception of classical and popular music is now negligible: "The differences in the reception of official 'classical' music and light music no longer have any real significance."[71]

Thus a critic working after Adorno should see through the niceties of these distinctions – among them "high" versus "low" – regularly foisted on the binary "popular music versus serious." Both repertoires sport enough instances of identity thinking to illuminate many such distinctions as illegitimate (and to frame legitimate ones). The remaining essays in this book, while they will observe distinctions legitimate and otherwise, are aimed largely at framing the illegitimate.

Smashing pumpkins. An inarticulate negative critique forms the basis of a large number of popular music repertoires by bands that our parents warned us were "just not nice." Suspicion of positivity accounts for a grand *ethos* in some forms of popular music. The Rolling Stones have a *chthonic*-like element: rude boys, suggestive of heroin, clumsy in demeanour, rebellious against the facade of *politesse* and social adeptness that the Beatles manoeuvred shamelessly. No doubt over the years (early on in the case of the Stones) this critique was appropriated by the industry to its own ends. But, as the dark cousin to Middleton's optimistic *struggle*, the negativity, the nihilism, the garage-band-smash-the-***ing-daylights-out-of-this-stupid-song rebellion persists. Such a negativity cannot really be done justice by positive means.

Today's Parent. The producers of the 90s group *Spice Girls* effected a negative critique of the consciousness of society on the subject of pre-pubescent girls, for whom the *Girls* served as eminent role models. By the use of musical conventions derived from big band repertoires formerly associated with the darker aspects of lounges, Las Vegas, and aging Mafiosi, these selfsame producers have set forth clearly what perhaps several million parents have found incapable of clear and forceful articulation: society's current conception of very young women does not correspond to the material reality of maturing girls without leaving some remainder, a deep-seated confusion of identity in young minds. This is not to suggest that the playing of recordings by the *Spice Girls* ought to be limited by parental discretion. That would be out of keeping with Adorno's negative project, which is purely critical. But it is to suggest that the rage for *Spice Girls* is a perfect symptom of fetish in a world of cultural commodities where anything less than an absurd construal of young womanhood is no longer possible. Adorno, in this sense, proffers hope to parents everywhere.

Whispering. Pines. On the outskirts of a rural Alberta town, the following advertisement: "Whisper Inn. Good Nights Rest." The letter o's are pierced by holes produced by a high-powered rifle. What remains of a good night's sleep?

The Houghton Library at Harvard University houses the Rudolf Kolisch Papers, including Adorno correspondence.[72] In a postcard, dated "Truckee," 23 September 1947, sent from the "Truckee Resort," Highway 40, California, Adorno notes that "everything went alright with the car" and that they will be back in Los Angeles on Monday. The front of the postcard shows a small motel-like structure with silhouettes of large spruce and pine trees behind, a sign "Sportsmen" on the roof, and an aging dust-encrusted sedan parked in front.

Berg to Wiesengrund-Adorno, Vienna, 29.9.27, Joint Card
Do you remember, dear doctor, how the 4 of us sat here? *Where might you be now?* We extend you our affectionate greetings
Yours Berg

I hear that you intend to invite (not ask!) me to come to Italy. Please do not say no
Yours Soma [Morgenstern]

Dear Teddy, we long to see you! Helene
[Original: picture postcard: Vienna XIX Schlosshotel Koblenz; stamp: 29.IX.2[7].][73]

121 BENJAMIN TO HENNY GURLAND [AND ADORNO] [PORT BOU, 25.9.1940]
Dans une situation sans issue, je n'ai d'autre choix que d'en finir. C'est dans un petit village dans les Pyrénées où personne ne me connait ma vie va s'achever. Je vous prie de transmettre mes pensées à mon ami Adorno et de lui expliquer la situation où je me suis vu placé. Il ne me reste assez de temps pour écrire toutes ces lettres que j'eusse voulu écrire. [In a situation with no escape, I have no other choice but to finish it all. It is in a tiny village in the Pyrenees, where no one knows me, that my life must come to its end. I would ask you to pass on my thoughts to my friend Adorno, and to explain to him the situation in which I have now found myself. I no longer have enough time to write all those letters I would dearly have written.][74]

3

The Work of Music

With regard to construction it will be decisive to identify the moment of
negativity in the perfection of the middle works, a moment which took the
music beyond this perfection.

Adorno, *Beethoven: The Philosophy of Music*

When I was a small child, I had a recording of Burl Ives singing
"Froggy went a courtin'" in his inimitable style. I grew attached to
that recording, claimed it as entirely mine (not to be shared with
siblings), and demanded to hear it with a frequency that tempted
parental censure. One day, I was taken to a playmate's house. There,
spinning on the tiny turntable in his bedroom was my record, with
Burl Ives holding forth in just as genuine a manner as he had in my
own bedroom on my own tiny turntable. Disconsolate, I could be
persuaded only with the greatest difficulty that my friend had not
surreptitiously visited my house, rifled my bedroom, and absconded
with "Froggy." The realization that there were in fact two (possibly
more!) copies of the recording in circulation was traumatic, eliciting
tears not merely at the loss of "Froggy" but at loss *tout court*. Burl
Ives never seemed quite as genuine again. Every time I put the record
on the turntable a tiny apprehension came over me: was another
child doing exactly the same thing, putting stylus to record, just at
that moment somewhere else in the world?

In this instance the knowledge that there were two such recordings (or more!) transformed my initial immediate experience of the
song into an experience broken up and then reassembled, and mediated by self-consciousness.[1] This reassembled wholeness did nothing
to elide the discrepancy between the parts – the fact of the two records – or override their distinction, his record and mine. Instead my
new-found consciousness acknowledged the fracture, with a know-

ledge that remains to this day implicit whenever I hold a record in my hands.

First hearings are immediate: the work is heard as new and thus newly whole; its audition is unprecedented, and thus no distinctions – between past and present, the self and the work – have been drawn. A new work comes as a complete, self-contained object, not yet a commodity.

Hearing a musical recording, or just a passage thereof, for the second time, however, the listener is presented with two objects: something heard once before and its repetition. The listener adds to this a third, synthetic element, a conscious awareness that "the two are different."[2] In essence, repetition mediates the first object by means of the second, and the two fuse into a new whole.[3] This transformation produces a basic objectivity,[4] a conscious awareness, something which Adorno calls (in the passage quoted below) an "objective result," a "result, something attained."[5]

In the *Poco sustenuto* introduction to the first movement of Beethoven's Piano Trio in E-flat, op. 70, no. 2 and the subsequent *Allegro ma non troppo* at the onset of the movement proper, the violin and cello introduce motifs that are imitated immediately by the piano. For Adorno, something in this pianistic echo – its mechanical character – is functionally different, a *frisson* that catches the breath and in doing so makes us aware of breathing. The piano's repetitions of the motif are mediating: "On the Trio in E-flat major, op. 70: the first movement contains splendid examples of 'mediation': the motifs first appear successively in the two string parts, then on the piano. The latter's mechanical character is used to convey the dialectical meaning. The objective and, as it were, smaller sound of the piano presents each theme as a *result*, something attained."[6] Repetition produces a conscious detachment from the music, a detached awareness, a moment of critical reflection in the wake of immediate experience. Adorno heralds the detachment found in the trio as the "decisive feature" in Beethoven's music: "The *detachment* of the piece: nothing is *immediate* just as it is. Especially the introduction and the second subject group connected to it. This detached, non-literal quality is probably the decisive feature of Beethoven's work as a whole."[7] Detachment of this sort involves not simply the memory of the first experience but also the awareness of that memory – *cogito ergo* in the mirror. Memories born of repetition thus become

self-awareness, and the unity of identity thinking is irretrievably
lost, negated through mediation.

Repetition, then, is a rhetorical figure that draws attention away
from the musical object as heard and moves it allegorically toward
a larger design, the object *and* the listener. Repetition implies that
"I have been here before," and thus "I," the subject, is folded into
the equation along with the object. Repetition draws attention to
both the object and the subject, and to their existence conjoined as
the self.[8]

Repetition serves a sociological end: it makes a self-conscious
listener out of a simple listener.[9] And if the listener should pause to
think, "Some of us are aware of this repetition and some are not,"
then repetition has made a social theorist out of a self-conscious
listener.[10]

Self-consciousness carries with it the human responsibility of
the self to the selves of others. The self-consciousness produced by
repetition is not freedom. Complete and unfettered freedom lies in
forgetting the self. But Beethovenian self-knowledge is binding: repetition holds up a mirror to the self, producing a reflection in which
all the obligations of the self in the climate of Late Capitalism are
crisply revealed. Beethovenian self-consciousness is a responsibility
from which there is no escape. In essence, through repetition I come
to know myself, and coming to know myself thus, I am obligated to
be true to my self.

In Adorno's thoughts on music, this kind of mediating repetition
is not confined to musical motifs. A coda, for example, is a mediating gesture that transforms the work into an allegory of thanks
and separation, as if the sentiment *Lebewohl*, farewell, could
take musical form: "In its thanking lies the turning backwards of
music – that which most deeply distinguishes it from brisk effi-
ciency. Beethoven's thanking is always related to leave-taking ('Les
Adieux,' close of the first movement, is one of Beethoven's decisive
metaphysical figures). In early Beethoven the expression of thanks
is quite pure at the close of the 'Spring' Sonata [op. 24] ... Thanks
and unhappy consciousness."[11]

Mediation produced by repetition is an essential component –
perhaps the essential component – of what Adorno calls the "fully
dialectical mode of composing," of which Beethoven is exemplary.[12]
Beethoven gravitates toward this mode (moving from what Adorno
calls the "intensive" to the "extensive" type[13]). Mediating repeti-

tion produces this gravitation – absent in the early work (the Violin Sonata, op. 30, no. 2), present in the later (the *Appassionata*, op. 57): "*On music and dialectical logic*. It can be shown how Beethoven only gradually attained a fully dialectical mode of composing. In the C minor Violin Sonata from op. 30 – one of the first truly Beethovenian conceptions, and a work of highest genius – the antagonism is still *unmediated*, that is, the thematic complexes are set out in splendid contrast, like armies or pieces on a chessboard, then collide in a dense developmental sequence. In the *Appassionata* the antithetical themes are at the same time identical in themselves: identity in nonidentity."[14] In the immediacy of op. 30, no. 2, thematic complexes contrast. There can be no possibility of mistaking them as similar and thus repetitive. In the first movement the contrast between themes is exaggerated, one theme *legato* and *piano*, the other *sempre staccato* and introduced by *fortissimo* strokes. The *Appassionata*, however, contains themes that, although superficially different (tonic minor, relative major), are in essential aspects remarkably identical: mm. 1–2 (tonic) and mm. 35–37 (relative major) share similar rhythms, the same triadic basis, and an inversional symmetry discernible in the overall shapes of the two themes. It is not that these measures enunciate the same theme (Adorno is no organicist), but rather that they are calculated to make one ponder that possibility. They provoke us to look for mechanisms of explanation, and by provoking they make us aware of ourselves and of our thought as applied to music.[15]

Mediating repetition extends to the use of convention – the repetition of things past – a hallmark of Beethoven's late style for Adorno.[16] Counterpoint serves here as an example *par excellence*. The association of a melody with a contrapuntal treatment will mediate that melody: "Insofar as all themes are adapted to counterpoint, they are no longer 'melodies,' self-sufficient formations," but they become instead contrapuntally conventional,[17] pointing beyond themselves to the antiquated, the learned, and the reserved.[18] Indeed anything sounding contrapuntal – through imitation or a suspension idiom, for example – will invoke the practice of counterpoint, refer outside itself, and thus interrupt immediate musical experience.[19]

Repetition, however, is not the sole vehicle whereby mediation is produced in late Beethoven. Compression (in Webern's *Sinfonie*, op. 21, for example) refers outside itself (to the category *symphony*) and thus derives its content in part externally. Adorno's catalogue of mediations includes what he calls "the tendency towards *compression* in late Beethoven; that is, mere indications often stand for groups in the formal schema."[20] Beethoven's mediating melodies can be formulaic – compressed to their algebraic essentials.[21] In certain works this is done to the point of self-erasure, Beethoven's melodies no longer manifesting themselves as "material," as musical objects in their own right, but existing instead as mere referents to external categories. The highly compressed adagio of the *Hammerklavier* actually dissolves its form, leaving nothing objective behind. Beethoven reduces the musical artifact, an operation Adorno calls "positive negation": he reduces "to such elementary forms that it no longer manifests itself as material at all ... Beethoven, the master of positive negation: discard, that you may acquire. The shrinkage of the Beethovenian adagio is to be seen in this context. That in the 'Hammerklavier' Sonata is the last adagio in music."[22] Repetition, recapitulation, counterpoint, compression – these are but a few of the stylistic elements in Beethoven's late works that produce mediation by disrupting immediacy.[23]

On this account, the principal aim of Beethoven's late style would seem to be the evocation of the world that lies beyond the confines of the musical work at hand (but in a sense quite the opposite of idealism). The late works unfold a world of extreme musical convention. The music of the late style expresses itself as if it were entirely conventional, as if listening were all *déjà entendu*, "The production of categories instead of individuations."[24] Consider the *Hammerklavier* sonata: "The melody loses its immediacy, appearing from the first mediated, and, moreover, 'meaningful.' It is not itself but what it means. It can hardly be heard and understood as a 'melody' at all, but as a complex of meanings."[25] Or the following description of mediated tonality (referring again to the *Hammerklavier*).[26] "At any rate, to say that the tonal material is ossified into a convention is only a half-truth. In its estrangement from the process and from identity, it juts out bare and cold, like a rock. In having become subjectively expressionless, it takes on an objective, allegorical expression ... The bare chord ... single chord, which 'signifies' tonality; the chord as allegory replaces the key as process."[27] In the middle period, harmony is a process – a narrative. But in the late style, harmony is allegorical, a process of generating import, carried out at length, albeit evoked sometimes by a single harmony.[28]

In this sense mediation does not depend necessarily upon repetition and an actual distinction drawn between two discrete moments. As Adorno puts it (with clear reference to Hegel) mediation is immanent in *the* moment, if one is thinking critically: "The truly Hegelian quality of Beethoven is, perhaps, that in his work, too, mediation is never merely something *between* the moments, but is immanent in the moment itself."[29] In other words, the listener to the late style will come to appreciate every moment as a vehicle of mediation. I shall call this "momentary" mediation a *categorical awareness*. At its simplest, as well as hearing individual repeated notes, lines, motifs, melodies, or lengthy phrases ("parts" as Adorno calls them), the listener hears a categorical imperative, the siren call to listen categorically, which marks an end to immediacy, to a lack of self-consciousness. The listener hears beyond the surface to a stratum Adorno compares again to "allegory": "Each individual part stands not for itself but as a representative of its type, its category, a situation which indeed comes very close to the allegorical."[30] Music of Beethoven's late style becomes an evocation of categories, and in this sense it becomes both artifactual (in the sense of referencing other times and other places) and allegorical (taking on a new life by means of these references).

With the late style, a decisive change came about in Beethoven's relationship to his music, a change brought about by a growing awareness of his self in light of his social class.[31] Like a wedge, this awareness lodged between the composer and his middle-period work. Music was no longer immediate for him; he could no longer divorce the social aspect of his self from it nor concentrate solely on the musical object to the exclusion of self. Instead music came to him bound up with self-consciousness and a consequent social responsibility, to declare that self in light of others. The representation of class became the object; the vehicle was a form of mediation that played upon the universal appeal of Beethoven's middle period. If the middle period fractured class distinctions in its ready appeal to all classes (aristocracy to working class), then the late period made an audible fact of that fracture.[32] To the musical mind made aware of itself through mediation, class distinctions become as contrived and artificial as the fugues of the *Missa Solemnis*.

The late style, then, is a reconstituted, fractured style, a mediated style. For something to be fractured, it must have its origin in a state of wholeness. For Adorno, Beethoven's middle period offers just such a state. As a moment of fullness or plenitude, the middle period becomes a point of reference for the mediation of the fractured late style. In the middle period, musical reason coincides with musical freedom so as to transform the human condition into a hitherto unknown wholeness, an immediacy never to be achieved again, "the free individual, a self-conscious human being with the freedom to determine his or her own destiny, above all as Kant defined freedom, through the exercise of moral choice."[33] The middle period on this account is an integral totality. But totalities do not necessarily mediate.[34] In Beethoven's middle-period music (the Violin Sonata op. 30, no. 2, for example), repetition is absorbed in the context of the musical narrative entirely without self-consciousness; in this sense, middle-period repetition is a form of identification – non-mediating.[35] Although Adorno describes and theorizes the epoch at length, the middle period is ultimately less important in and of itself, and more important as a horizon against which the late style is put into perspective.[36]

The customary reception of the late style holds it to be radically innovative, wilful, expressive if not expressionistic, an uninhibited subjectivity. Correcting this notion, Adorno describes the late style in fact as virtually "expressionless" and extremely conventional (this in the full sense of an oxymoron).[37] The late style is filled with formulae and conventions, scattered like barren seed onto "some of the flintiest strata of the polyphonic landscape, the most restrained stirrings of solitary lyricism."[38] The late style, in other words, turns away from hubris and subjectivity into self-conscious reflection and mediation.

Thus Adorno observes a formal law of the late style: the musical work must be about something other than itself (for example, about the conventions of fugue, aria, theme and variations). Little in the late style, then, is immediate; almost everything is informed by supplementary meaning and thus refers outside itself. Mediation is sown into the fabric of the late works – the sudden pauses as if conversation lagged abruptly and uncomfortably, the inordinate repetition of a rhythm or a motif as if the work itself became self-conscious and began to stutter.

Adorno refers to the late style (in terms reminiscent of Lukács and Benjamin) as bare, the product of an "*inorganic* element," unadorned and dead, and "allegorical" in lieu of "symbolic."[39] It is "merely" functional: the function of referring beyond itself becomes its true theme. Thus it avoids any accusations of subjectivity.[40] Late-style harmonies, for example, often stretch out for great lengths – the antithesis of what dynamic harmony should do. Harmony becomes categorical; having heard it all before, "one already knows all about it,"[41] since the harmonies make the same utterances repeatedly. Whereas middle-period harmony functions internally to give the work tonality, an integrity, a wholeness, late-style harmony "signifies" – makes reference to something outside itself. Late-style themes are more thematic possibilities than actual worked-out melodies (like fugue subjects devoid of realization).[42]

After Adorno, the late style becomes a finely focused mirror in which one can study in exaggerated and self-conscious form the conventions implicit in the middle period and in high classicism, as if when shaving one noticed wrinkles for the first time.

Rose Rosengard Subotnik draws attention to the potential artificial status of the middle period in Adorno's thought, that the perfection of the middle period is nothing but a logical possibility. If the late style is a kind of second nature writ large in musical terms (a style of dead conventions, cyphers, and allegory), then it is possible, following Lukács, to look skeptically on the traditional account of the middle period's integrity and see therein a *first nature* – a phony nature, whose origins lie solely in *second nature* given to nostalgia. The much-acclaimed integrity of the middle period, in other words, could be no more than a phantom, a phony integrity and wholeness. In Subotnik's words, Adorno never said that dialectical synthesis was "achieved by society in Beethoven's lifetime."[43] Synthesis was possible, at least plausible enough to suggest itself as a formal possibility to the artistic mind. Ultimately, Subotnik disavows the link between the middle-period music and society, except as a phantom extrapolated from the late style. The late style thus becomes the "most realistic," the most critical in Adorno's sense of the term.[44]

Seen from this view, classicism is a deception. Adorno calls it the "'self-deception' of totality [*der "Selbsttäuschung" der Totalität*]."[45] Only the works of the late style are truly objective: "Beethoven's last works are *the* objective answer."[46] Beethoven's middle-period work is a manufactured falsehood, a coercion, a product of violence and sleight of hand, epiphany achieved by a diminished seventh chord.[47]

For Adorno the late style responds to a suspicion sown by mediation: "To the musical experience of the late Beethoven the unity of subjectivity and objectivity, the roundedness of the successful symphony, the totality arising from the motion of all particulars, in short, that which gives the works of his middle period their authenticity, must have become suspect."[48] As Adorno puts it, "He saw through the classic as classicism. He rebelled against the affirmative element, the uncritical approbation of Being, inherent in the idea of the classical symphony ... He must have felt the untruth in the highest aspirations of classicist music: that the quintessence of the opposed motions of all particulars, which are annulled in that quintessence, is positivity itself."[49] Here lies a thorough revision of thought about middle-period Beethoven. If we adopt it, then there are no Beethovenian islands in music left above the flood line of negation through late-style mediation.[50]

This conception of the middle period affirmation through renunciation becomes important not just for Adorno's work on Beethoven but for his criticism in general. He is sometimes accused of an inordinate prejudice in favour of Beethovenian classicism (at the expense of popular music). Such is not the truth. Were the middle period seen by him as ideal, a Utopia immune to the negation to which Adorno submits every other form of music, then he might justifiably be dismissed as prejudiced, and his reception of repertoires such as jazz and popular music dismissed along with it. But if the middle period is itself subject to negation through the mediating locus of the late style, then all forms of music (from classic to popular, including the late style) are treated equally in Adorno's critical eyes. Negation transcends prejudice; all music is affirmed negatively through renunciation.

What kind of work is musical work? Caught in a world of musical commodities, we think customarily of the *work of music* as a thing[51] – a score, a performance,[52] a recording. This is to forget two things after Marx: first, the labour – the work – involved in producing music but, more important, the actual work performed by music itself, and thus the thing accomplished by music.

No doubt for most of us music works to entertain, soothe, distract – the list of functions served is, it seems, endless if not perennial. But in his Beethoven critique, Adorno ascribes another kind of labour to music – the work of philosophy. Some forms of music, indeed some repertoires, work to produce self-awareness through mediation.[53] These works of music will function – *work*, as a verb – to disrupt our immediate and thus unmediated self-absorption with musical commodities. They do so internally – immanently – through repetition or, as in the case of late Beethoven, compression or convention. Or they do so externally through repetition of the commodity (as in "Froggy," or through the mass marketing of a recording). Or they do so by evoking auxiliary types of musical labour, as in Schoenberg's audience, who must work for their leisure.

When referring to Adorno, however, we must qualify *philosophy* if we are going to talk about the work of philosophy. His is not an Idealist philosophy of musical works, a notion that posits an autonomy of the musical thing-in-itself.[54] We mean instead a historical-materialist philosophy: the philosophical work accomplished by music is to draw attention to and thereby illuminate the contradictions of capitalism.[55]

Setting Adorno to one side briefly, I extrapolate from a treatise written in 1935 by an Austrian musicologist, the late Kurt Blaukopf, under the pseudonym Hans Wind, with the imposing title *Die Endkrise der bürgerlichen Musik und die Rolle Arnold Schönbergs*, or *The Final Crisis of Bourgeois Music and the Role of Arnold Schoenberg*.[56] Wind describes in the form of a dialectic the meeting of two styles – monophony and polyphony – when a medieval conception meets the Renaissance spirit. On Wind's simplified account, medieval monophony in the form of chant is the music of servitude, ultimately to the Church; Renaissance polyphony is the music of rising aristocratic power, including a secular power that breaks with the dominance of the Church. Monophonic chant, the vehicle by which the dominion of the Church is spread, is itself universal in application: appropriate to everyone, it makes no class distinction between master and serf. Polyphony, however, flourishes in the growing and exclusive aristocratic courts, wherein the secular spirit of the Renaissance begins to flower in forms of individuality – the professional musician being one instance thereof. In this sense, a specialized polyphony negates the universality of monophonic chant. By its very complexity, polyphony requires a system of individuation – patron, composer, professional musician – and produces the birth of the commodity in, for example, the exchange of musicians between secular courts and, with the growth of musical typeface, the musical score. Musical *work* in the sense of a commodity becomes a thing of commerce.

Monophony and polyphony function as polar opposites during the rise of secular polyphony but are brought together dialectically in a

later development. Out of polyphony grows a style of harmonic texture, called *homophony*, capable of sustaining a single monophonic
line against a polyphony congealed in a chordal accompaniment.
Initially antagonistic, monophony and polyphony (transformed as
"voice leading") are brought into an unlikely synthesis in homophony. The element of dialectic in this synthesis elevates it beyond
these technical details: the homophonic style becomes the hallmark
of a growing bourgeois music, and of a musical amateur to succeed
the Renaissance specialist. These amateurs, by their anonymous
membership in a new class, the bourgeoisie, will negate ultimately
the class structure of their predecessors – the division between lord
and serf, and between duke and *Kapellmeister* (if only to replace
it with another class distinction – between the bourgeoisie and the
musical labourer).

This particular historical-materialist conceit is no doubt a crude
oversimplification. But I take it as a materialist thought experiment.
As Wind expresses it with the hindsight of history, as a superstructure, the dialectic changes of musical style accompanied certain
changes in base – presumably the rise of a new mercantilism that
both produced a secular aristocracy and led to its downfall. To the
listener of the day, these changes must have demanded a remarkable
change in consciousness, a reorientation of the self to new practices
of making music, this accompanying a reorientation of the self to
the structure of society at large. Of the two reorientations, I call
the first the *work* or *labour* of a musical historical-materialist philosophy; the latter can be called simply in and of itself a historical-
materialist philosophy.

The growth of the public music concert, the advent of Italianate
opera in Central and Western Europe, the birth of urban rock and
roll out of a miscellany of Black musical styles both urban and rural,
the congregation of an intellectual elite in Schoenberg's *Vereine für
Privataufführungen* – in each of these instances, music provokes a
reconsideration of the relationship between the musical classes, in
particular a reconsideration of music as the vehicle of a fully bourgeois musical identity, to follow Wind's thought.

This, then, is the historical-materialist philosophical work – task
– of music, by means of which a critic after Adorno might describe
Beethoven's late style as a negation of the middle period: the late
style exemplifies the work of negation; the late style is musical work,
in the sense of labour. The late style works to draw attention to

the commodification of the middle period and thus to the historical material fact of a rising musical commodification that puts capital on equal footing with (soon higher than) aristocracy. To the Viennese burghers of Beethoven's day, resplendent in the gains of their industry, this fact must have been emblazoned over the entrance to the *Theatre an der Wien* as an indelible truth that not even the entrance of Don Fernando at the denouement of *Fidelio* could erase.

This, after Adorno (and Wind), is the work of music as a philosophy: to draw our attention away from the identity-thought of musical individualism toward a comprehension of the self in distinction to others.[57] As a philosophy, it runs against the grain of both capitalism and philosophical idealism. For this reason, it manifests itself indirectly, wherever music will not allow commodification (Beethoven's late style), or where, in succumbing to commodification, music spawns contradictions and juxtapositions which thereby produce mediation (as in much jazz and popular music, when seen from Adorno's critique). Since historical materialism is not a staple of philosophy in much of the West, this kind of musical philosophy is a rarity, not easily understood by either musicians or philosophers. Or, to apply the lyrics to a well-known tune by Gershwin, "Nice work if you can get it."[58]

Errors in Mahler Scores. Dover, in republishing the score of Mahler's *Seventh Symphony* (original publication by Bote and Bock, Berlin, 1908), has generously provided a glossary of German terms with English translations. As a thought experiment, we might tabulate the frequency of occurrence for each term. In all likelihood, the word occurring most frequently would be *nicht* [not], followed by *ohne* [without], and thereafter *aber* [but], and then surely *noch mehr* [still more]. The use of the exclamation mark, while it lies outside the pale of a glossary proper, might be tabulated as well, well outnumbering the usage of any given term.

Admonitions and cautions – *Nicht Eilen*! [Don't rush!], *Nicht Anschwellen*! [Don't get louder!] – are scattered all over the landscape of Mahler's scores. The composer, of course, knew well how an orchestra might swerve from the path of fidelity to one's intentions; Mahler learned this in the pit and on the podium. There is no composer after Berlioz whose scores witness such a vision of musical sublime negated by such a profound mistrust of the common, everyday musician.

The customary study of orchestration teaches the ranges of the orchestral instruments, their timbres, the foibles composers sometimes succumb to, all combined with a menagerie of "hints" and "tricks" designed to reassure the student that the task at hand – coordinating a small array of instrumentalists moving in milliseconds so as to produce a lengthy series of precise musical sounds – is capable of mastery. To this end, score excerpts taken from middle-period Beethoven and from Tchaikovsky are still foisted on the student as exemplary.

Mahler symphonies are clearly unsuited to the task of "instruction" in at least two regards. None of his orchestrations are "normative" but instead seemed designed to destroy – to negate – the very notion of norm itself. And for this reason he must constantly watch over – as archangel – his errant flock of musicians with admonitions and cautions lest they stray into orthodoxy. To the student of orchestration, Mahler scores are both the worst and the very best vehicles for instruction: if the student, having been shown with astonishing frequency just how things can go wrong – "*Nicht schleppen!*" – still persists in composing, then a teacher's work is surely done.

The musical sublime in Mahler is sometimes hailed by musicologists as a synthesis of divine inspiration mated with despair straight out of Hades. The gold-tinged synthesis this produces is ornamented further: Mahler is a product of the modern condition (with emphasis on Hades), then the postmodern condition (with a wink at heavenly resurrection), and then various post-post derivatives (narratology, musical phenomenology, etc.). These syntheses are all negated, however, by the cautionary tales in Mahler's scores – the *nicht* and the *ohne*. As never before in a composer's work, the epiphanies derived of Mahler's scores are overturned by a kind of musical labour – not labour by proxy (the manufactured effort of the conductor for whom a four-gram baton has suddenly taken upon itself Atlas's burden, or the perfumed beads of sweat on the concertmaster's brow). Instead, Mahler's scores are filled with simple, albeit often shrill, instructions for musical labourers and written out in the sort of detail that a shop foreman might dispense: "Do this now, no not too loud, and now try this softly, softly I said, and damn!, did I say you could speed up? Did I?"

The unobtrusive second movement, *Serenade*, of Mahler's Seventh is a case in point. Sprinkled perhaps even more liberally than the exclamation mark across the score is *sempre* [still], administered in the sense of "keep it up," and "stay focused." The *Formenlehre* would tell us that from the entry of the first theme at rehearsal number 72(+1),[59] a large ternary design is unfolded: A [72(+1)] then B [79(-3)] then A' [86(-3)]. Within the initial A, a smaller ternary is nested: a [72(+1)] b [74(+2)] a' [76(+1)]. (And nestled within the small 'a' is yet another ternary form with a sentence of eight measures – the horn at 72(+1), with the cello stretto.) The A' section will bring back the nested ternary design but modify it by postponing the return of the small 'b.' Many of these seemingly placid formal indications, however, carry certain anxiety for Mahler. For example, at 69(+4), the clarinets are instructed to remain ever a little stronger than the oboes, as if their volume, and ardour, is in danger of flagging before the principal theme of the movement is introduced. So too, at 71(+1), still before the start of the ternary design proper, the orchestra is instructed "*Nicht Eilen! Nicht Anschwellen!*" It seems as if the mood in anticipation of the first theme must be expressed negatively by cataloguing potential errors, rather than by setting the scene positively: "Keep a steady tempo and dynamic ... idiot."

The "content" of the movement thus devolves into the number and degree of temptations – the lapses – avoided by musical labourers. The appearance of the small ternary 'b' at 74(+2) provokes another insecurity – again a "*Nicht eilen*" – as if, confronted with a change of musical idea, the orchestra might be tempted to hurry along nervously. The crescendo in the strings at 75(+5) is a "poco" crescendo – a "little" crescendo – not just to a mezzo forte from pianissimo, but expressly only "little," as if one might somehow get carried away and make a crescendo to mezzo forte sound somehow "big." In the reverse sense, the crescendo in the upper strings from piano to the fortissimo of 77(-1) is marked "molto," as if one might be tempted by avarice to skimp a bit of effort and withhold our due. (This is not helped by the divisi desk where one player bows and the other plucks away with pizzicatos.) And the piano espressivo's that follow in the first violins a measure later – how could you think not to make these espressivo? How could you? Why do I have to remind you? Twice!

After about 78(+1), the *sempre*'s begin to crowd in, mostly *sempre pp*, and *sempre p*, as if gravitation might drag the orchestra back to the bland centricity of the mezzo forte. This nervousness bursts out in the new grand indication above the score at 79(-3): *Sempre listesso tempo. Nicht eilen, sehr gemächlich*," or "Always the same tempo. Don't rush. Keep it loose, there." Presumably the reason for anxiety is at root the *Formenlehre* design, for 79(-3) marks the entry of the large B. But at this moment the predominant sense of the score indications, one of anxiety and nervousness, is quite the opposite of the smoothly idyllic cello line over which this breast beating is transpiring. Signs of formal anxiety diminish at this point (although the *sempre* indication remains perennial), but give way to concerns about musician competence and trustworthiness. The contrabasses are cautioned at least twice: "*Nicht eine Oktave höher spielen* [Don't play this an octave higher]," even if it is easier to do so. The trumpets are given mutes at 92(+1) and told to play piano, "*aber stehts deutlich* [but stay audible]," the *deutlich* underlined for emphasis. (Those trumpets!) And the clarinets at 90(+1), given mock trumpet calls, are told not to play legato, this in a passage over the clarinet's registral "break," which would be next to impossible to pull off legato, would be impossible to produce at an audible level without a crisply tongued separation of each note.

All the scholastic anxiety about Mahlerian "musical ideas" – the dissonance, the radical rethinking of musical form, the innovative scoring, the epiphanies – seems to exclude the humdrum workaday world of the score and the labour of realization; they swath Mahler in much the same winding sheet applied to Coltrane. Mahler makes explicit thus (and elsewhere in the finicky precision of all his scores) a materialism, the fact of musical labour, a fact by which the most effusive conductor, the fawning radio announcer, the superlative-riddled liner notes are all negated. The indicated errors – albeit only potential errors anticipated by cautions and exhortations – break apart the absolute facade of Mahler's scores.

4

Technique

The truth is that Schoenberg was a naive artist, above all in the often hapless intellectualizations with which he sought to justify his work. If anyone was guided by the tide of involuntary musical intuition it was he.

Adorno, *Prisms*

A basic knowledge of musical notation is necessary to observe an important pattern in the first eight measures of Beethoven's F Minor Piano Sonata, op. 2, no. 1, reproduced in example 1, below. The first two complete measures (including the upbeat) are what Schoenberg called a "tonic form" – built rhythmically of rising quarter notes, a dotted quarter, a triplet, and two detached quarter notes. The same rhythmic pattern (minus the upbeat) returns in mm. 3–4 but shifted to new pitches: Schoenberg called this a "dominant form," and said of the technique of variation involved here, "This kind of repetition, through its slightly contrasting formulation, provides variety in unity."[1] Again a basic knowledge of harmony is needed to add to the observation: the harmony of the first two measures outlines an F-minor chord; the harmony of the next two measures outlines a dominant chord with C as root. Schoenberg referred to themes that begin with this particular kind of harmonically contrasting form as "sentences."[2]

After m. 4, the rhythmic pattern begins to come apart: Beethoven excises the rising quarter notes, compressing them into single grace notes, the dotted quarter note is extended to a full half note, four descending eighth notes lead to the last remnant of the triplet, and the two quarter notes now lead smoothly to a half cadence at the fermata. Schoenberg called this taking apart process "reduction," and its goal "liquidation" – the gradual elimination of any remaining restive energy before the stasis of the cadence.[3]

Example 1. Sentence form in the first theme of Beethoven's F minor Piano Sonata, op. 2, no. 1.

The whole procedure – statement of tonic and dominant forms, reduction, cadence – is referred to by analysts as a theme "type."[4] As noted, Schoenberg called this particular theme type the "sentence form." Theme types of this sort – the principal counterpart to the sentence being the "period form" – serve a logical purpose. By repetition, they draw the work together conceptually and audibly: motivic variations of the tonic form in a sonata (such as a Beethoven symphony) can be referred back to the theme as a model, so that everything in the work can be said to derive from a germinal cell, or "germ," as Schoenberg put it.[5] Contrast, on the other hand, lends the work a dynamic sense of opposing musical entities put together in an energetic succession.

There are three conclusions to be drawn from this thematic procedure, the traditional study of which is called in German the *Formenlehre*, to which we shall return in discussing Adorno's Schoenberg reception.[6] First, the sentence-form scheme antedates the composition of any given piece of music; although it may be expressed individually in a given instance, the actual scheme itself is a predetermination worked out, as a formal genre or *typus*, prior to the composition of the piece. In this sense, there is a history to a putatively "absolute" music work such as the Beethoven piano sonata op. 2, no. 1 – the history of the sentence scheme, its development as a nascent form (with roots in the subject-answer pairing of the fugue), and its rise to maturity. The history of the scheme (alongside its generic application in other works) undermines the often final impression of the sonata as a self-contained, individual, absolute, and thus ahistorical work.[7]

Second, the processes involved in the sentence form have been called from time to time *dialectic*.[8] Along this line of thought, the tonic form is negated by the opposing harmonic extreme of the dominant form. The two are then synthesized into a unity by means of subsequent development and the cadence. Schoenberg is not innocent in the promulgation of this dialectic idea: for him, the tonic and dominant forms are necessary for the unitary expression of the key (and thus they sublimate themselves individually to the greater purpose of the cadence), tonic and dominant being pillars of Beethovenian tonal unity. Key contrast, then, is subordinated to an elevating – *Aufhebung* – function, the unitary purpose of key expression.

Third, the contrast leading to key expression in the sonata form as worked out in the textbook *Formenlehre* formula arises as a contrast between two themes – a principal theme in the tonic, and a secondary theme heard later in a contrasting key, often the dominant. On this account, a whole movement works dialectically: the key contrast of themes is developed over the course of the movement – exposition, development, and recapitulation – so as to express one single, unified key. All the keys touched upon during the course of a work are thus to be seen, Schoenberg said, as merely facets of one unitary key, or more properly one tonality. Schoenberg called this kind of unitary key perception "monotonality."

Much the same principal of key expression by means of contrast is to be observed regularly in Schoenberg's work (for example, the opening measures of his op. 2, no. 1, the lied "Erwartung" [anticipating the better known monodrama of the same name by several years]).[9] At the very beginning of his compositional career, Schoenberg drew on well-established historical schema – rhythmic, harmonic, and formal – in composing music, which he then rethought to meet the needs of an evolving, highly chromatic musical style.

Schoenberg's Piano Pieces op. 11 would seem to break the link to precedent. The first piece of the three seems to come fully constructed out of a different formal conception, as if in complete defiance of the Beethovenian models in Schoenberg's earlier work. So this work in particular has been received by Adorno, who said it

Example 2. Sentence form in the first theme of Schoenberg's Three Pieces for Piano, op. 11, no. 1. Reproduced with permission of the Estate of Arnold Schoenberg.

"destroys" the "illusion of spatial depth" proper to tonal harmony[10] and that it "abandoned ... entirely" the art of thematic work.[11]

The opening to op. 11, no. 1, however, is not entirely free of the sentence form, but rather redistributes the component parts of the form: the dominant form – similar in rhythm to the tonic form – comes at the end of the sentence (see example 2, the last measures thereof being the misplaced dominant form). The effect the opening measures produce on most audiences is one of consternation. To those aware, however, of the remnants of the sentence form, the effect is startling: an almost malevolent will seems to be at work here, as if Schoenberg were tearing apart his Beethovenian inheritance and reassembling it in a distorting fashion designed deliberately to confuse. Consciously or otherwise, Schoenberg would seem to render a verdict on the relevance of a Beethovenian *Formenlehre* here, at the beginning of the twentieth century – relevant but only with dramatic modification that challenges the consistency of musical *Formen.*

As if he had broken with extant form in this manner, Schoenberg's immediately subsequent works have less and less to do with the Beethovenian model, the acme of this renunciation being the Piano Pieces, op. 19. But when Schoenberg takes up the twelve-tone method, he takes up the *Formenlehre* again.[12] The Gigue from the Piano Suite, op. 25, is almost slavish in its return to the sentence form, with tonic and dominant forms carrying different forms of the tone row, and the sacred order of the row itself coming apart with reduction to the cadence. In the Gigue and other pieces from this period, the twelve-tone method (with its twelve-tone tonality based on repetition of the row in its derived forms) is sublimated to the by now antiquated design of the sentence form.

It is important to note that both form and row are preconceptions – the form revived from an earlier era, the twelve-tone row first conceived in its manifold forms (prime, retrograde, and their compound forms) prior to actual composition. This is a development not without importance for Adorno's Schoenberg critique. Before moving to that discussion, however, a brief parenthetical analysis of Adorno's prose needs to be made along lines just laid out in the discussion above.

The structure of Adorno's prose is directly related to the negation in his thought.[13] The basic layout of Adorno's negating ideas is often expressed in witticisms, in German *Kernspruche*, wherein meanings collide like tiny kernels. The result is not a logical syntactic succession of subject and predicate (although syntax is usually observed) but a juxtaposition of disparate meanings so as to produce new meaning. In other words, when looking for a consistent single unitary meaning in Adorno's prose, we are often confronted with unanticipated meaning.[14]

In the following highly compressed passage, Adorno combines a common merchandising caveat often encountered in stores (no returns of merchandise) with the idea of giving gifts, and in turn with the principle of exchange (that commodities have an exchange value quite apart from their use value). To this he adds the thought that awareness of the exchange value of a commodity has sifted down to contaminate the minds of children. These elementary kernels are juxtaposed in a way that makes no linear sense, and yet the essence of the idea is conveyed with the force of an argument twice its length.

Articles may not be exchanged. — We are forgetting how to give presents. Violation of the exchange principle has something nonsensical and implausible about it; here and there even children eye the giver suspiciously, as if the gift were merely a trick to sell them brushes or soap.[15]

This passage can be teased apart and then recombined: gifts (birthday presents for example) are not like commodities. Commodities are priced and thus should be capable of being returned and exchanged for articles of the same price. A gift, on the other hand, is priceless, and thus cannot really be equated with commodities. We are losing sight of that distinction in two ways. Some stores will not allow returns, and thus the articles they sell are to be viewed with suspicion. Being thus suspicious of articles that cannot be returned, the receiver of a gift – a child in particular – is naturally suspicious of all such exchanges. Adorno, even in translation, expresses this with much greater precision and eloquence than my linear attempt at standard prose.

Some of this prose style was surely carried over from Adorno's understanding of the musical *Formenlehre*, which he studied, in all likelihood, either on his own or with his teachers, among them Alban Berg. Henri Lonitz notes how Adorno himself compared his prose to music. In a letter describing his essay on *Wozzeck* from 1925, Adorno describes his satisfaction with a prose style, in which the logic of his argument does not pursue a string of surface associations but reflects the simultaneity of Berg's compositional intentions. Citing Berg's thought that for musical analysis to be adequate a compositional mode of expression is necessary (taken from Berg's essay "*Warum ist Schönbergs Musik so schwer verständlich*," 1924), Adorno recounts the debt his prose owes to musical composition.[16] The letter is dated 23 November 1925, and the important passage is the following: "My most secret intention was to make the essay's use of language correspond directly to the way in which you compose, for example in the quartet [Berg's op. 3]."[17]

In this sense, Adorno's prose is *musical prose*.[18] Schoenberg used the term in the chapter "Brahms the Progressive" in *Style and Idea* to describe two prose-like qualities of a musical work, first its "precision and brevity," which "presupposes the alert mind of an educated listener." This listener "in a single act of thinking, includes with every concept all associations pertaining to the complex. This enables a musician to write for upper-class minds, not only doing what grammar and idiom require, but, in other respects lending to every sentence the full pregnancy of meaning of a maxim, of a proverb, of an aphorism. This is what musical prose should be – a direct and straightforward presentation of ideas, without any patchwork, without mere padding and empty repetitions."[19] Second, a work of musical prose has an asymmetrical quality, the musical work "consisting of a number of phrases of various lengths and characters, each of them pertaining to a different phase of the action and the mood." This loosely woven style (as opposed to the easily comprehended symmetrical prose found in much classical music built on the four-measure phrase) allows itself to be understood as an idea capable of being taken apart and recombined in developmental form: "loosely joined together, and ... simply juxtaposed, thus admitting to be broken asunder and used independently as motival material for small formal segments."[20] But whereas Schoenberg, by *musical prose*, meant prose-like music, I mean here music-like prose. In literal and figurative senses, Adorno's prose is like music, like Schoenberg's op. 11 in particular – compact (like a maxim or proverb) and asymmetrical (seldom balanced).[21]

Consider the following excerpt from the essay "Bach Defended against His Devotees," from *Prisms*.[22] Adorno's prose retains something of Beethovenian form here, but the sequence of ideas is complex and compact, and thus facile clarity is avoided. Here, the initial idea of Adorno's prose is like a *tonic form* – an aphorism, a self-contained, highly compressed expression of an idea. It is restated as a *dominant form*. In essence, Adorno's subject is revealed immediately from two complementary perspectives, these compressed into the smallest syntactical space possible.

[Sentence 1, *tonic form*] The view of Bach which prevails today in musicological circles corresponds to the role assigned to him by the stagnation and industriousness of a resurrected culture. [Sentence 2, *dominant form*] In him, it is said, there is once again the revelation – in the middle of the Century of Enlightenment – of the time honoured bounds of tradition, of the spirit of medieval polyphony, of the theologically vaulted cosmos.[23]

I try to straighten this out in standard prose:

[Sentence 1] In our day (in current musicological circles), Bach is assigned the role of industrious stagnation, like that of a resurrected culture. [Sentence 2] From that perspective, Bach appears

to play a comparable stagnant role, embodying a culture resurrected from medieval polyphony, tradition, and theology.

The common temporal element of stagnating culture (the equivalent of the common rhythm in the tonic and dominant forms of the
Beethoven example above) is broken apart as a discrepancy in time:
in sentence 1, our time assigns Bach the stagnant role of a culture –
Enlightenment – resurrected; but in sentence 2 the resurrected culture
is in fact the stagnant culture that Bach revived – medieval culture.
Much like *tonic* and *dominant forms*, then, one element stays the
same (temporal stagnation), while the other changes (Enlightenment
for medieval). The global theme of the two sentences is temporal, in
essence the telling of *history*, how the story of Bach-in-his-time is
told in our time. The two time frames (today and Bach's time), however, do not go hand in hand despite attempts by musicologists to
make them do so. We are not resurrecting Bach with the vibrancy he
applied to resurrecting medieval polyphony (the many-voiced tex-
tures of medieval mass and motet that find new life in Bach's work,
both vocal and instrumental). Ours is a stagnant culture: little or
nothing of the vitality of Bach will be revived – instead only the
hoary notions of tradition, polyphony, and theology.

In the *Formenlehre* as noted above, the theme will return in whole
or in part from time to time, interspersed with developmental episodes where its elements are taken apart. In a similar fashion, after
an episode, Adorno brings back a complementary statement of the
theme of sentences 1 and 2, expressed now in two contrasting sentences (numbers 9 and 10 of the passage):

> [Sentence 9] His work, which originated within the narrow con-
> fines of the theological horizon only in order to break through
> them and to pass into universality, is called back within the
> boundaries it transcended. [Sentence 10] Bach is degraded by
> impotent nostalgia to the very church composer against whose
> office his music rebelled and which he filled only with great
> conflict.[24]

Here the idea of time reappears but in new guises, blended with
the ideas of confines and boundaries, impotence and rebellion. The
central idea is that of boundaries in Bach's time and in ours: in
Bach's time, his music broke through boundaries; in ours his music

is bound again. In Bach's time he rebelled against the impotence of the church composer. In our time he is made to assume that same impotence; his devotees would return him to the nostalgic category of Leipzig *Kappelmeister*, church composer and musical handyman.

Between sentences 2 and 9 lies a little developmental passage, taking up aspects of the theme but setting to one side the principal idea of time. The third and fourth sentences are linked in common-tone fashion by the notion of Being. The fourth links to the fifth by the notion of the immutable (thus returning to time), the inexorable, and the secure:

[3]His music is said to be elevated above the subject and its contingency; in it is expressed not so much the man and his inner life as the order of Being as such, in its most compelling musical form. [4]The structure of this Being, understood to be immutable and inexorable, becomes a surrogate for meaning; that which cannot be other than its appearance is made the justification of itself. [5]This conception of Bach draws all those who, having lost either the ability to believe or the desire for self-determination, go in search of authority, obsessed by the notion of how nice it would be to be secure.[25]

The central term in sentence 3 is *Being*. It becomes the "common tone" between sentences 3 and 4[26] – in sentence 4 as the "order of Being" as the state "above the subject and its contingency." Via *Being*, sentence 4 links to sentence 5, as "the structure of this Being, understood to be immutable and inexorable." If something is "immutable and inexorable," then it lies far above the quotidian fray where meaning is determined. Superior *Being* appears thus as a superior "surrogate for meaning." Adorno barely conceals his distaste for this rarified development: this is just posturing by those who, incapable of finding security in their own being, treat Bach as a "surrogate" for security. Bach has become a surrogate for those bereft of the ability for self-determination.

Whether talking of Beethoven or of his own work, Schoenberg referred to a principal called the "tendency of the smallest notes,"[27] the tendency of the rhythm in the latter part of a musical sentence to become filled with notes of shorter and shorter duration, which like the small waves produced long after one drops a rock in a pool of water, carry less and less energy until the surface is restored to smoothness at the end of the phrase. The length and choppy rhythm of Adorno's sixth sentence, followed by the short, pithy seventh is reminiscent of this principal. The rhythm reduces to prose molecules – six molecules in the English translation of sentence 6, these indicated by slashes in the quotation below – and then slows to a halt in the balanced phrases of sentence 7, like the reduction and cadential phases of the musical sentence form. (To grasp this musical effect, it would help to read aloud both the English translation and the German original below.)

[6]The present function of his music/ resembles the current vogue of ontology,/ which promises to overcome the individualistic condition/ through the postulation of an abstract principle/ which is superior to and independent of human existence/ and yet which is free of all unequivocally theological content. [7]They enjoy the order of his music/ because it enables them to subordinate themselves.[28]

Die derzeitige Funktion seiner Musik ähnelt der ontologischen Mode: durchs Versprechen, den individualistischen Zustand kraft Setzung eines den Menschen übergeordneten, dem Dasein enthobenen, zugleich jedoch eindeutigen theologischen Inhalts entratenden, abstrakten Prinzips zu überwinden. Sie genießen die Ordnung seiner Musik, weil sie sich unterordnen dürfen.[29]

The developing musical rhythm of the two sentences is more readily apparent in the German. The rhythm of sentence 6 is chopped up into small and disjointed prepositional, accusative, and dative chunks (virtually impossible to translate literally):

Die derzeitige Funktion seiner Musik / ähnelt der ontologischen Mode: / durchs Versprechen, / den individualistischen Zustand / kraft Setzung / eines / den Menschen übergeordneten, / dem Dasein enthobenen, / zugleich / jedoch / eindeutigen theologischen Inhalts / entratenden, / abstrakten Prinzips / zu überwinden.

Sentence 7, however, splits neatly down the middle around the parallel "Ordnung" and "unterordnen," like a perfect authentic cadence V–I:

Sie genießen die Ordnung seiner Musik, / weil sie sich unterordnen dürfen.

The effect of the whole prose passage is musical – literally musical
prose. The sentences march forth in clear rhythm. Gradually the
rhythm grows more complex and asymmetrical, dividing into
smaller and smaller phrases. Ultimately Adorno conceives a long,
head-breaking sentence built of tiny components, over which the
mind stumbles, thereby losing momentum. Finally the whole comes
to rest on a simple assertion that seems unprepared in terms of the
logic of a normal prose paragraph but makes perfect sense, in both
musical and conceptual terms. Adorno begins by saying that Bach's
devotees elevate his music to debase themselves. He concludes with
a logical residue: we do not elevate Bach to an absolute but only
subordinate ourselves: "They enjoy the order of his music because it
enables them to subordinate themselves."

Not all Adorno's prose is so tightly wrought or susceptible to a
quasi-musical analysis. But a large part of his prose has a musical
grace, if by *grace* we mean that graceful atonality of Schoenberg's
op. 11. Adorno's prose has as well a kind of musical developmental
logic, where subjects are broken up developmentally and recombined in taut nets of interlacing logic. If we are to read Adorno for
understanding, we would do well to attend to the morphology of his
phrases, and bear in mind their potential as music. His prose in turn
will appear much less "difficult," if still not nice.

This is not to suggest, however, that Adorno could or would
have brought an extant prose scheme to his work in the way that
Schoenberg mined the *Formenlehre* and Beethoven's op. 2, no. 1.
There is no equivalent to the musical *Formenlehre* in the German
prose stylistics of Adorno's day.[30] If musical prose does indeed char-
acterize Adorno's writing from time to time, it draws upon neither
a historical precedent nor an ahistorical natural model, for to do
so would raise certain problems for Adorno's conception of technique; some of these problems will be addressed below in light of
the twelve-tone method. Instead Adorno seems to have brought to
some of his prose a sensibility to construction derived from music
(learned perhaps in his composition studies), and then applied this
in a freely inconsistent manner, along lines Schoenberg adopted in
op. 11.

The ground over which Adorno's critique moves in both the Schoenberg essay in *Prisms* and in the first chapter of *Philosophy of New Music*, "Schoenberg and Progress,"[31] is the twelve-tone technique, which for Adorno lends Schoenberg's music much the same critical interest as jazz, popular music, and Wagner; they serve as good symptoms of a badly uncritical world.[32] For Adorno the technique was produced by certain social and historical tendencies; Schoenberg's role was to give these tendencies form, doing so unwittingly and thus naively. In this manner he entered spontaneously and unawares into one of the sharpest critiques of society ever delivered by music. Adorno speaks of Schoenberg thus: "The truth is that Schoenberg was a naive artist, above all in the often hapless intellectualizations with which he sought to justify his work. If anyone was ever guided by the tide of involuntary musical intuition it was he."[33] With comparable naïveté, Schoenberg insisted that he was on equal footing with all the great composers before him and thus supremely equipped to transmit the absolute compositional forces that drove him. Adorno agreed with Schoenberg that the composer was a conduit, but not for supreme absolutes (of which Adorno was eternally suspicious).

What does it take, then, for Schoenberg to compose in the era of Late Capitalism? Adorno responds to this question in two clauses: it takes a penetrating insight into the mechanics of musical composition, combined with the naïveté of a child, a lack of sophistication in thought and deed. Although Adorno grants Schoenberg this naïveté, he suspects him of dissembling. Schoenberg did his naive best either to deny responsibility (claiming destiny was thrust upon him) or to slough it onto the shoulders of an absolute such as his "Supreme Commander." Describing his compositional ability with reference to Beethoven, Schoenberg said, "The original form, *a*, 'Muss es sein,' appears in *b* inverted and in the major; *c* shows the retrograde form of this inversion, which, now reinverted in *d* and filled out with passing notes in *e*, results in the second phrase of the main theme. Whether or not this device was used consciously by Beethoven does not matter at all. From my own experience I know that it can also be a subconsciously received gift from the Supreme Commander."[34] Master dialectician, Adorno draws our attention to the difference – the remainder – between the artist's vision and the real state of the art. When Schoenberg thinks of himself as the vehicle for some absolute compositional force – his "Supreme Commander" – this is simply naive. He is, instead, the vehicle of a musical intuition that penetrated to the very essence of music in Late Capitalism, doing so without any awareness of itself.

How would Adorno have one compose, then, in Late Capitalism? Like Schoenberg, one chooses a technique such as twelve-tone composition, a technique powerless, bankrupt, illusionary, and thus immanently contrived to reflect society, to bring its normally "subcutaneous" truths to the surface, no matter how painful. But while doing so, unlike Schoenberg, one must shoulder complete and utter responsibility in the matter.

"Schoenberg and Progress" is a wholesale refutation of musical absolutes such as those Schoenberg relied on in justifying his work. The refutation takes the form of six propositions.[35] Propositions 1 through 3 establish the work of art not as absolute but as the product of "historical tendencies" exerted upon its composer. Proposition 4 establishes the possibility of an ahistorical interior absolute in a musical work (with its own dynamic sense of time and history). Proposition 5 postulates the demise of that absolute where its objective musical frames (tonality, thematic variation) crumble under the weight of dynamic forces (developing variation, expanded tonality). Proposition 6 posits the possibility of relocating the dynamic sense of a work's interior time and history either on the surface of the work (as in Schoenberg's op. 11) or through precompositional determinations (such as the twelve-tone row). At the end of the chapter, these six propositions are brought together in a narrative extending from pre-Beethoven (propositions 1 to 3), through Beethoven's middle period (proposition 4), to late Beethoven, Wagner, and Brahms (proposition 5), and ultimately Schoenberg (proposition 6).

The first proposition states that there is no pure and immediate absolute experience of a work. On Adorno's account, a pure and immediate experience presupposes the existence of an impure and mediate experience and in doing so logically invalidates itself. Adorno quotes Hegel: "Pure insight ... is in the first instance without any content; it is ... the sheer disappearance of content; but by its negative attitude towards what it excludes it will make itself real and give itself a content." [36] There are three ideas here: first, something absolutely pure has no apparent content. It is like a vacuum. Second, lacking content, something absolutely pure cannot define itself without reference outside itself, to its opposite – impurity. But reference to impurity would give purity content (as that which is not pure) and thus purity as a self-contained absolute would invalidate itself. And third, the putatively absolute work takes a "negative attitude" to itself; it negates itself by reference to impurity. This "negative attitude" – it has no content but that which it is not – becomes its sole content. The idea of a polished work – a pure work, an absolute work – is invalidated by the necessary logical consequent, the impure, the unpolished, the sullied, with which it must combine. The acknowledgment of this implicit contradiction – purity defines itself only as absence of impurity – becomes an "objective logic" for Adorno: "Under the constraint of its own objective logic, music critically cancelled the idea of the consummate artwork and severed its tie with the public."[37]

The objective logic of the idea of purity is thus conceived by Adorno along the lines of negative dialectic. As antonyms, the terms *pure* and *impure* should be equal partners in a synthesis, but the latter invalidates the former. Whereas impurity can be defined with reference to purity (as absolute purity corrupted with impure content), absolute purity cannot be defined as absence of impurities, for impurity is unthinkable to absolute purity. Dialectics is made here to sublate the very notion of purity.

The negative difference between *purity* and *impurity* becomes in Adorno's hands a sociological index. Any pure community or culture must either logically negate itself,[38] or vehemently suppress the very idea of an alternative, an impure culture. To purify a community, it would be necessary to root out and purge impure art, *entartete Kunst*. Purity resides in gated communities.

Schoenberg, however, commits himself exclusively and thus absolutely to pure art: "One thinks only for the sake of one's idea. And thus art can only be created for its own sake. An idea is born; it must be moulded, formulated, developed, elaborated, carried through and pursued to its very end. Because there is only 'l'art pour l'art', art for the sake of art alone."[39] A central pillar in his notion of pure art is the *Formenlehre*, which, as we have seen, operates as if it were based on purely musical phenomenon of forming and shaping, despite the fact that it has a history. No doubt the original *Formenlehre* was merely a pedagogic device, and it retains this function in Schoenberg's hands. But it also takes on the status of a precept: if musical works have this kind of form, then they can be treated in these terms as self-contained entities. This notion of a self-contained entity will be an irritant for Adorno when he turns his critique to the twelve-tone method.

Adorno's first proposition, then, is a refutation of Schoenberg's musical *l'Art pour l'Art*. Following from the first, the second proposition asserts that a composer cannot make pure and absolute decisions about suitable musical materials. A "historical" process (based on observation of "historical tendencies") regulates the relationship of suitable to unsuitable. Adorno tells us that in traditional musicological accounts the composer is free to choose from a wealth of musical material. This is a misconception contradicted by historical materialism. The actual material available is a fraction of the potential material, and the precise relationship of the actual to the potential is determined historically in light of a development such as Late Capitalism: "The presumption that the musical means themselves have a historical tendency contradicts the traditional interpretation of the material of music. It is defined physicalistically – in any event, in terms of a psychology of sound – as the sum total of sounds at the disposal of the composer. From this, however, the compositional material is as different as speech from the inventory of its sounds. Not only does it contract and expand in the course of history. All of its specific traits are marks of the historical process."[40] In order to distinguish a sound as suited to music, then, one cannot fall back on psychology or physics for justification. Exceptionally, Schoenberg says much the same thing about "non-harmonic tones" in the *Harmonielehre*: since all tones are suitable for harmony – all tones can create harmony – how can some be "non-harmonic" except by a historical process of determination?[41] An absolutely "pure" conception was responsible for the rejection of Schoenberg's *Transfigured Night* based on a "spurious" inversion of a dominant ninth chord (which aroused the ire of adjudicators attached to the concert society of the Vienna *Tonkünstlerverein*). The contradictions implicit in the adjudication are expressed by Schoenberg as follows (with a trenchant irony reminiscent of Adorno's prose): "Only now do I understand the objection, at that time beyond my comprehension, of that concert society which refused to perform my Sextet on account of this chord (its refusal was actually so explained). Naturally: inversions of ninth chords just don't exist; hence, no performance either, for how can one perform something that does not exist."[42] Again, purity as opposed to history is the question: the adjudicating committee did not recognize the chord since its usage by Schoenberg was an innovation (an impurity within the pure realm of harmony); within its absolute and ahistorical conception of harmony, the committee had no vehicle for comprehending history and thus innovation.

If, however, Schoenberg rued the lack of a historical sensitivity on the part of the adjudicators, he did not supply a history in the presentation of his *Formenlehre* (although historical elements begin to appear in the late chapters of his *Harmonielehre*). And even when accounting for history, Schoenberg left much wanting. Certainly the standard Second-Viennese-School explanation of historical change in musical material and technique falls well short of the kind of history Adorno had in mind. The standard explanation is articulated clearly in an essay by Anton Webern, *The Path to the New Music*, wherein he describes a natural evolution (*natural* in the sense of a socially neutral history) up the partials of the overtone series toward more and more complex sonorities.[43] This explanation falls well short of meeting Adorno's historical materialist needs. For Adorno, the suitability of a given harmony, a form, or a technique can be determined only in a dialectic relationship with unsuitability (since any pure and exclusive notion of suitability is logically invalid). Musical suitability is determined according to the histories of the composer, performer, and audience. Being historical, they are impure; they point outside themselves to other times, places, and people – and thus to other conceptions of musical form, harmony, and technique. There is nothing absolutely pure, in other words, when it comes to musical materials.

In essence, Adorno's critique is aimed at a music theory devoid of historical materialist reference. A harmony such as the "Tristan chord" is often taken out of context in theory treatises and studied as a "purely" harmonic phenomenon. But the chord expressed a moment in time, presumably distinguishing itself from all previous chordal usages by both its inherent shape and its application in the first measures of a Wagner opera; it would have been out of place in Mozart, and its usage since Wagner's time – in Berg's hands, for example – cannot help but invoke *Tristan und Isolde*. When studied as things in their own right (or when used as idioms or harmonic tricks), such chords can lose their historical context – "historical traits," as Adorno calls them. But the historical necessity of a chord is never truly lost; it must be borne by the chords around it. In this regard, Adorno speaks of a process of inversion. In the case of chords bearing a high degree of historical necessity such as the Tristan chord, the attention of the listener focuses on the chord itself, and thus its historical context recedes: "The more they bear historical necessity in themselves, the less they are immediately legible as historical traits." But that receding legibility leaves a vacuum: "In the moment when the historical expression of a chord can no longer be discerned, the chord demands that the sounds surrounding it do justice to its historical implications."[44] Attempting to describe the chord as a thing in its own right, Schoenberg excised it from its historical context and treated it as a singular entity, as if it were a sort of universal currency, to be plugged in here and there according to its "possibilities," not its necessities: "It can come from everywhere." But in the same breath, he restored its dependence on context and application: "What is essential for us is its function, and that is revealed when we know the possibilities the chord affords."[45]

Proposition 2, then, posits that all musical materials are governed by historical process. It follows, as proposition 3, that the suitability of musical materials for composition is determined by history, and a composer cannot help but compose under historical influence. In capitalism, musical material may seem to "self-locomote," operate absolutely and purely as if above the sway of history and human consciousness (in ways that hearken back to the mystique of Marx's commodity fetish). The V-I cadence would seem to carry its own sense of kinetics – tension on the V, resolution on the I. But what would appear as a self-standing kinetics of music is framed ultimately by a social history that prefers one form of chordal resolution at one moment and another form at another: "Of the same origin as the social process and ever and again laced through by its traces, what seems to be strictly the motion of the material itself moves in the same direction as does real society even where neither knows anything of the other and where each combats the other."[46] What is so purely natural and thus ahistorical about the V-I cadence, if it can be supplanted by other cadential gestures and ultimately suspended as the means of tonal punctuation in Schoenberg's opus 6 songs, notably the famous "Lockung"[47]?

History cannot be ignored. If a composer should try to pass off outdated material from another era as fresh and appropriate to its time, the audience will respond historically, detecting its "shabbiness and tiredness" as Adorno puts it.[48] On the other hand, if the composer tries to introduce a novelty, the audience will demand to know the historical and social forces behind it. The measure of a sound or a form is taken relative to sounds and forms that came before, this measured by a sense of progress both technical and social: "The most advanced level of technical procedures prescribes tasks compared to which the traditional sounds prove to be powerless clichés."[49] History renders a verdict, in other words, even on apparently pure musical harmonies. Every harmony has a historically appropriate moment determined by a horizon, the level of technique of a given time. Adorno goes into considerable detail in this regard (taking aim implicitly at Schoenberg's *Harmonielehre*) with reference to the diminished seventh chord: "What is decisive in the truth and falsity of chords is not their isolated occurrence. It is measurable exclusively by the total level of technique. The diminished seventh chord, which sounds false in salon music, is correct and filled with expression at the beginning of Beethoven's Sonata op. 111. Not only is the chord not patched in here, not only does it emerge from the constructive layout of the phrase, but the *niveau* of Beethoven's technique as a whole, the tension between the most extreme dissonance that was possible for him and the consonance, the harmonic perspective assimilating all melodic events, the dynamic conception of tonality as a whole, all confer on this chord its specific weight."[50]

The historical "specific weight" is written on the chord in indelible ink: it cannot be erased. Such a weight can only be deciphered within a context: "The defunct diminished seventh chord itself represents a state of technique that as a whole contradicts that of today ... No chord is simply 'in itself' false, because no chord exists in itself and because each chord bears in itself the whole, indeed the whole of history."[51]

Situating Beethoven's use of the diminished seventh chord against a materialist historical horizon, Adorno describes three aspects – its dissonance, its modulatory potential, and its dynamics. First, the chord lies historically on a continuum reckoned between dissonant and consonant chords. In Beethoven's day, the diminished seventh chord is extremely dissonant. By the time of the palm court orchestra it is much less so; in some repertoires it becomes almost consonant. Second, in Beethoven's music, the diminished seventh can be used to modulate to the most remote keys in abrupt and energetic fashion. By the time of the palm court orchestra, the modulatory energy of the diminished seventh chord is rendered innocuous if not

superfluous by other, more extreme forms of modulation and by
an expanded tonality. Third, the dynamic power of the diminished
seventh was confined to particular expressive situations in Beethoven's day. By the time of the palm court orchestra, more energetic
chords – the augmented triad, for instance – are required to revive
the flagging energies of innovation hitherto fed by the diminished
seventh. Chordal usage is to be understood as a social contract, its
horizon understood as socially determinate. For Adorno, no chord
is an island. The same holds for all aspects of musical material and
technique – including those manifestations of the *Formenlehre* discussed at the beginning of this chapter.

This is borne out with great clarity in Beethoven's late style. On
Adorno's account, the late style marks a clear blow to the preten-
sions of absolute and ahistorical music theory: music "loses that
freedom on a grand scale which idealistic aesthetics is accustomed
to grant the artist." Instead of being absolute, pure, and thus timeless, Beethoven's late music (as noted above) relies excessively on
the exaggerated use of conventions – fugue, aria, recitative, vocal
polyphony reminiscent of the Renaissance. But these conventions
qua conventional are negated by exaggeration. Convention is
contradicted by, as Adorno puts it, "disobedience, independence,
and spontaneity."

In other words, in the late style, technique demands a historical
accounting: Beethoven cannot use conventional techniques as if
they were still fresh and spontaneous (as he attempted to do in the
middle-period works); instead he must acknowledge their conven-
tionality through exaggeration, for example by extremes in dynamics and register and by unusual articulations. Through exaggeration,
then, technique acknowledges a historical determinant, in Beethov-
en's case a history pared down to the demands of "technique at any
given moment":

> Thus the image of the composer is at the same time transformed.
> He loses that grand-scale freedom that idealist aesthetics habitu-
> ally attributes to the artist. He is no creator. Society and the era
> in which he lives constrain him not externally but in the rigorous
> demand for correctness made on him by the composition. The
> state of technique presents itself to him as a problem in every
> measure that he dares to think: In every measure technique as a
> whole demands of him that he do it justice and give the one right

answer that technique in that moment permits ... What he does is located in the infinitely small. It is accomplished in the execution of what his music objectively demands from him. But for such obedience the composer requires all possible disobedience, all independence and spontaneity: The movement of the musical material is just that dialectical.[52]

Neither the self-sufficient composer nor the self-sufficient work of art is possible after the end of middle-period Beethoven (if they ever were). Dialectics has voided all possibility of self-sufficiency: "Today, however, this movement has turned against the closed work and everything it implies."[53]

The works Schoenberg composed after programmatic early works such as *Transfigured Night* and before the advent of the twelve-tone technique serve as test cases for Adorno's historical materialist theses. As a case in point, Schoenberg's op. 19 piano pieces are so expressive, so apparently "pure" in and of themselves, that they demand a historical accounting. Negating dialectically their putatively pure content, they make perfect sense historically, as an act of avoiding the slightest reference to moribund practices. An apparently absolute work such as op. 19 – a house without windows – places itself thus within a historical perspective.

Adorno's fourth proposition would seem to invalidate the first three: if the treatment of a theme through successive thematic variations is of a strength sufficient to create an absolute sense of time and history internal to the musical work, then the external pressures of time and historical tendency which invalidate such absolutes might be eclipsed temporarily. In the battle between idealist compositional subjectivity and historical and material constraint, Beethoven's middle period stands as a temporary victory for subjectivity. For Adorno, Beethoven appeared to create an internal musical narrative, and in doing so he perfected the notion of a "work in itself" that might have such an interior. Around this time and with Beethoven's oeuvre as a point of reference, the idea of an absolute work of art eclipses, however briefly, the notion of a socially determined work.

For Adorno, then, middle-period Beethoven presents the possibility of a music absolutely free of constraint and obligation.[54] This internal freedom was secured by means of thematic variation, a process whereby a theme (such as a sentence) undergoes transformations apparently of its own accord. Variation, however, led to freedom's demise. To put this into a grand historical perspective beginning prior to Beethoven: unvaried thematic repetition (of which the fugue is exemplary)[55] is superseded by varied thematic repetition or "developing variation" (typical of Beethoven's middle period, the development section of the sonata form in particular), and then by total variation (to Schoenberg via Brahms). When listening to a fugue, the listener recognizes the artifice of repeating a theme whole-sale between contrasting fugal episodes. This recognition imparts a certain mediated objectivity, allowing the listener to distinguish between the work as a thing created and themselves. By means of varied repetition of the kind found in middle-period Beethoven, however, artifice is replaced by the impression of naturalism, as if the work were to locomote of its own accord. If this variation is progressive – a perfect fifth becomes a perfect fourth, becomes a major third, becomes a minor third – then the listener's full attention is taken in hand by a musical narrative, as if musical development were an engrossing prose story. The *Eroica*, for example, is hermetic, its perception almost voyeuristic, as if the listener were watching the personal destiny of the motif. Adorno describes this state as dis-interested perception, by which he means perception turned away from historical and social self-interest; the listener surrenders the sense of self with which she would normally separate from the art-work: "The closed artwork was not an act of knowledge; rather, it made knowledge disappear into itself. It made itself an object of direct 'intuition' and enshrouded every fissure through which think-ing could escape the immediate givenness of the aesthetic object."[56] This "escape" becomes ever more difficult, as developing variation encompasses more and more of the work.

Ultimately total variation leads to works like Schoenberg's op. 19, an indecipherable mass of squirming variation wherein the actual theme has been eliminated as redundant. The distinction between theme and variation cannot function here. The only tenable formal distinction is the division between the self and the work's artifice – the fact that one is faced with a work created as if to avoid for-mal narrative. On this account, however, total variation produces a mediated self-awareness by alienating the self from any spellbinding musical narrative; the act of creation through composition – musical labour – becomes intelligible again, where it was obscured before (in middle-period Beethoven). This marks a return to the sense of self as elicited when listening to the fugue.

Adorno accounted historically for these three stages in the life of developing variation. In early practices (Bach and Mozart), themes could be developed by the composer only after they were stated securely for the benefit of the listener. Thus the composer was constrained to acknowledge the listener (certainly, in the case of Mozart, his patrons), and indeed the listener expected to be acknowledged as a participant in musical creation. (And thus listeners both aristocratic and bourgeois came to play a decisive role in the stylistic determination of classical music.) But Beethoven in his middle period, freeing himself from such constraints, made development rather than thematic identification the focal point of his work. Thus musical works with their self-contained narratives lent themselves to commodification, and the participating listener became instead a spectator and a consumer. Adorno makes middle-period Beethovenian variation the *prima causa* of new forms, forms that seem to work autonomously without acknowledging the participation of the listener: "At the start, in the eighteenth century, development was a small part of the sonata. Once themes were stated and adequately established in the music, they were modified by subjective illumination and dynamism. In Beethoven, however, development, the subjective reflection of the theme that decides its fate, becomes the center of the form altogether ... In music before Beethoven, with hardly an exception, variation was counted among the most superficial of technical procedures ... Now, however, conjoined with development, variation serves the production of universal, concrete, nonschematic relationships."[57]

Middle-period Beethovenian variation, then, draws the listener's attention as a consumer (rather than a creator) into the musical matter at hand, so much so that the work appears to take on a dynamic life of its own to which the listener's presence is at best secondary. Certain formal consequences devolve from this. Beethovenian variation involves a sense of time internal to the musical work – a temporal distinction between the theme and each of its variations. This sense of purely musical time (and a sense of internal history and historical tendency) seems to reside absolutely within the work. Music is internally "no longer indifferent to time," as it was in Bach's day. Instead music takes time in hand through a temporal process of development: "Music is no longer indifferent to time, for in time it is no longer arbitrarily repeated; rather it is transformed."[58]

In the late works, Beethoven can barely restrain the dynamic forces thus conjured. Variation spills over into the exposition and recapitulation, and even into the coda, so that the whole work evolves into a grand scene of a narration. (Presumably, this happens in contrast to the use of convention and repetition to produce mediation, as described elsewhere in this book.) After Beethoven, the process of variation is extended formally (alongside the continued resurrection of convention) by Brahms so as to make the whole sonata a framework for dynamic temporality. The result is a confusion of the subjective with the objective:

> For this reason, the intervening variation in the most authoritative works of Beethoven's so-called classicism, such as the *Eroica*, contents itself with the development of the sonata as with a "part" and respectfully prescinds from the exposition and the reprise. For later music, however, the empty course of time becomes ever more threatening precisely by virtue of those dynamic powers of subjective expression that demolish all conventional residues. The subjective moments of expression detach themselves from the temporal continuum. They can no longer be mastered. To counteract this, the development – based on variation – unfurls across the entire sonata ... In Brahms, development, as thematic labour, had already utterly seized possession of the sonata. Subjectivization and objectivation intertwine.[59]

In other words, subjectivity allows itself to be swept along with the musical narrative, and having done so, "intertwines" with objectivity, presumably capturing objectivity in its coils.

In retrospect, Brahms's sonata forms – and his other allusions to musical convention – appear as stopgap measures aimed at containing and harnessing a dynamic process raging out of control. Rising dangerously alongside Brahms is the Wagnerian spectre of leitmotivic variation and thematic development-at-any-cost, development "at the expense of objectivity and binding force in the music itself." Wagnerian endless variation drives the listener mercilessly. Without the objective distinction between theme and variation the listener is put entirely at the mercy of the composer's scruples (or lack thereof): "The transformation of language was achieved along the lines of the Wagnerian romantic tradition, to the detriment of the objectivity and bindingness of music itself. It broke up the motivic-thematic unity of the art song and surrogated leitmotif and programmatics."[60] Unfettered development shatters the distinction between essential and unessential and thus it invalidates the distinction between "theme" and "transition," as ultimately it invalidates "development" and even "form": "There is no longer any inessential transition between essential elements, the 'themes'; consequently, there are no longer any themes at all or, in the strictest sense, any 'development.'"[61]

With total development, the musical narrative that ensnared the listener's attention dissolves. There is no story, after all, if there is no plot. And thereby the "absolute" moment in music history – with middle-period Beethoven as its apogee – comes to a dissolute end at the feet of Schoenberg, perhaps coincidentally at roughly the same moment that the economics of Adam Smith come to rest at Lenin's feet in Petrograd in the late fall of 1917.

The fifth proposition takes the fourth to its implicit consequent: if every moment of a musical work is given over to variation, then logically the theme or subject of the variation is thereby eradicated and the variation form itself is invalidated, or as Adorno put it, "If musical nominalism, the annulment of all recurring formulae, is thought through to the end, differentiation tumbles."[62] In other words, if variation and theme become indistinguishable, then the basic form of the musical work is destroyed and with it any interior absolutes of time and history. The work of art reverts to being entirely determined by historical tendencies external to the work. What seems like the purest of the pure – the work of total variation, op. 19 – is thus transformed by its very purity from an absolute into a historical artifact subject to the kind of analysis Adorno practises.

Schoenberg sought to avert this development by means of the twelve-tone row. The contrasts and variations to which the row was subject would replicate the internal narratives of Beethoven's middle-period forms. High classical form would be thus "restored," to use Adorno's term.

Schoenberg's solution was fatally flawed, however. In middle-period Beethoven, the narrative of developing variation is expressed entirely within the work through the manipulation of the work's own motivic and thematic content. A twelve-tone composition, however, develops a row through its row forms, all of which are pre-determined externally to the composition of the actual work. The

actual use of the row proceeds in the work as if it were taking part
in a middle-period-Beethovenian narrative, but this follows only
after all its possible forms have been worked out on the composer's
sketch pad. This working out takes place in a sense absolutely, without necessary reference to the final work; one and the same row,
after all, can be applied to two or more works. In this sense the row
is never developed as a true theme per se: the first actual statement
of the row as a "theme" (the first row form stated in the piece) is
in fact already a variation of the precompositional row; this theme
statement is referred to as "prime" or referential only because of
being heard first.

Addressing this abstraction, Adorno calls the objectivity of the
row "an omnipresent construction," omnipresent in both spatial
and temporal terms, everywhere at all times. In a twelve-tone work,
any sense of musical time interior to the work must of necessity be
"dissociated" from its moment of birth. Thus musical time is funda-
mentally invalidated, and music, at least in the internal dimension
of the work, "no longer recognizes history," a history internal to the
work. The interior dynamics of the musical work lapse back into
the stasis – "statics" – of total variation. As a corollary, composition per se falls into stasis at the hands of the twelve-tone method:
"Twelve-tone technique contradicts dynamics."[63] Or, "The elements
of the course of music are, like psychological impulses, juxtaposed
sequentially, first as shocks and then as contrasting figures. The continuum of subjective experiential time is no longer believed to have
the power to integrate musical events and, as their unity, to give
them meaning. Such discontinuity, however, kills the music dynamic
to which music owes its own existence. Once again music masters
time – but no longer by guaranteeing its fulfilment, but rather by
negating time through the suspension of all musical elements as a
result of omnipresent construction."[64] Omnipresent construction –
the predetermination of the row, which hovers above the work like
Schoenberg's Supreme Commander.

Adorno describes the limitations of the twelve-tone technique
elsewhere from social perspectives, a matter beyond the scope of
this book. Noteworthy, however, is the brief assessment – brief
but brutal – in "The Aging of the New Music," which carves out a
very small territory for the technique, while it casts the rest away:
"Twelve-tone technique has its justification only in the presentation
of complex musical contents, which cannot otherwise be organized.

Separated from this function, it degenerates into a deluded system."[65] The importance of his twelve-tone critique as a critique of
systematization must have been particularly pressing to Adorno,
having himself partaken of the procedure in his own compositions.[66]

In terms of this interior stasis, Adorno equates the twelve-tone
works of Schoenberg with jazz and Stravinsky: "Late Schoenberg
shares with jazz – and, incidentally, also with Stravinsky – the dis-
sociation of musical time."[67] Thus, as noted, Schoenberg's twelve-
tone attempt at restoring a dynamic interior to a musical work, a
work's "own self-development," is invalidated: "Thematic labour
becomes merely part of the composer's preliminary labour. Variation
as such no longer appears at all. Everything and nothing is variation; the process of variation is itself relegated to the material and
preforms it before the composition properly begins."[68] Variation,
in other words, takes place primarily on the composer's sketching
table, well before the actual writing of the work.

Instead of becoming absolutely resplendent in the freedom of
developing variation, Schoenberg's music becomes the perfect symptom of musical delusion.[69] The row has all the trappings of commodity exchange value – to be used one day in this particular work or in
this manner, and on another day in an entirely different manner or
in different circumstances. This whole development – the demise of
variation and of internal musical dynamic– is itself produced by a
grand historical tendency, the bourgeois suspicion of rampant subjectivity, a suspicion which much prefers logical objectivity to magic:
"A system of the domination of nature results. It answers to a longing arising out of the primordial age of the bourgeoisie: to seize all
that sounds in a regulatory grasp and dissolve the magic of music in
human reason."[70]

The sixth proposition renders a verdict on the aspirations of a
composer such as Schoenberg: any attempt to reconstitute the
internal absolutes of the musical work, along the lines of middle-
period Beethoven, by means of a dominating system – in terms of
technique, the system of composition with twelve tones – is simply naive. The system takes over and sublimates any semblance of
freedom that might be compared with the subjective freedom of
Beethoven's working method. Normally the composer is free to treat
the material systematically. But in the instance of the twelve-tone
technique, the system takes over and subordinates that freedom:
"The subject rules over the music by means of a rational system

in order to succumb to this rational system itself. Just as in twelve-tone technique – in the composition proper – the productivity of the variation is forced back into the material, so it turns out for the freedom of the composer in general. Whereas this freedom is [normally] achieved in its disposal over the material, [the system] becomes a determination of the material, a determination that confronts the subject as something alien and in turn subordinates the subject to its constraint. The composer's fantasy made the material entirely malleable to his own constructive will, but the constructive material hamstrings fantasy itself."[71] Thus naïveté becomes Adorno's verdict on Schoenberg's music and implicitly his verdict on the composer's capacity for self-delusion.

These six propositions can be telescoped, brought together in the viewfinder of a single historical perspective. Propositions 1 to 3 describe the state of affairs prior to middle-period Beethoven: musical material – its suitability– is determined by historical tendency, and neither work nor composer is an absolute, above the material wiles of history. Proposition 4, however, describes affairs at the time of Beethoven's middle period, where musical materials are used in such a way that they appear to take on internal histories and internal temporalities that lend them a self-contained, absolute quality. External history would appear to be irrelevant on this account. Proposition 5 addresses the demise of the middle-period Beethovenian absolute. Variation, like narration, depends on form (a sense of tonality, or a theme as a starting point). This sense of an absolute form can be destroyed – made too patently conventional (as in late Beethoven), or softened by a technique of extreme variation (in Brahms) or invalidated by *Leitmotiv* (in Wagner). When form is destroyed, the internal objectivity of a work – internal absolute musical time – crumbles, as Adorno puts it. A composer such as Schoenberg will be forced to relocate objectivity outside the work, either through total variation (as in op. 19) or through the twelve-tone technique. In the case of the latter, the precompositional nature of the row and its properties invalidate any subjectivity that might otherwise produce a dynamic narrative internal to the work. As proposition 6 states, the twelve-tone technique is, in and of itself, a creative cul-de-sac.[72]

Reactionaries in Adorno's day claimed that the work of composers such as Schoenberg is decadent, individualistic, and asocial in character. For Adorno, nothing could be further from the truth; ironically, Schoenberg's work carries too little of these qualities. The music is anything but decadent: as timely (and as perennial) as capitalism, Schoenberg's work responds precisely to the needs of commodification; even Mahler's jackass will sense the social implications of Schoenberg's work – that it reflects perfectly a world where individual existence is shaped by determinate forces well beyond our comprehension (even that of a sublime jackass). And to this end, Schoenberg is hardly individualistic – making instead grand sacrifices, wandering Moses-like in his wilderness without full comprehension of the greater design. Given its twelve-tone organization, charges of formlessness must fade before the all too patent organization of the work – the determination of the row and its forms. Schoenberg's twelve-tone works are exemplars of bourgeois culture in Late Capitalism, produced by logic carried out at the ultimate expense of subjectivity. In this regard, they are perfectly formed.

The reactionaries have it all wrong, then; nothing could be more reactionary than Schoenberg. Seeking freedom in his music, Schoenberg produced a method by which it was transformed into a model of the very world against which it protests: "The determinate freedom in which music attempted to reconceive its anarchic situation reversed before its very eyes into an image of the world against which it rebels. It flees forward into orderliness."[73] Schoenberg's music becomes thus a vehicle of truth. As functionless art (in contrast to functionally repressive music such as Wagner's), it "delineates the image of total repression."[74] The twelve-tone method redeems itself as a barometer of historical materialism (and not as an absolute thing, *l'Art pour l'Art* as its composer naively suggests).[75]

Adorno's principal accusation of naïveté is set forth in the following quotation. Destroying compositional authority in his twelve-tone music, Schoenberg naively clung to a phony authority in his self-awareness and his work: "While inflicting the most deadly blows on authority through his work, he seeks to defend the work as though before a hidden authority and ultimately to make it itself the authority."[76] This clinging to a false authority had detrimental consequences for Schoenberg's music and sparked Adorno's harshest critique. Whatever revolutionary nature the twelve-tone music retained from the period of op. 19 (the striking dissonance, the rhythmic complexity) was compromised by the retention of naive anachronisms such as the dance idioms of the Baroque suite and the *Formenlehre* constructions found in works such as Gigue of op. 25.

Schoenberg "continued to speak the idiom and to strive for the kind of musical texture which is inseparably tied to the means he eliminated ... Even in his most advanced works he remained traditional; he excluded the material of musical language which had provided musical structure with its basis since the beginning of the seventeenth century, and yet retained the structural categories ... the familiar categories of musical structure, like theme, elaboration, tension, resolution, [which] no longer suit the material he has set free."[77]

Schoenberg continued to believe in a composer's subjective freedom. He attempted by sheer stubborn determination to create a subjective synthesis in his musical work in an era when the synthesis of subjectivity and objectivity was simply no longer possible. To do so, he devised a technique that assured the fracture of subjective synthesis. As Adorno described the situation, "The break between the substantiality of the ego and the over-all structure of social existence, which denies the ego not merely external sanction but its necessary preconditions as well, has become too profound to permit works of art a synthesis."[78] Any attempt at objectivity is "futile."[79] The twelve-tone technique, accordingly, is an exercise in futility.

Adorno's ultimate verdict, however, redeems Schoenberg's music, if not the composer's sense of self. Schoenberg's art contradicts his naïveté: "Against his will, that which crystallized in his work embodied immanent musical opposition to such socially naive conceptions." Schoenberg's music itself is thus remaindered and made objective by this very naïveté. Success despite the best of intentions.

5

Wagner, Terrorist

For people who want the kind of effortless suppression of awareness they get from music, there is a wonderful recent discovery which far surpasses that art. We refer to ether and chloroform.

Eduard Hanslick, *On the Musically Beautiful*

The ultimate object of Adorno's Wagnerian study in social character would appear to be pathology.[1] Adorno gravitates to the dark side: the psyche split, Wagner is denied the normal psychological correctives that produce integrity in most humans.[2] Whatever he accomplished for the good of humankind is negated by the service it rendered Wagner himself. Wagner's "ego"-centricity blankets his altruism like smog.

Adorno uses the term *terrorist* sparingly in the Wagner essay and yet it encapsulates what I take to be essential to his diagnosis of a Wagnerian pathology. One of the central undertakings of the Frankfurt school in the 1930s was the analysis of terrorism.[3] (The extent to which this served to counter terrorism is debatable.[4]) In the later essay "Freudian Theory and the Pattern of Fascist Propaganda," written in 1951, Adorno draws together much of his thinking on fascism from the 1930s and 1940s and makes explicit many of the Freudian underpinnings found in the Wagner essay.[5] Indeed, while there is no mention of Wagner in the 1951 essay, the *Versuch über Wagner* (published in 1952) seem like the 1951 essay writ large and pinned on Wagner. As Adorno attests in his preface to the *Versuch*, and as Nicholas Baragwanath has shown in detail, the Wagner study is linked closely with Max Horkheimer's "Egoism and the Movement for Emancipation: Towards an Anthropology of the Bourgeois Era."[6] The *Versuch*'s other debt is to anti-Semitism, which surfaces notably in Wagner's treatment of the conductor Hermann Levi and Wagner's "characterization of Jews" in chapter 1. Not coincidentally the collective project *The Authoritarian Personality*, in which both fascism and anti-Semitism are critical objects, was published in 1950; Adorno became a participant in 1944.[7]

On first blush, then, terrorism would appear a secondary matter in the *Versuch*, the echo of work carried out elsewhere. But in truth it lends continuity to Adorno's "micrological" treatment of operatic character in the first chapter. He describes the social character of Rienzi: "the last Roman tribune and the first bourgeois terrorist [*des letzten römischen Tribunen und ersten bürgerlichen Terroristen*]."[8] And Wotan's dispatch of "Hunding, the primordial husband": "the contemptuous wave of the hand with which Wotan dismisses Hunding is itself essentially a terrorist gesture."[9] In describing Wagner's own character and work, however, Adorno makes frequent comparison with tyranny and terrorism, in particular the character of fascism, its leading personalities, and their mode of operation: "Self praise and pomp – features of Wagner's entire output and the emblem of Fascism – spring from the transient nature of bourgeois terrorism."[10]

The term *social character* as Adorno applied it to Wagner evokes the term *physiognomic*,[11] as if the character of a society could be read off the face of the man.[12] Implicit here is analysis – *physiognomy* as a process of analysis – and thus a debt to Freud. Adorno, however, makes explicit reference to Freud only twice in the *Versuch* (although the *Versuch* owes a Freudian debt to both Horkheimer and the earlier essay on fascism).

First, Adorno links Brünnhilde's wilfulness to an "attenuated form" of an "internal impulse" expressed by archaic man originally in violent action, an impulse expressed now, however, "only in dreams and madness" as deciphered by Freud.[13] Henry Klumpenhouwer, in a review of Deborah Cook's *The Culture Industry Revisited: Theodor W. Adorno on Mass Culture*, and other books, puts the matter succinctly: "Central to Adorno's working out of an appropriate social-psychological critique is his intention to isolate and describe the appearance not only of the psychological pathologies of individuals, but also (and more importantly) the emergence of what might be called public or social pathologies."[14] This is accomplished by means of the "'weak father thesis,' developed earlier by Horkheimer"; Klumpenhouwer adds, "The individual psyche generated under these conditions is characterized by both Adorno and Horkheimer as 'narcissistic.'"[15] The backdrop for this idea – with the "individual" as a horizon – is sketched thus by Cook herself: "The individual is antagonistic to capitalism because of its ungratified biological instincts which have a potentially resistive force."[16] Brünnhilde, then, embodies as a dramatic characterization this resistive force (no doubt resistance to Wotan, who, in turn, embodies as a dramatic character his own repressed resistive forces to the force of Law annunciated throughout the *Ring*). The notion is suggestive – Wagner anticipating Freud by means of Brünnhilde – but it steers away from Wagner's character itself as the subject of Freudian-underpinned inquiry.[17]

Adorno's second Freudian citation in the *Versuch*, while it is likewise concerned with dramatic characters, is directed more at Wagner himself. Adorno states that Wagner transforms Schopenhauer's "metaphysical concept of the will into the more manageable theory of the collective unconscious."[18] Adorno takes up the opposition of Freud and Carl Jung made in a preceding passage (hinting at the fascist implications of collective will implicit in Jung's collective unconsciousness): "Ultimately this turns into the 'soul of the people,' in which a brutality borrowed from the overbearing individual combines in an explosive mixture with the amorphous masses who have been solicitously protected from any thoughts of an antagonistic society."[19] This observation sets up much of the critique of Wagner in chapter 1 of the *Versuch* as an overbearing individual exercising an uncanny control over the amorphous masses at Bayreuth. Subsequent references to Freudian constructs (as well as Jungian) make sense as diagnoses of the individual instinctive terrorism worming its way through Wagner's life. Terrorism on this account is a social entity, not merely the psychic wreckage of an individual.

By *social character* then, Adorno denotes the relationship of Wagner's individual conduct to the important "tendencies" at work in society, the gravitation toward terrorism and totalitarianism being particularly important in Wagner's case. In this sense, physiognomics as a tool of social diagnosis can be applied, after Adorno, to human conduct (to Wagner's or Mahler's), or a literature (musical or otherwise), or the attributes of a larger entity whose social character is read by a special form of observation focused on the individual.[20] In drawing a distinction between *social character* and *physiognomics*, I presume that the former is a subset of the latter, *social character* being thus a type of physiognomic analysis applied to humans in a broad sense so as to discern those elements of a human character that point in indexical fashion to aspects of society.[21]

A study of social character along Adorno's lines is a biographical examination of the individual as an "exponent and locus" for society: "social character – the private individual as the exponent and locus of social tendencies ... If the connection is not made between the power of artistic production that was concentrated in [Wagner] and the society, whatever accusations are made against him are pure philistinism, not far removed from the contemptible genre of fictionalized biographies."[22] The goal, after Adorno, is not a sketch of character per se but character as a lens for viewing social context.

The character study of an individual, on this account, is similar to the criticism of a work of art where the latter is understood as a social diagnostic. The study assumes that a work of art reflects, in a particularly Adornian fashion, the society within which it locates itself. As Lambert Zuidervaart puts it, citing Adorno's *Aesthetic Theory*,

> When Adorno writes on art, he tends to develop tensions within particular works that echo tensions in society as a whole. Obviously this description must be qualified; Adorno does address the social position of art as a whole, and he does comment on the production and consumption of art. Nevertheless his focus remains on tensions within the work of art. The main claim in the section titled "The Mediation of Art and Society," for example, is that works of art express the social totality: "The process that occurs in art works and which is arrested in them has to be conceived as being the same as the social process surrounding them. In Leibnizian terminology, they represent this process in a windowless fashion ... All that art works do or bring forth has its latent model in social production."[23] To ask about the structure of Adorno's model of social mediation, then, is to ask about the structure of the artwork as a social monad whose internal process brings forth the social process surrounding it.[24]

In this regard, Adorno concentrates on tensions – in Schoenberg, for example, the tension between insight and blindness – as these reflect the social circumstances that give birth to character. In this manner he describes Schoenberg, who, while adhering to a vision of the world in keeping with the remnants of Hapsburg Vienna, cultivated nonetheless a hostility to that world by means of a latent, chthonic force: "In the eyes of the Viennese composer, coming from a parochial background, the norms of a closed, semi-feudal society seemed the will of God. Yet this respect was linked to an opposing element, although one no less incompatible with the notion of the intellectual. Something not integrated, not entirely civilized, indeed hostile to civilization, kept him outside the very order of which he was so uncritical. Like a man without origins, fallen from heaven, a musical Caspar Hauser, he hit the bullseye unerringly. Nothing was allowed to recall the natural milieu to which he nonetheless belonged, and the result was that his undeveloped nature became all the more evident."[25]

Adorno is not concerned, however, with just any character or just any piece of music. Colin Sample sets forth a basic principle of autonomy, as applicable to character as it is to a work of music, in a review of Adorno's fragmentary *Beethoven, Philosophie der Musik*: a "most basic principle of Adorno's aesthetics, which could be called *the principle of the formal mimesis of social reality*, can be summarized as follows: The greater the autonomy of an artwork from social or institutional imperatives, the more precisely will its formal constitution depict the structure and conflicts of the society in which the artist works."[26] In this regard, Schoenberg and Wagner stand out as special instances of autonomous characters, precisely suited to studies in social physiognomy.

Adorno's broadest critical perspective takes in the production and consumption of character – how, for example, Wagner's character was both produced and consumed by his bourgeois audience. But this is not the stuff of social biography – a narrative in which the writer assumes that events in a given society produced a directly corresponding reaction in character. Instead the evocation of the monad entails an indirect relationship between character and society, a relationship inscribed internally on the character, the nature of which is brought forth as the character operates. This kind of character expresses social circumstance as if it were written on the face. Consider the notion touched on above: Schoenberg made his audience work for their leisure. In doing so, Schoenberg expressed a notion of musical labour appropriate to his own character – the naive composer forced ever more strenuously (a form of labour) to defend his naïveté through works of greater and greater sophistication.

Tracing Wagner's character, Adorno begins with the early, lesser known operas, as if searching for the first symptoms of an ailment that manifests itself later in full-blown pathology. He starts with an autobiographical note, penned by Wagner in later years, on *Das Liebesverbot*, whose libretto is based on Shakespeare's *Measure for Measure*. A contrite Wagner offers a self-criticism: in composing the opera he downplayed an element of Shakespearean justice rooted in the conflict of opposing social forces and the duties of good government, the "element of dramatic 'justice' that alone made possible the development of the opposing forces in Shakespeare."[27] In lieu of treating justice, he concentrated on an element of "free sensuality" by which he sought to overturn something of the puritanical hypocrisy of his day.

The substitution of sensuality for social justice in Wagner's first opera is ironic. This substitution – unbridled passion in lieu of ethics – is the kind of social tendency Adorno finds characteristic of Wagner's whole life and work, a substitution that, in erasing justice and ethics, produces a full-blown demonic aspect in the composer's character. For Wagner to confess such an infraction is shamelessly self-serving: the old composer confesses to a sin of his youth, thus drawing attention away from its continuance to the present day.

I shall call the sin in question a *Wagnerian contrition* since it is the kind of self-serving activity many of Wagner's characters, Wotan in particular, engage in throughout the operas. Wagnerian contrition falls far short of doing justice to the sin. Absolving only the youthful error, it leaves its mature continuation intact.

The plot of *Rienzi*, wherein physiognomy is much easier to read, is an example of what Adorno calls *bourgeois terrorism* – a terrorism produced by the people for the people. With their permission, Rienzi usurps the power of the bourgeois establishment, whom he then oppresses. Propping up the appearance of shared power, he builds an empty shell, again with complete bourgeois collaboration: youth dressed in snappy togas, a dictator's sense of concern for the welfare of the poor (read National Socialism), and a universally acclaimed end to a libertine style of life (read "family values"). The Tribune makes a character transformation from plebeian to tyrant.

Bourgeois terrorism of this tyrannic ilk carries an awareness of its own excess and anticipates its own demise. Requiring an act of Wagnerian contrition, Rienzi, the bourgeois Tribune, must fall.

Unfortunately his self-sacrifice will take others with him. Calling this the "death instinct," Adorno sees therein the recipe for Fascism as well as a pencil sketch of Wagner's *Ring*: "Self-praise and pomp – features of Wagner's entire output and the emblems of fascism – spring from the presentiment of the transient nature of bourgeois terrorism, of the death instinct implicit in the heroism that proclaims itself. The man who seeks immortality during his lifetime doubts that his achievement will survive him and so he celebrates his own obsequies with festive ceremonial. Death and destruction stand behind the Wagnerian facade of liberty: the historic ruins, which come crashing down on the costumed heroes of freedom, are the models of metaphysics, which engulf the powerless Gods and the guilt-ridden world of the *Ring*."[28] The bourgeois bystanders are spared no mercy but instead form part of the ritual sacrifice anticipated in Rienzi's transient victory. Comparison to the demise of Hitler is patent: "The Hitlerian statement that if his regime should ever collapse he would slam the door so that the whole world could hear it, is indicative of something much farther reaching than it seems to express ... The Germans permanently anticipated, as it were, the revenge for their own downfall. This may suffice as an example for speculations on the innermost secrets of Nazi mentality and Nazi reality as suggested by the Wagnerian work."[29] A foretaste of Berlin, late April 1945, Rienzi falls and drags with him Irene and the other misguided plebeians who supported him.

In *Rienzi*, as in *Liebesverbot*, social justice is set aside, this time for a petty bourgeois death. Incapable of self-criticism, the hero debases himself and everyone standing in his shadow; thus all are made equal – the hero included – and all differences erased, all the hero's sins cleansed in debasement, again a Wagnerian contrition that deflects the full weight of justice from the hero to his entourage. Social justice is thus violated, as it will be again in the *Ring*; the drama celebrates only the characters and their psychoses. By way of comparison, the drama of Shakespeare's *Coriolanus* has a truly allegorical component to it: Coriolanus the hero becomes a dramatic category that will not be encompassed by a mere play, and thus *Coriolanus* extends beyond itself as a moral lesson. *Rienzi* could have been a noble allegory, but the Wagnerian obsession with character pathology forbade it.

The seeds are sown in *Rienzi*, but in the operas that follow, Adorno tells us, dramatic "harmony is achieved [only] in the name of death,"[30] the death of the innocent. Tannhauser, for example, having been reconciled in death, must drag the pious Elizabeth down with him, thus cleansing his crime with her blood, as Faust is cleansed by Margaret. For Adorno, innocent death becomes the Faustian price Wagner pays for achieving dramatic harmony.

From *Rienzi* onward in Wagner's oeuvre, the common people – the Gibichungs, Isolde's nation, the working stiffs in *Meistersinger* – bear the brunt of state-sanctioned terrorism: "The insignificant are punished, while the prominent go scot-free."[31] The middle classes– "knights, guild-masters and all figures from the middle of the social hierarchy" – become collateral damage; they shoulder the liberties, they pay for the "dispensation from middle-class obligations" their superiors in the operatic Politburo enjoy.[32] Rhinemaidens and norns soak up the commitments of an upwardly mobile meritocracy and thereby characters such as Wotan receive dispensation. Wotan, who will not commit to written contract but instead moves about in the manner of a covert intelligence agency, "appears to defend rebellion, but he does so only in the interests of his universal imperialist design and in terms of the categories of freedom of action ... and breach of contract."[33] Thus he disenfranchises the very souls he would set free and then calls a holocaust down upon himself and them. The reader is at liberty to draw analogies with regimes closer to home, but comparison to the Nazis is implicit once again in Adorno's case. The plots of the operas are parables of terrorism, physiognomic in their reflection of nascent Central-European fascism.

With a passing reference to Marat (whom Wagner once discerned in a photograph of himself), Adorno turns his focus directly on the composer, holding Wagner up to much the same mirror of dramatic justice he has held to Rienzi and Wotan. Wagner has lost psychological integrity. A virtuous sentimentality – perhaps a sympathy engendered within us by a momentary human weakness or error – allows us to forgive other human beings. But the two parts of Wagner's character, virtue and sentiment, do not add up to integrity as they would in another human. The virtue rings hollow, the sentimentality is disingenuous. Adorno calls it *begging*: "This sentimentality assumes sinister features in Wagner's make-up: those of the man who begs for sympathy."[34]

A sentimental mask of virtue – like the cloth of Roman good draped across Rienzi – allows Wagner to achieve a superficial integrity. For Adorno, however, Wagner is the man on the run, the rebel with no cause but himself. His family is virtual – anyone who will listen with sympathy. The listener, however, gains nothing and loses much by the interaction. Adorno describes Siegmund in these Wagnerian terms: "As a restless wanderer he appeals for sympathy and uses this as a means of acquiring a woman and a weapon."[35] There is little to separate Wagner from Siegmund (or Brando): their apparent virtue appeals to the libertine in women and to the revolutionary comrade-at-arms in men. Hunding recognizes all too well what this vagabond Siegmund entails and yet succumbs like a drugged man to the terrorist's appeal for shelter. His nocturnal draught is merely an ironic token of the toxic sedation Siegmund exudes.

The fissures in the psyche of Wagner's characters project the physiognomy of the composer himself. They indicate, for Adorno, a state of lost integrity and dissipated virtue, a blend of envy, sentimentality, and destructiveness. Wagner's social character foreshadows a widespread rupture in the bourgeois social character, a psychic split that lays the groundwork for the music and the totalitarianism of the future. Schizophrenic, lacking integrity, the bourgeois characters in the operas – and the Weimar Republic – are rendered susceptible to the first totalitarian who happens by. Wagner, in terms of physiognomy, is a foreshadowing. Bourgeois moral decay as expressed in Wagner's terms is a prototype for totalitarianism: "For the focal points of decay in the bourgeois character, in terms of its own morality, are the prototypes of its subsequent transformation in the age of totalitarianism."[36]

In these ways, Wagnerian portraiture takes on a physiognomic quality – in Adorno's text, first in the characters in the operas, second in the composer himself. After Adorno, the method of physiognomic portraiture becomes a spontaneous comparison between object, be it music or man, and its setting, principally the social tendency toward terrorism. The task of reading off social character is made all the easier by the latent pathology of the object under study. (And while no composer is an angel, one wonders how Bach's physiognomic might have been read off his work – certainly the *Passions* – and in comparison to the man himself.) Following Adorno the phrenologist, we feel the bumps and indentations on Wagner's skull, as if they were anticipating pathology-producing lesions on the interior. Nowhere is mode of operation made clearer than in Adorno's analyses of Wagner's scores.

The fact remains, however, that score analysis appears only haphazardly throughout Adorno's *Wagner*, as elsewhere in Adorno's writings, frustrating modern scholarly sensibilities raised in an era of abundant and detailed score analysis.[37] The situation is made all the more frustrating because Adorno himself draws an emphatic link in principle between Wagnerian social character and what he calls musical analysis: "A minute musical analysis of Wagner's works yields insight into the repressive, compulsory, blind and ultimately anti-individual way of his composing in a very concrete and tangible sense. His music itself speaks the language of Fascism, quite apart from plots and bombastic words."[38]

Adorno is engaged, however, in a very different form of score analysis. The object is not an ideal structure such as the Schenkerian *Ursatz* but a form of musical labour in the sense discerned in Adorno's treatment of Beethoven's Late Style. In the latter, as I sought to demonstrate in an earlier chapter, music performs philosophical labour; it draws its listener's attention to themselves, thus illuminating the self through a form of musical mediation. In Wagner's case, music performs the work of physiognomy: it provokes the listener to make a minute analysis of social circumstance in terms of the character of the composer and his work, to measure the conformity of Wagner's character to its society (and to the Central-European society that follows after Wagner's death).

One of the principal objects of Adorno's Wagnerian physiognomy-as-social-analysis is the *leitmotiv*, which is made a vehicle for Wagner's demonic social character. The leitmotiv cannot be argued with. Its caprices forbid any logical analysis and thus any resistance: "Confronted with [the leitmotiv's] irrational superiority, its seal of unmistakability, the individual subject has no alternative but to capitulate."[39] Like Schoenberg's audience, Wagner's listener is driven by the music, made to work – to resist and then capitulate. The leitmotiv produces an effect like that of a totalitarian speech, substituting sheer brutal force for logic:[40] "The audience of these giant works lasting many hours is thought of as unable to concentrate – something not unconnected with the fatigue of the citizen in his leisure time. And while he allows himself to drift with the current, the music, acting as its own impresario, thunders at him in endless repetitions to hammer its message home."[41] By means of leitmotiv, then, an act of terrorism – agitation – is carried out in the musical text: "The musical logic ... is softened up and replaced by a sort of gesticulation, rather in the way that agitators substitute linguistic gestures for the discursive exposition of their thoughts."[42]

Thus Adorno draws an analytic link between Wagner's character and the particulars of his music: because of the leimotiv, Wagner's music is formless, devoid of logic, lacking a technical content that might lend itself to customary score analysis. The fact of this emptiness is the starting point for social analysis.[43]

Emptiness in the musical score, however, is not due to a creative lapse on Wagner's part. Produced as if by a conscious or a pathologically unconscious design on the part of the composer, the score's aim appears to be as empty of true substance as was Wagner himself. Like Rienzi and later Siegmund, he offered nothing material in return to the bourgeoisie and aristocracy who provided for his existence, and his works give nothing in return for the listener's attention. The listener is put to work, made to labour, not the music (and not the composer). Substituting leitmotifs for logically developed themes, Wagner evacuates musical content: as Adorno put it with more than a touch of sarcasm, there is a "grain of truth contained in the charge of [Wagnerian] formlessness."[44] Like the self-destructing record of a perfect crime, Wagner's scores liquidate themselves through performance, leaving nothing that a customary analysis of musical content might trace: "The formlessness is the product not of chaos, but of a false identity. Identical materials put in an appearance as if they were something new and thereby substitute the abstract succession of bars for the dialectical progression of substance."[45] And all this exacts a toll on Wagner's listener, who must labour to provide musical connections, to fabricate substance, just as Schoenberg's music (but to different ends) forces the audience to work for their leisure. The physiognomic comparison to capitalism – the commodity fetish – is almost too patent to be remarked.

The relationship of this kind of analysis-as-physiognomy to customary score analysis is encapsulated in Adorno's judgment of Alfred Lorenz and his grand analyses of Wagner's operas. Lorenz's analyses are as static as the music itself: "It is no accident that Lorenz's analyses can be tabulated, for in principle a table is as inimical to the passage of time as Wagnerian form itself. For all their meticulousness they are nothing more than a graphic game, without power over the actual music."[46] Here too musical labour comes into question: Lorenz is Wagner's expert listener writ large, forced to make the most tenuous assertions about musical form, to which he clings with a ferocity in direct proportion to the obscurity of the assertion. It is perhaps, then, no coincidence that Lorenz's work – so devoid of substance – should have endeared itself to the Nazi intellectual *apparatchik*. Substantial analysis, especially a critical social analysis, can be resistant, and neither the Nazis nor Wagner brooked that sort of resistance.

What appears as musical freedom (based in large part on the unregulated nature of the leitmotiv) is superficial; the music lacks strictures to transcend, lacks shaping form, spins its wheels at endless length. Wagner's leitmotifs are the melodic equivalent of the chromatic scale, which by its very richness in artificial leading tones overwhelms the essential, tonic-defining leading tone and thus leaves the tonality completely indeterminate. The use of the leitmotiv produces its own fate – a sameness devoid of drama. In doing so, it records the material progress of society toward reification:

> Wagner's music, which – in contrast to traditional music that
> works with solid, extant forms – defines itself as dynamic, as
> continually in a state of becoming, ultimately turns static, in
> the final analysis because its absolute dynamism lacks the other,
> antithetical element against which it could become genuinely
> dynamic ... In Wagner unceasing change – both an asset and a
> liability – ends in constant sameness. This is already embodied
> in his most striking musical material. For chromaticism – the
> principle par excellence of dynamics, of unceasing transition,
> of going further – is in itself nonqualitative, undifferentiated ...
> One might go so far as to surmise that Wagner's compositional
> process prophesied the dawning horror of the transition from a
> society that had reached the apogee of its dynamism to one that
> had again turned rigid, become utterly reified.[47]

Passages like these are physiognomic analyses, reading the social off the face of the music, at times crudely. The propositions are derived from the basic physiognomic conception that the music is like the man, a vacuum that takes rather than gives, for Wagner's bourgeois audience were only too willing to give in exchange for nothing. In thus giving they supplied Wagner's every want. The desire to do so became a fetish, a scar rubbed and itched. The social character of the music, then, is like that of the man – sugar masking as nutrition.

Wagner's music is internally dysfunctional, a fact that becomes the starting point for analysis after Adorno.[48] Mahler's scores, on the other hand, will answer internally to analysis. Indeed, they would seem to analyse themselves. Thus in similar terms, they too are physiognomic.

The basis of Wagnerian pathology lies in his identification with bourgeois values, an identification combined at the same time with rejection, a fear of oppression – smothering – by those selfsame bourgeois masses. But Mahler, on Adorno's account, has a true empathy for the masses, not this exploitive Wagnerian pseudo-sympathy. Empathy is made manifest in Mahler's music through extremes that fracture, a fractured state of affairs that corresponds to the state of the masses. Mahler's music is the opposite of the smooth Wagnerian facade mounted by leitmotifs woven into endless melody.[49] From this opposition, Adorno draws a social analysis: Mahler's music, being fractured,[50] poses a challenge to the concept of a pure, unmediated art, and thus constitutes a rebuke of identity thinking and the social consequences such thought may bear.

For Adorno, Mahler's disruptive use of popular or folk melodies (in the First Symphony, for example) is not a form of pastiche or potpourri, as Mahler's critics, confining themselves to a positivistic reading, would suggest. Instead, the abrupt, often disturbing insertion of these melodies serves to critique seamless Wagnerian musical form and, by implication, the terrorist impulse that lies behind it. Wagner dissolves musical logic by substituting the narcotic leitmotiv. When Mahler dissolves musical logic, he puts scraps of popular trash in its place, the better to reflect upon disruption of logic in both music and the broader social sphere, a disrupted logic that would deny to some the privilege of culture: "The parade step of musical logic is disrupted by reflection on the social wrong that art-language irrevocably does to those denied the privilege of culture."[51] Fractured internally, Mahler's music reflects the fissures in the smooth facade of cultural privilege. For Adorno this kind of observation constitutes analysis.

Adorno's analytic object, then, is not merely to praise Mahler but, as in his appraisal of Wagner, to connect character to social context by a description of music's internal form. The connection is not programmatic, not made through association with a musical theme or motive: Mahler's music is not representing – *Idée fixe* – the denial of the privilege of culture, any more than Wagner was representing anti-Semitism by means of a particular theme. No mere representation, Wagner's music *was* anti-Semitic; its work was to produce a state of collective somnambulance, a general anaesthetic applied to the population like ether, rendering people incapable of perceiving the rising forces of anti-Semitism. And so too Mahler's music was a disruption of the privilege of culture, not just a programmatic description of the deprivation of an uncultured class.

As a vehicle for music labour, then, Mahler's symphonies are the very antithesis of absolute unity in music. They never point in a programmatic sense outward from themselves but, by their exoticism, they require their audience to situate itself outside the work, to "listen ... against" the work for a mediated comprehension:

> In flagrant contradiction to everything familiar from absolute, program-less music, his symphonies do not exist in a simple positive sense, as something granted to the participants as a reward: on the contrary, whole complexes want to be taken negatively – one should listen, as it were, against them ... The brutally intrusive passage in the coda of the first movement of the mature Sixth Symphony is heard directly as an irruption of the horrible. To conventional thinking this seems literary and unmusical; no music ought to be able to say no to itself. But Mahler's music is receptive precisely through its stringent capacity to do so, which extends into its selectively indiscriminate material, a content that is both non-conceptual and yet incapable of being misunderstood. Negativity for him has become a purely compositional category: through the banal that declares itself banal; through a lachrymose sentimentality that tears the mask from its own wretchedness; through a hyperbolic expression in excess of the music's actual meaning.[52]

Anticipating Schoenberg, Mahler's music negates leisure by demanding this kind of labour of its audience – to listen against the familiar.

A musical force opposing Wagner appears in Mahler's symphonies, then, a critique of self-enclosed Wagnerian music by means, ironically, of what had hitherto been the epitome of the self-enclosed – the autonomous, non-programmatic symphony. The conceptual counterpart to this musical opposing force was developed by Eduard Hanslick, whose name, however, does not figure profusely in Adorno's writings on music and does not figure at all in the Wagner monograph, a fact that seems on reflection remarkable for at least two reasons.[53] Many of the conceptual issues of music criticism that Adorno raises are anticipated in general aesthetic terms by Hanslick (with at times an acidic wit comparable to Adorno's). And Hanslick identified some of these issues specifically as Wagnerian, in particular the trance-like quality of the musical reception afforded Wagner's operas (see the epigraph): "Richard Wagner's *Tristan* and *The Ring of the Nibelungen*, along with his doctrine of endless melody, i.e. formlessness raised to the level of a principle, and the sung and fiddled opium-trance for whose cult, if you please, a temple all its own has been dedicated in Bayreuth."[54]

In his treatise, Hanslick spoke of a pathological form of musical engagement, one that would not have been lost on Adorno. Hanslick discerns two opposing categories of engagement – aesthetic and pathologic. The first is an engagement embodied in listeners for whom feeling is united with and thus tempered by aesthetic contemplation: "This feeling, which in fact to a greater or less degree unites itself with pure contemplation, can only be regarded as artistic when it remains aware of its aesthetic origin."[55] Such listeners are capable of discerning Hanslick's famous aesthetic musical content, whose axiom reads "*Der Inhalt der Musik sind tönend bewegte Formen* [The content of music is tonally moving forms]."[56] While the sense of the locution has yet to be deciphered fully in light of Adorno's thought,[57] I equate it with the form of Mahler's symphonies as Adorno discerns it – a process of internal musical shaping[58] that a listener can engage with consciously (but not necessarily linking it to their social situation).[59] Second, Hanslick posits a listener who lacks such a critical aesthetic awareness but instead engages music on a level that precludes aesthetics, a level Hanslick calls "a fuzzy state of supersensuously sensuous agitation." Thus he describes the populace at Bayreuth: "awareness is lacking ... there is no free contemplation of the specifically musical beauty ... feeling thinks of itself as only involved in the natural power of tones ... [the listeners] subside into a fuzzy state of supersensuously sensuous agitation determined only by the character of the piece. Their attitude toward the music is not contemplative but pathological."[60]

The concept of the pathological raised in this second category calls to mind Adorno's description of Wagner's victimized audience. They ensnare themselves in the chains of his elemental leitmotifs, congratulating themselves on having done so. Hanslick describes this as feeling without defences: "It is the elemental in music, i.e., sound and motion, which shackles the defenseless feelings of so many music lovers in chains which they rattle quite merrily."[61] Hanslick's description equates easily with Adorno's analysis of the Wagnerian listener: "unable to concentrate" while the music "thunders at him in endless repetitions."[62] Too intoxicated to recognize the distinctive features of musical works, Hanslick's pathological listener is incapable of distinguishing between them: "If we play a few similar pieces, perhaps of a noisy, cheerful character ... he will remain under the spell of the same impressions. Only what these pieces have in common, the effect of noisy cheerfulness, penetrates his awareness, while that which is special in every composition, namely, its artistic individuality, escapes him."[63] This kind of listener resembles as well Adorno's jitterbug and encompasses several entries in Adorno's typology of listeners in the *Introduction to the Sociology of Music*. Consider its opposite, however, which Hanslick calls the *musical listener*: "The musical listener will proceed in precisely the opposite manner. The characteristic artistic construction of a composition, which in effect marks it off from a dozen similar compositions as a self-subsistent artwork, so dominantly occupies his attention that he considers its similar or dissimilar impressions upon the feelings to be of trifling significance."[64] This category anticipates Adorno's *expert listener*: "The *expert* himself ... would have to be defined by entirely adequate hearing. He would be the fully conscious listener who tends to miss nothing and at the same time, at each moment, accounts to himself for what he has heard ... Spontaneously following the course of music, even complicated music, he hears the sequence, hears past, present, and future moments together so that they crystallize into a meaningful context."[65]

If Hanslick's description of a capable musical listener is carried forward, then, to Adorno's expert listener, surely this kind of listening is made concrete in Mahler's music. Mahler's symphonies would be inimical to the pathological listener (sublimely so to Adorno's jackass), but the rupture of the symphonic logic would be readily discernible by the expert musical listener and would demand the kind of aesthetic contemplation that Hanslick and Adorno require of the expert. While he lacks the historical materialist background of Adorno's sociology, Hanslick sets forth a comparable sociology under the guise of aesthetics: the consciousness of a capable, indeed expert listener is based on the auditory understanding of a fractured reality after Mahler; the consciousness of a poor listener is determined by the fetish of a phony unified reality, like that spun by Wagner. The former is capable of understanding a social physiognomy. The latter is not.

In the *Versuch*, Adorno's ultimate concern is with the flaws that appear in social character. Pathology, be it in character or in biology, is a social ill. Studying Wagner, Adorno's aim was like that of such early biological pathologists as Jenner, Wendell Holmes, Semmelweis, and Freud. He sought not merely to treat an individual case, Wagner in this instance, but to decipher the traces of a disease in the general musical character, the better to define it, predict its spread, and thus equip the world with precaution.

Dollar store. When did "nickel and dime" become a term of abuse? Dollar stores, ubiquitous in recessions, emit a melancholy attraction, like bingo halls and the midway at county fairgrounds: no currency exchange of any import will transpire here, and thus the customer is made free to spend without fear of extravagance and penury. Like nickels and dimes before it, the dollar becomes toy money and dollar store transactions devolve into make-believe, as if buying remaindered CD's – *Opera for People Who Hate Opera* – were a stand in for the real thing, La Scala, Covent Garden, Bayreuth. The CD has twelve tracks: four unobnoxious overtures, the Bridal Chorus from *Lohengrin*, two arias (maximum two) – "Summertime" from *Porgy and Bess*, and something from *Barber* – and at its central core, tracks 4 to 8, a selection from *Pirates of Penzance*. Combined, the selections yield an antidote for opera as a remainder: one might develop a fondness for the genre by not liking it.

As adolescents, a friend and I saw the premier of *2001: A Space Odyssey*. Smitten, my friend bought an LP of *Thus Spake Zarathustra* from the small profits of his paper route. He was crestfallen, expecting at least a full hour of trumpet and tympani. When last I taught *Rheingold*, an undergraduate approached me: "When does that Prelude thing come back?" On the score I traced the return of the Prelude's *Hauptmotiv* through the remainder of the opera. He said, "But when does the Prelude come back just like at the start, the whole five minutes without the singing?"

Mahler on ice. I knew a music professor from Austria, sturdy and handsomely ugly. After making a general point about Mahler (or Strauss, or Schoenberg) he would remove his heavily black-rimmed glasses in his right hand, hunch his tweed shoulders, push out his lower lip, and address his gaze to the distant corner of the room, where two walls meet at the ceiling, as if the point where the three planes met were a tiny Euclidean crack through which infinitude might be being conceived. He would pause for a fraction of time as if to say, "This is very important." Then with a flourish, after running the fingers of his left hand through his hair, the glasses would be replaced on his sturdy face, and rubbing his hands together, he would return to work: "Now, where were we?"

Skating to the Adagietto of Mahler's Fifth, Canadians won gold in the doubles competition at the Vancouver 2010 Winter Olympics. Unlike skating, ballet reveals the whole body, tip to toe, as a thing of aesthetic beauty – an object of a pure contemplation undisturbed by matters of utility. Not so ice skating, where the top nine-tenths of the body, elevated in beauty well beyond dance by the velocity and grace of movement on ice, are compromised by the business end of the matter, the feet cast in rigid plastic and clad with a steel rail. Astigmatism is an asset when watching figure skating, or, lacking astigmatism, the ability to squint so as to retain the overall shapely beauty of the bodies while obscuring the ugly quotidian solidity of the skate-bound feet. No doubt the Mahler was chosen for its epiphanies, but running counter to such raptures, the play-by-play voice-over television commentary, like the skater's foot, is strictly utilitarian: "And now, a two-point turn, followed by ..." Ordinary people, after all, might fidget were they forced to listen to Mahler without verbal guidance and some visual aspect: how do you like your Mahler? On ice? Not liking Mahler would seem thus to be produced as a remainder when his music is brought together with sport. Being a competition, the proceedings are framed by a panel of five judges with score sheets who sit on a perch behind and above the ice surface in judgment: "Nein," "Nein," "Nein," "Nein," and "Nein."

6

Spätstil Zappas

Wowie ... Zowie ...

Frank Zappa, *Freak Out*

"The present day composer refuses to die!" Edgar Varese, July 1921
Frank Zappa, *Freak Out*

The two epigraphs delineate the extremes of Frank Zappa's world. The first calls to mind the pop-art canvases of Andy Warhol and the photographs of Dianne Arbus, where the bathos of middle-America is transformed into a critical subject matter. The second evokes the struggle of recalcitrant, self-designated "serious" artists against this very same bathos. The serious composer knows that by his death his music will attain a respectability denied him while living. The subrosa text to Zappa's citation lies in the thought that the rock composer shares precisely the same aspiration.

Subrosa aside, the two epigraphs delineate what are customarily taken as polar extremes in twentieth-century Western music: popular and serious. Zappa died before he could fully examine the dialectic potential of this delineation by subjecting serious music to the same kind of acidic critique he applied so brilliantly to the insipid "teen" music of the 1960s. As a result, his engagement with serious music had about it much the same kind of naïveté Adorno discerned in Schoenberg's engagement – the belief in an absolute category, the Great Composer (the "present day composer" in the words of the epigraph). Had he lived, Zappa might have seen through this mythic category and discerned how the two extremes, popular and serious experimental, are but emblems of the same alienation.

Discrepancy and immodesty are the very essence of Frank Zappa. He delighted in pointing out the discrepancies between the vision of Lyndon Johnson's "Great Society" and the injustices it wreaked upon the less enfranchised. In doing so, his best work operates in the finest dialectic sense. Those who attended consciously to his music were conducted to an insight not unlike that which Adorno achieves dialectically.

On stage and through remarks on recordings, however, Zappa's immodesty establishes itself. It contributes to the growth of the Zappa icon – a frozen persona, the object of a "cult of personality" to use the pre-Perestroika term. He never shrank from hectoring his audience, a practice one can engage in for only so long before the bludgeoned listener lapses into the kind of worship practised by victims (and therein Zappa's audience has much in common with its alienated counterpart at Bayreuth). For a large number of his adherents, Zappa became an icon of weirdness but not a "present-day composer" in the heroic style of Varèse, the mentor of his superego.

Perhaps Zappa's lack of modesty prevented a normal corrective in his developing self-image (much as the same lack did in Wagner's development). In this regard, Zappa fits the two criteria of the "expert listener" established by Adorno in *Introduction to the Sociology of Music*. The first is expert technical ability: "The *expert* himself ... would have to be defined by entirely adequate hearing ... the fully conscious listener who tends to miss nothing and at the same time, at each moment, accounts to himself for what he has heard ... Spontaneously following the course of music, even complicated music, he hears the sequence, hears past, present, and future moments together so that they crystallize into a meaningful context."[1] The second is pathology. Late Capitalism will foster expert listening (and, presumably, expert composing and criticism) only as an extreme, and this will take its toll on the psyche of the expert. Highly concentrated specialization distorts reality, producing neurosis, psychosis, disorientation and "pseudo-orientation," which is simply another term for naïveté: "The expert listener needs a degree of specialization as probably never before, and the proportional decrease of the 'good listener' type ... might well be a function of that specialization. And the price paid for it is often a seriously disturbed relation to reality, including neurotic and even psychotic character deformations ... such defects occur precisely in the most highly qualified musicians. It cannot be an accident, but must lie in the course of specialization itself, that many of them, faced with questions beyond the realm of their own expertise, will seem naive and obtuse to the point of total disorientation and deviant pseudo-orientation."[2]

Zappa's signature critical failure occurs in his late attempts at serious music, and it is a failure in terms of both modesty and discrepancy. Before addressing his early, successful music and the late style, however, something of Zappa's developing psyche needs to be established.

Fully aware of the limitations of popular music fame, intrigued with a notion of persecution and isolation that he derived from his youthful adoration of Varèse, Zappa devised the spectre of the Great Composer: "The present day composer refuses to die!" So his biographers describe it: "From the beginning, and throughout his life, Zappa's intention was to pursue the career of 'the present-day composer,' and in the 1960s, adopting the guise of a rock 'n' roll musicians was one – albeit an unusual – way to do that."[3] They overlook the fact, however, that although vernacular "rock 'n' roll" was a language he parodied, Zappa lacked the sophistication or the insight with which to parody serious experimental music. As a consequence, the serious-music side of the equation lacks the critical acumen of its popular counterpart. Instead of parodying, Zappa attempted naively to identify with a category of serious composer, a category that, from a perspective derived after Adorno, was not entirely accurate.

A growing imbalance between critique and naïveté, between teen music and the category of great composer, lies at the heart of the developing *enigma* of Zappa. In rock music he developed a cutting analysis throughout his career, leaving no sacred cows anatomically intact. In serious and experimental music, however, he seemed ultimately reconciled to an unsophisticated image. In terms of conduct and demeanour in a rock milieu, he behaved in an increasingly outrageous manner, one that spread his reputation far beyond the effect of his music. But as a serious composer of experimental music, his persona never progressed beyond modesty, like that of an interloper, foreigner, and supplicant.

Zappa's conception of serious experimental music could have been gleaned from courses in harmony and composition at Antelope Valley Junior College in 1958,[4] and at Chaffey Junior College in Alta Loma and Pomona College in 1959,[5] where he was introduced to the basic texts of introductory music appreciation. Or Zappa might have formed this conception in conversation with musicians such as Buzz Gardner, brother to Bunk, Zappa's long enduring reed player. Don Preston, another Zappa sideman, recounts the impact of Buzz Gardner's largesse: "In the days in the army, Buzz Gardner was like a teacher for me ... He turned me on to all kinds of new composers – I'd never heard Bartok before I learned about string quartets, Schönberg, Alvin (sic) Berg, Anton Webern and on and on. He also turned me on to all the Russian authors plus Thomas Mann – and all these things I had missed because I quit school in the 10th grade, so I really never got exposed to that stuff."[6] Preston, and presumably Zappa like him, seems to have had an unqualified reverence for the category of serious experimental "Great."[7]

Preston's notion of an evolving musical tradition is easily traced (presumably via Gardner) to Webern's pamphlet *The Path to the New Music*.[8] Esoteric for the 1950s, the pamphlet and its ideas nonetheless made the rounds of amateur and learned musical circles in North America. A musical myth, it occupied one of the central explanatory pillars of experimental music, but like most myths it was seldom examined critically. Presumably Zappa partook of this mythology and others like it.

There are signs that Zappa appreciated the absurdity of the Great Composer category. In his Varèse reception, he likens the composer to a mad scientist, one who likes such simple pleasures as growing grapes and writing songs about deserts. Varèse becomes a *mélange* of the correct and the weird:

[In a telephone conversation] Varèse told me that he was working on a new piece called "Déserts," which thrilled me since Lancaster, California [Zappa's residence at the time], was in the desert. When you're fifteen and living in the Mojave Desert, and you find out that the World's Greatest Composer (who also looks like a mad scientist) is working in a secret Greenwich Village laboratory on a 'song about your hometown' (so to speak), you can get pretty *excited*. I still think "Déserts" is about Lancaster, even if the liner notes on the Columbia LP insist that it is something more *philosophical*.

All through high school I searched for information about Varèse and his music. I found one book that had a photo of him as a young man, and a quote, saying he would be just as happy growing grapes as being a composer. I liked that.[9]

This is a promising dialectic built on a discrepancy: grape growing as a qualification for writing serious music. As a dialectical remainder, however, the discrepancy produces Frank Zappa, who did neither.

The potential for an accurate critical understanding of serious music on Zappa's part is most evident in the chapter "All about Music" from *The Real Frank Zappa Book*.[10] While laced with absurdities, the chapter is an erstwhile attempt to come to terms with the division of rock and serious music, and it points to Zappa's growing realistic awareness of the latter's true state. These passages show signs that Zappa had attained something like a nascent critique of serious music. The critique, however, did not make the transition from Zappa's prose into his serious music itself. To demonstrate that fact, I juxtapose in dialectic fashion his teen music parodies to his late serious work.

The 1950s and 1960s saw the rise of a set of genres termed variously "teen music," "bubble gum," "teeny bop," or even "teen-dance music," labels that reflect both the music's substance and its principal audience. Despite its tremendous financial success under the aegis of the baby boom, the genre was a pariah in the eyes of musicians whose skills allowed them to discern its all too evident limitations. The genre received due diligence on Zappa's part, from his first album, *Freak Out*, forward. In the acidic lyrics of his work, Zappa seized on four aspects of Middle-American society made explicit in teen music: the hypocritical, smug, and self-serving elements in the psychological makeup of adolescents; the cultural industries that feed and in turn feed on these elements; the atmosphere of trivia – the climate of fetish – produced in Western societies by a growing fascination with adolescence in the 1960s; and consequently a naïveté, a general ignorance of repression (censorship in particular), material excess, and corruption to which American society succumbed through the neglect of mature paradigms.

Zappa's critique often takes the form of a pastiche of easily recognized characteristics drawn from the musical style espoused by popular teen television programs such as *American Bandstand*. His early albums are a theme park for this music, a net of trivia into which serious issues are woven, albeit as discordant threads. The whole blends Disney fantasy with the Schumannesque – cute and grotesque at the same time. The effect produced is that of a magic fairy-tale, a *Märchener fantasie* replete with dwarves and weirdness, set in a suburban shopping mall. The play with eroticism is subtle – a parody of adolescent clumsiness, blended with whiffs of aggressive masculinity. The eternally conflicted object of desire known as Suzy Creamcheese serves as a locus. Added to the whole is a glazed Kafkaesque paranoia about the police and the Establishment ("Bow Tie Daddy," from *We're Only in It for the Money*), which becomes static and then cartoon-like as the years go by and the American Left becomes impotent.

Freak Out is not flawless. Among its warts is an intensely moralizing tone, which Zappa kept for the rest of his life. His sense of superiority is often nauseating, a blend of sophomoric righteousness and 1960s politico. And Zappa name-drops shamelessly. The jacket to *Freak Out*, for instance, cites among other experimental composers Arnold Schoenberg, Robert Craft, Alois Haba, Leo Ornstein, Mauricio Kagel, and Vincent Persichetti. These names are tossed in among such unlikely confreres as Lenny Bruce, David Crosby, Bram Stoker, and Joan Baez, and the list is prefaced with the sophomoric, "These People Have Contributed Materially in Many Ways to Make Our Music What it is. Please Do Not Hold it Against them." Zappa's music reveals that he knew these names by more than mere report, and in this light he played the superior to his audience, whom he sometimes shamed for their ignorance. The sophistication of the album and its youthful intensity presumably saved Zappa from complete dismissal at the hands of the recording executives he so mercilessly pillories. The most characteristic quality of the album, however, is a position of indignant superiority.

Zappa's best parodies carry this tone of indignation to the extreme. Cover bands – bands that perform better-known bands' tunes night after night – grow to despise their tediously "classic" repertoires, referring to them often with scatological substitute titles. Rehearsals are marked by mockeries of these loathsome canonic works – spontaneous critiques, in essence, cutting assessments heard (unfortunately) seldom beyond the confines of backrooms or musicians' conversations. In this vein, the appreciation seldom rises above disparagement and often outright cynicism, an aesthetic of loathing. Instead of confinement to rehearsal, however, this attitude is paraded front and centre in Zappa's live and recorded performances.

The song "Wowie Zowie" from the album *Freak Out* is an excellent case in point. Its parody targets are readily recognized, those evoked in the coda being clearest – the songs "Sherry," by the Four

Seasons, replete with a falsetto by Franki Valli, and "You've Lost That Lovin' Feeling," by the Righteous Brothers, with the dusky masculine voice of Bill Medley. Both targets figured prominently on radio play charts in the early 1960s, during the Camelot years preceding the death of Kennedy and later years of the escalation of the Vietnam War, an epoch that Zappa subjects to deep scrutiny.

Zappa's texts evoke the actual lyrics of teen pop songs, cliché phrases such as "so fine," "be mine," "love me do," and "be true." Sewn into these, however, are references to teen agonies such as bodily hygiene, references that are inappropriate to the style – in "Wowie Zowie" to shaving legs and brushing teeth (depilatory agents and dental paste being particularly prominent advertisements in these Great Society years). The result is a masterful schizoid quality to the text, where the naive is eviscerated and then devoured by critique.

While lyrics and album designs (particularly *We're Only in It for the Money*) play principal roles, it is the style of Zappa's sound and the quality of its execution that convey the critical essence. The readily apparent technical ability of his musicians lends an uncanny sense of immediacy and force. In "Wowie Zowie," the band is tight and expert, the timbres especially worthy of note for their crispness and sharply recorded presence. The musicians take a not entirely benign interest in what is evidently a musical material far beneath the limits of their abilities. The technical limitations of teen music – the steely guitar slightly out of tune, the snappy drum kit – are made palpable by overkill. The abiding impression lies in the sense of something almost but not quite right – like Snow White about to accept the apple with the curious sheen from the elderly lady. A finger-snapping passage is a little too vehement; the voices, even the falsettos, emanate from men with beards, not from juvenile cherubs such as Herman and the Hermits. In total, there is something brilliantly incorrect here, albeit subtly so. A discrepancy between the way things 'sposed to be and the actual state of affairs is meant to seep into the already hormone-stupefied teen brain like an illicit intoxicant. The discrepancy is immediately evident when one compares the teeny bop originals to Zappa's parodies. Recalcitrant and fractious like its composer, his work will not flow with the tide of teen music.

Zappa and his teen parodies become artifacts of a dialectic that opposes the fleeting to the permanent. Teen music and musicians will come and go (nothing being as ephemeral as success in this genre);

Zappa endures. From *Freak Out* onward his music accumulated at a rate of about two albums a year. By the appeal of its critique, it remains the perennial residue of a music it negates. Authentic teen music is washed away by regular tides, but in Zappa's parodies it endures, if only as a remainder arrived at through negation.

Adorno's *Minima Moralia* are tiny constellations in which various sharply focused images are arranged as ordered stars – not a definite and eternal order but rather a kind of ad hoc arrangement that points beyond itself to a distant, barely discernible truth. Take as example an excerpt from one of the *Minima Moralia* pertaining on first blush to matrimonial relations. Like a number of the *Moralia*, it ends with a little "kicker"; the cluster or constellation of ideas that indicate a concept are arranged in a form that takes the reader well beyond the expected:

> *Philemon and Baucis.* The domestic tyrant has his wife help him on with his coat. She eagerly performs this service of love, following him with a look that says: what else should I do, let him have his little pleasure, that's how he is, only a man. The patriarchal marriage takes its revenge on the master in the wife's indulgent considerateness, which in its ironic laments over masculine self-pity and inadequacy has become a formula. Beneath the lying ideology which sets up the man as superior, there is a secret one, no less untrue, that sees him as inferior, the victim of manipulation, manoeuvring, fraud ... False nearness incites malice, and in the sphere of consumption the stronger party is the one who controls the commodities ... In demystifying the husband, whose power rests on his money-earning trumped up as human worth, the wife too expresses the falsehood of marriage, in which she sees her whole truth. No emancipation without that of society.[11]

Adorno sets forth a concise constellation of images:

1 The customary view of things: the tyrant and the servant, the overbearing patriarch and his servile matriarch
2 the inverted order (à la Molière): by indulging his childish whims, the matriarch is transformed into the seat of authority
3 which produces a kind of veracity: the wife sees the truth of

her own power through the facade of her husband (whom she
"demystifies")

4 but this veracity is false, since she mistakes it (as her little epiphany) for an essence, the essence of matriarchal fidelity

And then Adorno adds

5 How can there be any emancipation at all (of the working class
or whatever) if it does not extend to encompass (and thus overcome) relationships such as these, which lie at the very core of
"society"?

The last line, the "kicker," lest we missed the drift of where Adorno
is heading, moves our focus beyond the question of matrimony to
the subject of society as an object. We might fool ourselves into
believing that the subject of Adorno's tale is spousal relationship;
the real subject is society. We might reconcile ourselves that Adorno
is merely spouting off again – pontificating – about society. But the
choice of marriage as poetic conceit, the constellation of images, and
their evaporation at the kicker is far too seductive to be ignored.
Adorno has his cake and eats it too: he lectures us about society,
but the constellation draws our attention away from Adorno to the
fabula and its moral. Thus Adorno makes his point with the height
of modesty, setting forth an Aesop's fable within which we discern a
lesson. The images and their alignment are all contrived by Adorno
to give the impression of spontaneous revelation, as if, like gazing at
a pattern of·stars and seeing a belt or lion's tail, we see through the
constellation of contrived matrimonial relations into the deep space
of society.

Constellations, both astronomic and Adorno's (after Walter Benjamin), are negatively dialectic: they dissolve subject into object and
then leave unanticipated remainders. Out of tiny pricks of light in
the night sky emerges a pattern (a crab, a fish, a hunter's belt) with
no evident cause, no necessary basis, and offering little verifica-
tion. Once the pattern of a constellation is internalized, it becomes
redundant; the component stars soon identify themselves without
it. While objects in their own right, then, stellar constellations serve
a more important role as vehicles of discovery, a means by which
to place fainter non-constellating objects in perspective. In terms of
amateur astronomy, constellations are tools as well as features of
the night sky.

Constellate thought as a negation of idealism was set forth at
length in Adorno's lecture of 1931, "The Actuality of Philosophy
[*Die Aktualität der Philosophie*]" given to the philosophy faculty
at the University of Frankfurt in May of 1931.[12] Here Adorno likens the search for an essence behind a phenomenon to the search
in a riddle for an exact reflection of a being or thing. Consider the
following riddle and its solution: "What paints its toenails red and
hides in cherry trees? An elephant." The point of the riddle is not the
answer, which is itself absurd, but rather the absurdity of the question. Once the absurdity of the question is appreciated, the details of
the question and its answer become redundant (they could be apple
trees and hippopotami). Idealist and analytic philosophers are like
the literal-minded who go away scratching their heads: "Elephants
are too big to hide in cherry trees." The joke is a release of literal
constraints; it illuminates itself as an absurdity and then disappears
in a puff of smoke as a triviality. Adorno states this as follows: "The
function of riddle-solving is to light up the riddle-*Gestalt* like light-
ning and to negate it, not to persist behind the riddle and imitate
it."[13] And, "The answer stands in strict antithesis to the riddle, needs
to be constructed out of the riddle's elements, and destroys the riddle, which is not meaningful, but meaningless, as soon as the answer
is decisively given to it."[14] The riddle is as flighty and self-negating
as a constellation.

Seen in this context, analysis, interpretation, and critique do not
illuminate a fixed and stable meaning (much as ideas are not the
illuminations of fixed and stable phenomena). Instead interpretation brings together disparate elements – "the singular and dispersed
elements of the question," "small and unintentional elements,"[15] or
"extremes."[16] These are brought into "various groupings" – constellations – just long enough to produce a consequent, "long enough for
them to close together in a figure out of which the solution springs
forth, while the question disappears."[17] In disappearing, the constellation leaves only a residual awareness, like the residual impression
of the absurdity of the riddle. The end product is not a finite and
precise knowledge but a kind of transcendence, if by transcendence
one can arrive at nowhere specific and nothing precise.[18]

Adorno, bearing in mind the anti-idealism implicit in Marxist
materialism, calls this a materialist thought process, the "thinking
of materialism." In his materialism, unintentional and real are methodologically alike. Both are distanced from fixed and implicit meaning. Both work by the juxtaposition of otherwise isolated elements:

"Interpretation of the unintentional through a juxtaposition of the analytically isolated elements and illumination of the real by the power of such interpretation is the program of every authentically materialist knowledge, a program to which the materialist procedure does all the more justice, the more it distances itself from every 'meaning' of its objects and the less it relates itself to an implicit, quasi-religious meaning."[19] Materialism works through constellations, in other words.

Consider now the constellate qualities of Zappa's "Wowie Zowie" as a case in point.[20] The exclamation *Wowie ... Zowie ...!* was uttered by young juveniles as a sign of approval, (roughly the equivalent of "Excellent!" in the first decade of our new millennium). It connotes skateboards, root beer, and innocuous youthful fun, blending these together in the sense of a positive dialectic as an icon of juvenile innocence, a state of consciousness entirely oblivious to the cares of elders.

But "Wowie Zowie" as sung by bearded or beardable men (the tone and the range of the Mothers' voices disclose their maturity) is a completely different matter. Who are these interlopers in the juvenile Garden of Eden? Are they bringing intoxicants with them? When beardless boys sing "love me do," good morals prevent them from meaning anything beyond "I'll be true." But when these bearded men of infinite invention sing "love me do," they mean "Motherly Love" in a sense anything but maternal. So why are they singing about shaving legs?

From the sound of their *American Bandstand* style, they should be having fun. But as noted above, these musicians are far too professional to be just mop-haired boys with instruments bought from the Sears catalogue. It shows in the tightness of their execution. They take the usual snappy back beat produced on a rock and roll drum kit and give it an extra snap, a crispness that a boy without a beard would not have had time to develop, let alone the maturity to appreciate. The voice shows some latent sophistication in technique: a boy must have at least a modicum of skill to sing expertly in falsetto. But singing expertly in falsetto is not sufficient to hide the libido in a Mothers' voice.

Individually, these negations of the customary order of things mean little. But as the song progresses, they accumulate until a constellation appears, a light turns on in the blunted recesses of the middle-American teenage mind: "Hey, there's something going on here. This isn't right!" Or better, "That's exactly it! Golly, what a piece of trivial s*** teen music is!"

The sum total of these diverse negations in "Wowie Zowie" is a *mini-constellation* like those of *Minima Moralia*, a constellation contrived in such a way that we would have to work particularly hard at our entertainment to avoid reaching the conclusion that teen music is essentially trivial. Zappa does this by showing the discrepancy between the ideal images projected in the genre – choirboy virginity, strict bodily hygiene, and the virtues of amateur music making – and their truly material counterparts (as parodied by the Mothers): emasculation, obsessive compulsion, smelly breath and oily skin, and bad technique. Once we come to the realization of the teen music constellation, we look beyond the song to recognize its traces in every teen music hit we come across thereafter. The negative dialectic remainder is an abiding impression that all teen music has a malevolent side hitherto unremarked.

Serious and experimental music – teen music's antipode in Zappa's work – appears in two forms, either as the principle style of the work, exemplified particularly in the two recorded collections *Boulez Conducts Zappa: The Perfect Stranger* and Billboard award-winning *The Yellow Shark*,[21] or incorporated in works that belong primarily to the genre of rock music (usually surrounded and thus framed by rock material), as in *Weasels Ripped My Flesh*. Firmly enshrined in the first category, the piece "III Revised" from *The Yellow Shark*, in its stylistic concentration and its resemblance to the central pillars of musical experiment in the twentieth century, is representative of Zappa's homage to Great Composition. Its style is "Uptown" contemporary as defined by New York composers resident at or associated with Columbia University in the late 1950s and 1960s. The style's origins are traceable to the string quartets of Schoenberg and his students and to subsequent developments in Central European experimental music that took Webern as a starting point. The composition earned Zappa considerable accolades; these came, however, at the end of his life, when he was burdened with an illness that forbade his complete enjoyment of these laurels.

The opening four notes of "III Revised" are dissonant; the metre is at best ambiguous; the harmony indistinct. In truth, what follows is good modernism, on par certainly with the work of lesser known Uptown composers. But those familiar with Zappa's rock music will not recognize him here. And those intimately familiar with Uptown music will recognize that he is not quite at home here either. Elements of his rock music bleed over into the piece – a certain looseness in the rhythm in particular (not unwelcome given the rhythmic stiffness of Uptown). Thus in both regards, rock and Uptown, he is out of his element – an interloper.

In the serious experimental string quartet, as it derives from Schoenberg and Webern, an opening series of four notes such as these become the horizon, the basis for a musical logic devoid of sentiment. Pretty, raunchy, funky – these attributes, so customary to the rock milieu, simply do not apply here. Instead, in the institutional Uptown reception of this compositional genre, the opening four notes (and those that come after) stand on their own, meant to be isolated and in this critical sense absolute. Affect is irrelevant. Without such an affect, "III Revised" eliminates the essential juxtaposition, the frayed correspondence between music and affect that is a central tool in Zappa's parodies. The work shows Zappa's ability to move right into the serious style, but nothing is expressed – not even by simple allusion – of the critical discrepancy or the parodies so characteristic of Zappa's richly critical pastiches in the rock genre. Certainly the material of "III Revised" would have offered Zappa no opportunity for hectoring his audiences, and thus, lacking in these clearly identifiable Zappaesque characteristics, the work comes across as anonymous.

This is truly unfortunate. The domain of serious experimental music is as in need of critical reflection at Zappa's hands as its more popular counterparts, if not more so. In truth, Schoenberg's music and that of his followers is neither absolute nor devoid of affect. But the dogma of the musical absolute was so deeply enshrined in its history and as a defence mechanism that it would haven taken an illustrious interloper such as a Zappa to break the spell. Had Zappa better understood the contrived nature of serious absolutes and their affects, he might have engaged in the kind of critique that was so successful elsewhere in his oeuvre.

Zappa's serious works, then, lacked critical perspective. The blending of serious and experimental styles in his rock music, however, achieved a critical force – parody achieved through the blending of styles being his strong suit. But either through failure on Zappa's part or weakness on the part of his audience, Zappa never carried out the project to the heights attained in his teen music parodies.

Unfortunately Zappa's audience was accustomed to being berated and belittled by him. They responded in kind and treated these fertile hybrids as yet more evidence confirming their own lack of understanding. For the greater part of his listeners, the allusions to serious music became just more mumbled and otherwise incomprehensible weirdness. This lack of insight is regrettable, since these hybrids encompass some of the best music Zappa produced, while giving us a taste of what he could have accomplished.

By way of example, the album *Make a Jazz Noise Here* contains a brief excerpt, about a minute in length, drawn from Stravinsky, the "Marche Royale" trumpet melody from *L'Histoire du Soldat*. The pretentious roots of the high bourgeois style implicit in Stravinsky are brought out delightfully in this polkacized stomp. The tinsel-and-tissue fairy tale style of *Soldat* is violently ripped asunder. In stomps a trumpeter – breathless, perhaps inebriated – from a polka band out of Milwaukee. The bass and percussion are merciless in driving him onward, a far more adequate portrait of the soldier cast-away on furlough, slouching toward Beelzebub, than Stravinsky achieved. Any Stravinskian pretext at tepid *fantasie*, the tidy fetish of *L'Histoire*, is coarsely overturned and crushed. In force and wit, this brief episode attains the critical acumen of Ravel's *La Valse*.

But it is all over in the space of a minute, and Zappa rips onward (to a much less inspiring take on Bartok). The impression we have is one of timidity and uncertainty: why this sudden departure just when things are getting interesting? Is Zappa afraid his audience won't comprehend Stravinsky (which seldom bothered Stravinsky), or is he afraid of Stravinsky himself? The answer is not clear, and the question arises again and again. In these rock parodies of serious styles, Zappa veers away from a sustained and integral critique.

The track "Weasels Ripped My Flesh," the final cut on the album of the same name, from the summer of 1970, begins with a minute and a half of wide-spectrum noise, an ideal amalgam of rock and *musique concrète*. The medium of comparison is the sound itself, a Jimi Hendrix wall of sound that Zappa's audiences would have found both familiar and eternally defamiliarizing. Noise of this sort is a turf occupied jointly by both rock fan and serious musician. Hendrix made a science of it, but Varèse gave it legitimation. Zappa should pause here, resplendent in the wake of this sonic *détente*, for here he has brought the antipodes together. But after a minute and a half, the sound abruptly terminates, and the track continues. We hear Zappa wishing his audience – "boys and girls" – a good night, in a voice approximating that of a viciously benevolent parent at the end of a crushing round of children's birthday celebrations. Zappa's interjection is as if to say "The noble weirdness is over now, boys and girls. It's time to go home and leave the obscure and enigmatic to your betters." This is not criticism, merely hectoring.

This kind of implicit self-deprecation is made particularly clear on the track "The Eric Dolphy Memorial Barbecue," also from the *Weasels* album. Zappa prided himself on metric complexities. During this piece, various members of the band are set in different metres, with the exception of the saxophonist, who is improvising a solo in the free-jazz vein of Albert Ayler or Pharoah Sanders. The stylistic distinction between the saxophone and the drummer is particularly acute: the drummer plays along in a wired pop-drum-kit style, while the saxophonist alternates between multiphonics and screaming high notes. But this attractive equilibrium between serious and pop is again disrupted by Zappa. In his vicious voice, he recounts the various complex and unusual metres being played at this moment, as if to take a sneering pride in the accomplishment of his capable musicians. And then he utterly dismisses the whole project as trivia by adding, "and the saxophonist is blowing his nose." His audience roars their approval, confirming the fact that this is only trivial weirdness.

In the end, the possibility of Zappaesque dialectic – in the juxtaposition of these hitherto disparate styles lies a revelation, be it positive or negative – is blown out of the water. The status quo is maintained. Serious music remains just weirdness. The audience cheers its incomprehension. The vacuity of teen-music consciousness grows up to become the conceptual vacuum of the stoned freak.

Zappa's musical physiognomy bears comparison to Schoenberg's. One serious, one popular – the two are antipodes. Zappa epitomizes a kind of musical informality that Schoenberg seemed dedicated to erasing. Zappa's work is patent if not blunt in its orientation to the politics of the day, while Schoenberg's political engagement is negligible.[22] Zappa grew more and more occupied with serious experimental music, while Schoenberg, after the hack-work enforced upon him by poverty in his early years, kept his distance from popular music.

These dissimilarities aside, the most fruitful comparison lies in their solitary nature as composers and the means by which they reinforced and sustained this solitude. In this regard Zappa and Schoenberg are profoundly alike: events of the day flow around them in a blur, while they remain as perennial and constant on the musical horizon as Gibraltar on the Mediterranean. This steady state has assured a continued interest in their music. Buttressed by the force of their personalities, the music was neither easily ignored nor easily assimilated. Their works are more than momentary, more than the dreams of obscure musical inventors (like Josef Hauer or Van Dyke Parks).

Bearing in mind the caveats raised earlier about the separation of popular and serious music, I treat the two – Zappa and Schoenberg – as comparable. They exhibit a naïveté in understanding their place in the grand scheme of music, the stumbling block in both instances being the category of great composer. As I demonstrated in the discussion of Schoenberg in the chapter on technique, Adorno decried a naïveté on Schoenberg's part. Schoenberg thought himself privy to a kind of absolute inspiration, the source of which he called the "Supreme Commander."[23] Similarly, Zappa stumbles over the absolutes of "Serious Music 101."

The cover of the CD jacket to Zappa's serious *The Yellow Shark* paints a compelling portrait of the visibly aging rock star. His face is wizened, his hair sports touches of gray, he seems tired, possibly ill with the disease that will take his life. Here is the spectre of the "aging rocker." The young men of rock seldom planned on growing old, preferring rye to retirement plans. In the rock genre there are myths of posterity, most of them as naive as the "Mr. Bojangles" incarnation, trivial in comparison with the scope of a *Winterreise* through which Schubert contemplated his future. The emphasis in the 1960s on childhood and adolescence – so essential to a generation of parents who lost theirs at the hands of a sustained economic depression and a half decade of war – left an imbalance in the psyche of their children.

Zappa simply did not know how to grow old musically while retaining the element of criticism found in the rich pop work. In *The Yellow Shark*, he goes to great lengths to isolate the heroic aura of the serious experimental composer, but this is done with reverence, not criticism. Missing is the critical distance so characteristic of his other work.

Schoenberg, born in 1874, was fully thirty years old before his work began to receive performance that merited critical attention, and he died in 1951 at the ripe age of seventy-seven, producing breathtakingly fresh work almost to his deathbed. At the age of thirty, Zappa was confronted with an audience, some half his age, for whom he was largely a museum piece, weirdness exemplified. Schoenberg was born into an era with a succinct and highly revered pantheon – Bach to Brahms – and thereby he inherited a host of "role models" for aging creativity. In the field of popular music in Zappa's youth, role models were either rapidly forgotten or accorded relic status at Las Vegas, while the pantheon passed on to fresher faces. Schoenberg took deliberate steps to ensure his creative legacy: he built a corps of expert adherents, most of them highly accomplished musicians, many of whom, through strategic placement in the creative and educational institutions of the day, were in a position to sustain the creative support of their master and his music. He badgered conductors and producers for performances, doing so with a will and perseverance that only renewed itself through adversity. And he negotiated an evolving self-image, first in his own mind and then in the collective mind of his adherents and supporters. To ensure his legacy Zappa developed an enormous committed and devout following, but the greater bulk knew little of the terms such a legacy might require. His music required a commitment to human welfare and not merely to mindless diversion. While he cultivated an elite following of musicians, he sometimes behaved to them as a tyrant.

Lacking in legitimacy, Zappa found that the doors to cultural and educational institutions were largely closed (when he bothered to knock) until the 1990s when the governance of these same institutions fell into the hands of a younger, more sympathetic generation. Early on, Schoenberg took matters into his own hands and arranged performances under the rubric of an elite society of his devoted followers and hangers on. Zappa's relationships with concert and recording producers (and with conductors and symphony orchestras) seems to have devolved into a kind of residual cynicism on his part, and this frustrated whatever attempts he made at shedding the image of a youthful and fractious rocker. Schoenberg, if he did engage briefly in cynicism, seldom did so in public (unless under the guise of the acerbic Viennese wit that transforms cynicism into pleasantries).

If Schoenberg constitutes a standard by which to measure a serious musical career in the twentieth century, then Zappa's career falls far short. The German term for *late style*, *Spätstil*, is normally applied with reverence. Zappa's late serious work elicits no such attitude.

The material issue behind Zappa's late style lies in the relationship of popular to serious music in the twentieth century. Hitherto, relations between the two domains have been characterized by a mutual suspicion across a yawning gulf of misunderstanding. People dance to popular music; people remain seated with serious music. Popular music entails sex and drugs; serious music evokes the noble and the spiritual, and coffee at best.

Both domains, however, have in common basic tenets by which they measure their mutual worth. One of these is the category of Great Composer. The category was revered by popular musicians of Zappa's ilk (but seldom deconstructed), for it promised a legacy secured by the participation of expert musicians and a devoted, knowledgeable audience, something their popular music milieu lacked. The category was equally revered by musicians of Schoenberg's ilk (again not thoroughly deconstructed) for it justified their music historically, in direct compensation for a lack of justification produced by a slowly disintegrating audience.

Neither side, then, has taken much time to illuminate mythologies like that of "Great Composer." Like the marital relationship in Adorno's little parable from *Minima Moralia*, both parties are content to live with their respective illusions of power.

Frank Zappa's physiognomy shows him to be a compelling by-product of the category of Great Composer and its mythology. Whether through myopia or early death, Zappa never mastered serious music by taking it to critical task. Instead it drove him, making him the subject of its own dialectic. His enigma forms a constellation that points beyond him; his life and work attest that the category of serious composer in the twenty-first century is markedly in need of examination from the perspective of its antipode, the critical rock star.

Both categories – great serious composer and rock star – are facets of the same social character, each a visage by which we might read off much the same social conclusions about music in a climate of commodification. And yet both categories remain resistant to analysis along the lines of physiognomy. This is unfortunate, for the two can be properly understood only in light of the social, as negative remainders derived from the detritus that falls out of the customary synthesis made by the various industries of culture – classical and popular. A real perspective on the social character of the musical creator would need to synthesize musicians as different as Coltrane and Dietrich and then study the fallout. That might lead to a much broader critique of music's place in Late Capitalism, and offer some insight into how a measure of balance might be obtained in our treatment of our musicians. To return to Adorno's little moral tale of matrimonial deception: "No emancipation without that of society."

Stars down from Heaven

Museums are like the family sepulchers of works of art. They testify to the
neutralization of culture.

Theodor Adorno, "Valéry Proust Museum"

The digital video disc recording of Marilyn Manson's world tour,
Guns, God, and Government, has about it a certain air of melancholia and gloom. By evoking *melancholy,* I am not necessarily
referring to the patina of death that Manson calls forth on stage –
blood, war, torture – nor the evocations of suicide discerned rightly
or wrongly in Manson's work in connection with the Columbine
murder suicides. Instead, I mean the perception of death as a textual issue – the melancholic aura of death that lends a stasis to the
text of Manson's work, its sounds and images, as if we were watching a drama deprived of vitality (in this regard it begs comparison
with Patrice Chéreau's Bayreuth production of Wagner's *Ring,* likewise on DVD). Instead of the apparent content of his work (where,
admittedly, the gloom of death is pervasive), I shall concentrate on
the melancholic form of the text, a textual living death, where melancholia is made explicit in the vehicle itself, quite apart from the
gothic gloom of its content.

Critics have dismissed the textuality I find so fascinating here:
"the more serious and comic realms of deathly baroque rock, where
black-and-white 'Parental Advisory Explicit Content' stickers incite
outrage and yawns."[1] While perhaps appropriate with other artists,
such a facile disregard is not merited in the case of Manson (unlike,
for example, Alice Cooper), where the contest for Middle-American
values is worked out in the presentation, not merely the subject matter. His stage presence, for example, has about it what I shall call,
after Adorno, a *saturnine* air; contrary to its apparent exuberance,

there is a self-conscious tedium to Manson's work, as if he were seeing through the whole spectacle qua spectacle, forcing himself thus to go through the motions of a ritual he had long ago dismissed as *inutile*. The origins of Manson's text as a text lie in tedium, a melancholic stasis that spawns the unity of Middle America, a unity no one, not even a spectre such as Marilyn Manson, will disrupt. In this textual regard, his oeuvre (like the vampire novels of Anne Rice) reflects certain truths about the relationship struck between works of popular art and their social context in the last decade of the twentieth century.[2]

To be more precise (anticipating my discussion of the DVD), there is a limpid and slippery quality to the text of both Manson's work and life, a facile ability to move between the personal and the impersonal, to claim and then evade responsibility (seen most clearly around the issues brought to the fore at Columbine). This same limpid and slippery quality describes both the Middle-American values he sets out to critique and the vehicle of Manson's critique itself. For example, the values of beauty and fascism are linked astutely in a stanza from "Beautiful People," where the "horrible people" are allied with anatomy, "the size of your steeple." "Capitalism" has caused "it" – made it this way. "Old-fashioned fascism" will provide a remedy – "take it away." To link anatomy with politics in this manner – to elide the customary distinction, honoured in polite society, between the size of one's crotch and the colour of one's shirt – attests an ability to glide between a lack and an excess of values, capitalism and fascism respectively. But the elision is as useless as it is cute: precisely who is being called a fascist here, Pat Robertson?

Manson's offstage character, certainly as projected in the supplementary tracks on the DVD, lives in limbo, half acknowledgment, half denial, entirely in keeping with the persona projected on stage, as half victim (the brunt of placard waving moralists) and half villain (taunting the same), half rock star and half social reject. This slippery liminal quality overwhelms Manson's stage persona: flirtation with violence alternates with self-congratulation, apology, and hand-wringing; moral outrage vies with titillation. The resultant confusion produces apathy: Manson's ability to shock having lost its value, "shock value" becomes merely textual, something to leer and shout at. In truth, after the reality of Columbine, Manson's evocations of death and suicide no longer provoke us; they are merely melancholic: "too bad about those kids, too bad." This sad fact of impotence seems to have been lost on the pulpit-and-right-wing-press, set in its moral outrage at the rock star. But Manson did not transform youth culture into a culture of suicide murder; rather, a culture of suicide murder attained youthful expression at Columbine. If Manson's role therein was that of handmaiden, then a bevy of maidens – doughnut shop Valkyries – attended the deed. Seen from the perspective of text, Manson's work and life express our capacity to have not much more than a meagre, melancholic effect on our brave new world.

Extant criticism in general (with rare exceptions, like Chuck Klostermann) does not do justice to the melancholy class consciousness expressed in Manson's work and by its audience. For critics coming to Manson's defence, his reputed role in provoking the two Columbine assassins is not to be taken seriously: any implication of Manson as a stimulant to violence – a moral intoxicant – is dismissed roundly. Manson has nothing to do, on this account, with a broad class consciousness, just as Columbine does not reflect anything more than a temporary aberration (not unlike the death of presidents) in the steady progress of a nation. There are, after all, arsenals in the average American neighbourhood, if not ingredients in the medicine chests of most American households, sufficient to bring about mayhem on the scale of Columbine, so who's to blame? What segment of society is responsible for this, if all segments – all social classes, all forms of consciousness – have at their ready disposal the same vehicles for pain. From the perspective of his defenders, the danger in Manson's work expresses itself only on the margins of society, through individuals who fall out of the normative centre, the weirdos; the substantive threat to a normative core consciousness lies only in its unstable children, who veer toward the margins in the process of maturation. Children that "make it" through the years of instability – fitful years when Columbine rests on the horizon as a point of reference – will be restrained ultimately by melancholic conformity and grow to rue both the excesses of their youth (after Alan Bloom) and the decision to give them up. On his defenders' account, Manson is marginal in this process of maturing consciousness, a horizon against which the relationship of local mayhem to the stable class centre of America is measured. "The kids are alright!"

At the heart of Alan Bloom's disparaging chapter on rock music in *The Closing of the American Mind* (a text that constitutes in its own right a kind of conflicted horizon in music criticism, however hoary) lies a melancholia like that described here. It is as if, for Bloom, reconciliation to a life of servitude were the melancholy destiny of all. Our parents bore the burden, and so must we, and reconciliation to that fact becomes the central exercise in the education of our youth, set off by only the briefest moments of utopia, none of which are sexual. Bloom exalts the university baccalaureate thus: "He has four years of freedom to discover himself – a space between the intellectual wasteland he has left behind and the inevitable dreary professional training that awaits him after the baccalaureate. In this short time he must learn that there is a great world beyond the little one he knows, experience the exhilaration of it and digest enough of it to sustain himself in the intellectual deserts he is destined to traverse. He must do this, that is, if he is to have any hope of a higher life."[3] Whew! Pressure's on! Bloom argues that maturity is best served by the surrendering of youthful instabilities (like those that produced, at their most extreme, Columbine). Rock music, like excessive intoxication, simply compounds that surrender, delaying if not ultimately preventing the attainment of a state of grace.

This is a dreary grace, however. Having escaped the clutches of youthful irrationality, the citizen is then permitted to spend the rest of her days contemplating her good fortune while yearning nostalgically for the vitality of her errant youth. Such a contradictory life is best served by music that, after Bloom, instills core values such as those of the "natural" family and service to the greater community and country. While Bloom had Mozart in mind, soft rock might do the trick – maybe Kenny G. As Manson himself attempts to make clear, with tediously predictable regularity, these core values and their melancholy class consciousness – the class of "Beautiful People" – are themselves deeply suspect.

Where Manson's defenders will not acknowledge the danger to class consciousness expressed in his music, Bloom acknowledges the threat posed by rock music (and we must forgive him his references to Boy George, Mick Jagger, and Michael Jackson, now faded luminaries). Rock music is a threat not merely to values (which, after all, can change or be made to change) but more so to the forming of a proper class consciousness devoted to family and state. Rock music threatens the very understanding of what a maturing youthful consciousness entails and it does so not merely through its lyrics (the unchecked sexuality) but through its very textuality.

Headphones and high volume become vehicles of class isolation and introspection, equivalent in danger to prolonged intoxication and thus a threat to active and responsible democratic participation. Antisocial, on Bloom's account they threaten the fabric of American class consciousness – drive great rents in the tissue of devotion to state and family through self-sacrifice. The Sony Walkman (the Ipod of the day) is the errant vehicle of the cult of the individual. In motion under headphones, the child is dead to the world – *Totentanz* – to their parents' injunctions to clean their room, to civil exchanges of greeting on the street, and to their friends and cohort who, in equal manner, tread the earth in benumbed fashion.

Two kinds of melancholy present themselves here. One is the melancholy of the middle-class American values of duty and devotion: a kind of sadness to be discerned as sacrifice in Bloom, it is accompanied by an odour of nostalgia – mildewy – hearkening back to an imaginary America, the sort of nostalgia that blankets Grover's Corners in Wilder's *Our Town* like the thickly sweet exhaust of a cornflakes factory. The other melancholy is that which we discern in Manson, a sadness at the inability to do anything but mock the hypocrisy of the former. We shall return to these melancholy twins when we pass on to Georg Lukács.

Two forms of class consciousness are at play here as well. Bloom is devoted to a class consciousness that bears comparison with the elites of Ayn Rand's dyspeptic American landscape: American values are going to Hell in a handbag; it's time to get back to the noble individualism of self-sacrifice, to the common good, no matter the pain entailed. This is a protective consciousness: self-sacrifice is necessary to protect our values, and if this entails loss of innocence (and often loss of life in the train of duty) then we must sequester that melancholy fact, keep it close and secret, as the essence that links "the way things were" inseparably to "the way things ought to be." Manson disparages this same class consciousness but, since his disparagement (bound to earth by Columbine) can achieve little, it takes upon itself the same whining infertility as the mind-set it seeks to critique. Both forms of class consciousness – the righteous class in the case of Bloom, the hypocrite class in the case of Manson – are locked in the sort of stasis that produces presidents by the most suspect of margins.

Last, two textualities are involved here. In Bloom, as we have noted, the medium of rock, the substance of the text – headphones and high volume – constitutes as much of a threat as the lyrics. Perhaps if they would just turn it down so they could converse with their parents, but then rock music would most definitely not be rock music without the sonic distortion that constitutes a text. In Manson too, the medium is the issue: while the songs are ingenious in both words and music, Manson's identity resides in the spectacle, the visuality. If he would just quit prancing around on stage in that sick hardware. But Manson would not be Manson without a theatrical text.

Again, Bloom and Manson are driven to images of stasis – to a text as flaccid as, well, let the imagination suffice. On Bloom's side, the communal experience of the concert hall is replaced by the Walkman and then Ipod, or Inodule, or Icell, with a memory capacity capable of encapsulating the complete programs of the New York Philharmonic since its inaugural concert. Who needs to share music, to enter the concert hall en masse as a class collective, when music is available to all as individuals in splendid acoustic isolation? On Manson's side, when all the indelicacies of de Sade have been worked through, interlaced with spates of William Burroughs, the theatrics revert to the very sort of tedium Manson sets out to pillory. Shock value is eviscerated by the need to sell concert tickets.

If historical materialism posits the alienation of the human factor from the institutions of capitalism, then we ought to be able to look to Manson as a latter day materialist: he takes apart – literally eviscerates, guts and blood – the institutions of capitalism. The content of his work traces the scope of alienation. Thus we should turn to him as a revolutionary figure and to his work as alienation writ large.

But there will be no revolution after Manson. The melancholy tint of his work – the encrusted glam gone sour like curdled milk, the chicken blood, the bodices after Monroe – has no revolutionary potential and seems designed only to point out that gloomy fact. No one will effect a revolution to the sound of Manson's anthems. Therein lies the essence of Manson's critical potential. If his work has any effect on class behaviour, its yardstick is the melancholy fact of Columbine, the "charnel house," to anticipate Lukács. The material substance of Manson's music – the material fact of concerts, CD's, and music videos – is as much a vehicle of alienation as the alienating institutions attacked therein. Manson's arch-demonic epiphanies succeed only by making this perfectly clear.

Manson's Lucifer falls leaden from the sky in an era otherwise grown static. The import of the fall is transformed, much like the "hypostasy of aesthetics into metaphysics" that Lukács describes in the *Theory of the Novel*.[4] The roundedness and plenitude of an original world (Greece in the case of Lukács, Middle-America in the case of Manson's youth) is fractured; the Gods driven away, Lucifer into exile, Jesus to the Church of the Winnebago. Bearing this grand fracture in mind, a full appreciation of Manson's work requires the prospect of a social aesthetic based in an alienated class consciousness and mediated historically. Much as Lukács's early treatise, in his later eyes, "came closer to the right solution than its contemporaries were able to do," so too Manson's aesthetic critique – a metaphysics of social decay in late twentieth-century bourgeois consciousness – comes closer to critical validity than the work of his contemporaries, and yet is flawed (if only from the perspective of *History and Class Consciousness*). While Manson has never achieved a total synthesis (and Lukács's was questionable), his work constitutes nonetheless a worthy attempt at a synthetic critique, broad in scope and framework. Hence we cannot dismiss his work with the moral superstitions of his detractors, nor defend it with the facile agility of his proponents. We can criticize its ineffectual results – espousing some kind of revolution, it produces nothing but entrenchment. But that aside, we praise it as a vehicle of criticism while remaining ever suspicious of its efficacy, except as negative dialectics.

To this critical end, the old Marxist tropes of spontaneous revolution are no longer satisfactory for Manson or his audience, who lack even the simplest necessities for a revolutionary proletarian consciousness. For those who can afford a Manson concert ticket, congealed labour time is not a pressing issue. Manson himself seems incapable of a profound critical self-reflection embodied in a truly critical self-consciousness, incapable of transcending the stage persona. Like the bourgeois consciousness described in Lukács's *History and Class Consciousness*, an accurate vision of Manson's predicament is inimical if not fully antagonistic to his consciousness. Only the pre-Marxist tropes of *Theory of the Novel* apply here; in terms of the image of the charnel house borrowed from that treatise, Manson's work describes a sedimented history, which in turn his own life and work live out as a text.

By drawing on Adorno's study of Proust and Valéry in *Prisms*, Manson's work can be seen as constituting a double trajectory. On the one hand, his work is a mausoleum wherein he is fully sedi-mented, buried in place by the very sort of constraint he rails against. On the other, his work is a textual act of disintegration, aesthetics into metaphysics. In both subject and saturnine expression, it consti-tutes an artifact to be placed behind glass in the lobby of the mauso-leum Lukács called the Grand Hotel Abyss.

The medium is the message, that hackneyed shibboleth of 1960s techno-optimism, has not outlived its usefulness in this regard. Despite robust antics on stage, *Guns, God, and Government* is essentially powerless to go anywhere. Furiously treading water, it is ideally suited to reproduction through the medium of television, threatening to never move out of the sight line. The ochre makeup, leather, repetitive head banging, raised fists, masturbation – they all suggest a speakable cruelty, a kind of miserly nastiness to no end. This is cruelty eviscerated and pallid, bored, a flirtation, like children taunting the neighbour's dog. The dull images of mutilation cast a pall over the lively stage machinations, as if we were watching yet another zombie rerun. Like pornography piped into the television in hotel rooms, the action seems regular and predictable, a kind of stasis in motion: a freshly robust Manson, the never-ending stream of pornographic couplings – if we turn the screen off, they will go on and on, like the drummer in the longer-life-battery commercial who just keeps drumming and drumming. A post-Hobbesian life: nasty, brutish, long, and cliché.

The medium of television is the principal message of Manson's DVD. The hype and spin, the unrestrained self and the glitter – the essence of Manson's tour is encapsulated by the solemn black box within which it uncoils. The ubiquitous television screen may be of varying sizes and capable of displaying a wide range of colours, but with uncanny frequency the television unit itself comes in funer-eal black.[5] Provided with appurtenances like separate speakers or with a wide screen, it may come flattened in depth and stretched in breadth. But in its basic form the television is nothing more than a small container reminiscent of a casket. Much is made of music videos like Manson's, which are touted to show the medium's ability to encapsulate the spirits of youth, youthful enterprise, and creativ-ity, no matter how riotous. But given Manson's funereal associa-tions, there is a certain irony resident in the television set, through which we come to know this DVD. Like the Gideons' ubiquitous Bible, the black box waits for tired, world-touring rock stars, a fixture in hotel rooms, a verdict upon the living death of industrialized popular culture. So the fleshy essence of Manson's global wanderings is torn from its bones, desiccated, and placed delicately into the resting place of the DVD; in much the same way, in Patrice Chéreau's video recording of Wagner's *Ring*, the monumental stage apparatus is rent from its Bayreuth fixings and compressed into a television box about the size of an urn suitable for the ash residue left after the conflagration at the end of *Götterdämerung*.

Thus Manson's video comes to us casket-like, as if detached from a vital world. So stylized in mode of production, it becomes a virtual artifact, as if separated from us by time and encrusted sentiment. Manson's work thus gives up its integrity as a self-contained artwork, pointing instead to the moribund social circumstances that spawned it. It eviscerates present-day commercial volubility despite marketing campaigns to the contrary: despite all the commercial trappings of a revolution in taste, the overall effect is one of "perennial fashion," as Adorno called it. Nothing truly changes, be it in the performance of the concert itself, from Berlin to Tokyo, or in the lives of the participants, who appear as global citizens of shopping malls, the same the world over, from Moscow to Manhattan.

Similarly, Chéreau's *Ring* pillories the sameness of Wagnerian operatic culture: global productions of the *Ring* – the old Bayreuth, the new New York Met productions, Berlin, Vienna, Seattle – all moribund in deference to a Wagner long gone, like a room long untouched in a novel by Dickens. Chéreau realizes this fact. By its tawdry industrial realism, Chéreau's production equates the operatic cycle with the industrial sameness of our commercial heartlands – clothed in concrete, filled principally with wastrel lives, misfortunates who come and go at the beck and call of ambitiously misguided leaders. One detects a residue of Beckett in the air like a fine industrial dust. The dramatis personae have the *esprit* of street people, *Lumpenproletariat*, at best the lower-class working poor driven mercilessly by the corrupted directors of bankrupt global corporations. Chéreau renders verdict on the appropriateness of Wagner to our time: Wagner is as perennial as capitalism.

Irony is hard at work in Manson: the drama of death (the black makeup, the staged blood spilling, the guns) becomes itself a living death. The excessive concentration on violence and dying, achieved through staging and costume, is encapsulated in the genesis of the name – suicide via Marilyn Monroe and murder at the hands of

Charles Manson, characters both long estranged from our world
and yet revived perennially. The clever juxtaposition of the two
names connotes classic modern American death, novelistic after Tru-
man Capote.[6]

Manson's staged persona is as tightly wrought as a death mask,
a figurine that cannot be interrogated but speaks, sphinx like, only
in riddles. But rarely (in offstage profile shots packaged as DVD
bonuses) do we catch a glimpse of the slack-gut-visibly-aging, dilapi-
dated middle-age frame of the actor behind the name. Onstage, the
mask is never changing, again the world over, tired horseman of
some apocalypse. His audience is attracted to this sameness, made
all the more palpable by the uniform of blackness, with associations
to Goth culture. Perhaps the audience is drawn in by this irony –
by death in youthful vitality. If so, they distinguish themselves as
astute, infinitely more so than Zappa's audience and its fetish for
esoteric weirdness.

Manson and audience. Discerned from the video evidence, *Guns,
God, and Government* is a round-the-world junket in which, by
their immoderate sameness, Manson's concerts come to resemble
endless nights in moderate-priced chain hotels. The sameness these
chain hotels sport denies them any vitality, offering instead merely
the assurance (questionable at that) of a good night's sleep. The
sameness of Manson's grim visage, be it in Santiago or Portugal,
denies his concerts any vitality; it offers merely the assurance (again
questionable) of a reliable show. Not only is Manson's dramatic
subject matter, its topoi, about death – the pallid complexions, the
black face, the skin-punctured hardware. So too the whole edifice of
production is mausoleum-like, set in enormous caverns – a Blakeian
illustration of the Final Cuming. As a critique of modern middle
North American affluence in the Wasteland, Manson's work is as
perennial as the sale of tombstones.

In similar fashion, the Chéreau *Ring* puts an end to the manufactured vitality, the bourgeois attempt to breathe life into the
moribund, the *nature morte*, that is Wagner. Wagner, on Adorno's
account, is timeless in the worst dramatic sense: his music is an eternal sameness; endless melody means world without end. In modern
terms, the fortunes of Wagner never seem to flag; his intellectual
appeal dies only to be revived generation after generation by new
productions aimed at contemporary timeliness. These include, for
example, the Disney World pseudo-authenticity of the Seattle *Ring*

in the early 1980s and the austere American modernism of the dimly-lit Met productions of the next decade. Chéreau's production, however, deliberates on the subject of operatic death, the dead life of an industrial heartland writ large in the death of opera as a genre. By excessive reliance on the very worst of material life, juxtaposing Gods and garbage, the production appraises the very same operatic mausoleum toward which Adorno bends his critiques of Wagner.

Like Wagner (as noted in the chapter devoted to the subject), Manson bears a pathological inclination toward the self-serving. Manson recognizes the embodiment of violence in the static medium of television. But he seems incapable of recognizing himself as a participant, let alone a protagonist. He puts it as follows, with reference to a third-person "they" that includes everyone and everything but his own work: "Times have not become more violent. They have just become more televised. Does anyone think the Civil War was the least bit civil? If television had existed, you could be sure they would have been there to cover it, or maybe even participate in it, like their violent car chase of Princess Di. Disgusting vultures looking for corpses, exploiting, fucking, filming and serving it up for our hungry appetites in a gluttonous display of endless human stupidity."[7] Whose appetites? Ours (including his)? On the one hand, he aligns himself passionately with the spectacle: "Tonight seeing six thousand people raise their fist to 'Beautiful People' is so Nero, so powerful, bombastic, fascistic, rock and roll. It's disgusting and I love it."[8] On the other, he disowns it, representing himself as a merely benevolent critic of organized religion, a kind and Fatherly Antichristian: "I see what I do as a positive thing. I try to bring people closer to themselves. That may be farther from God but that's closer to themselves."[9]

Is this real violence, or just more titillation: what did those six thousand fist raisers do afterwards? Burn Rome? No. They went home, perhaps with a hamburger on the way. Were they closer to themselves? With their Ipods on, they were, or perhaps it only felt that way. Klosterman thinks he sees through Manson's persona: "One obviously suspects Manson's true quest is to parlay outrageousness into fame, and then sell that fame to consumers. His ultimate aspirations are almost stupidly transparent. However, his *modus operandi* is more sophisticated and non-linear – at least when compared to the guileless metal satanists from the '80s."[10] Although Klosterman gives Manson more credit for premeditation than I am willing to lend here, it seems true now that the metal Satanists were merely show-*Meisters*, akin to professional wrestlers; they were not prepared to confound offstage person with onstage persona and certainly not to do so in as deliberate and sophisticated a manner as Manson does. On other hand, they recognized clearly the relation of base to superstructure: outrage sells, in a climate of Late Capitalism, either onstage or on Fox news. There is nothing to suggest that they confounded parlaying outrageousness into fame with sophisticated non-linearity so as to produce a grand machine destined to go nowhere, as Manson did. The Metalists kept their acts clean and linear; Manson messes up.

Part of that mess has to do with mixing up work and life. The onstage identity appears heavily scripted, but Manson insists on a continuity with his offstage life. As Robert Wright puts it, "Manson refuses to distinguish between himself and his persona, and takes great delight in playing upon this ambiguity ... [He] has constructed for himself an elaborate autobiographical mythology in which his personal transformation from obscurity into a superstar is simultaneously prophesied and fulfilled."[11] Elsewhere Manson confesses, "I will never admit this to anyone, but I'll write it here: The reason I haven't copped out in an interview and said, 'Yeah it's just a character, this is just a concept album,' is because to me it is so much more. But in a sense it is. That's why when people asks, 'Well is it an act or isn't it?' it's both. I mean my whole life is an act, but that's my art."[12]

Why this ambivalence – act or reality? To judge by the autobiography, *The Long Hard Road out of Hell*, there was always a continuity – the stasis of Manson's existence. In Canton and Fort Lauderdale, the continuity of life was assured by four constant walls of banal repression, within which Manson gyrated and spun, ever the model, and thus stereotypical, rebel. Our Manson of the Video is assured that selfsame continuity with his rebellious youth by actions brought about in the United States District Court of New Jersey and elsewhere on behalf of the Minnesota Family Council, Senator Joseph Lieberman of Connecticut, the American Family Association. The list seems endless, tediously so.[13]

Physiognomy is written across the face of Manson's autobiography: a character who spots the death motive in the society all around him, but who, mired in solipsism, cannot detect it within himself. The pseudo-violence of Manson's work combined with its conflicted account in his mind illuminate what a Marxist might call the real violence of Late Capitalism which, obscuring us to our-selves, misrepresents our perennial sameness as vitality.

Manson's video is furious, a living death, Hannibal Lecter at his clavichord. Umbilicals connect instrument to amplifier – Manson's band constrained by electronics much like accident victims on hos-pital life support. The audience too, fixed in motion, swarms like bees over the hive, restrained only by an instinctual devotion and by burly security guards. And the wall of sound – little escapes it. Nothing but music shall escape these four walls; no cries, be they of pleasure or distress, shall be let stray from this acoustic crypt, except for a high wail, its words indiscernible, emitted by a blissfully tormented throng.

This is titillation – the violence of the surging crowd and Manson's apparent self-mutilation and abuse – a flirtation that will extend on the part of the audience not much further than fashionable body piercings and torn clothes, than the occasional smashed car win-dow or graffiti on a shop wall. This is not the music of revolution. Revolution today is accompanied by music, not goaded on. Quiet and sinister revolutions are accomplished by much older men and women in boardrooms that stretch across continents and are under-taken with the kind of global capital that makes Manson's assets look like a penny tossed in a tin cup. Revolution today is accom-panied by the strains of ABBA and played out on the leather seats of a Mercedes Benz, by the Beatles piped into corridors of hotels in world capitals, or by Tony Bennett over whisky at golf courses in Scotland or Thailand. Manson's audience, surging against the stage fences, might call to mind violent revolution but theirs is an impo-tent sameness, a torpor that extends now to the four corners of the world. Having shelled out the price of admission, they will go home to a short, ineffectual sleep and next day's work. Last night's concert will retain but a little remnant of heat, as if emitted from a residue of ashes – twilight of gods. Responding to this titillation, the audiences flirt with Manson's *outré*, thereby transforming the worldly same-ness of their lives into the barely palatable.

Manson's audience is entombed in a kind of living death. They will leap and fall in frenzy, rush the stage, flash power fists, but they have given up a certain vital spirit. They acknowledge in a miserly way the pissiness of life, that which Manson himself acknowledges both inside and outside the concert hall. Death is enshrined in our consciousness, as Manson puts it, even if it is a sacred death: "A half-naked dead man hangs in most homes and around our necks, and we have just taken that for granted all our lives. Is it a symbol of hope or hopelessness?" Or merely a secular death: "In my work I examine the America we live in, and I've always tried to show people that the devil we blame our atrocities on is really just each one of us. So don't expect the end of the world to come one day out of the blue – it's been happening every day for a long time."[14]

The death element in capitalism as described by Marx is not an abstraction. Rather it is the melancholy backdrop – the factual basis – against which Marx unfolds the concept of alienation as applied to the condition of the working classes (and even more so, those who become surplus to it). In *Capital*, Marx notes a marked division in average life expectancy between the labouring and the upper-middle classes in Manchester and Liverpool, between roughly fifteen and thirty-eight years respectively. Ironically, these ages – fifteen to thirty-eight – circumscribe the predominant ages of the attendees at a Manson concert, as if his audience, some of whose ancestors worked themselves to death before they were out of their teens, now succumb to a living death with apparent free will: "Dr Lee, Medical Officer of Health for Manchester, stated that the average age at death of the Manchester ... upper middle class was 38 years, while the average age at death of the labouring class was 17; while at Liverpool those figures were represented as 35 against 15."[15]

The passage just cited forms part of the chapter "The General Law of Capitalist Accumulation." Therein Marx cites Bernard de Mandeville, from *The Fable of the Bees*. Entomology aside for the moment, Mandeville's argument for the accumulation of a surplus labour force prefigures Adorno's analysis of the culture industry by some two centuries: "It is in the interest of all rich nations, that the greatest part of the poor should almost never be idle, and yet continually spend what they get ... Those that get their living by their daily labour ... have nothing to stir them up to be serviceable but their wants which it is prudence to relieve, but folly to cure ... In a free nation, where slaves are not allowed of, the surest wealth consists in a multitude of labourious poor; for besides that they are the never failing nursery of fleets and armies, without them there could be no enjoyment."[16] The full extent of what Mandeville means by "enjoyment" is not entirely clear. Here he means no doubt that enjoyment depends upon the accumulation of surplus value (turned to luxuries

such as entertainment), and this entails no enjoyment by the surplus "non-workers" (as Marx reminds us parenthetically) who drive
down the value of labour in the calculation of profit. The mixture of
"never be idle" and "no enjoyment" reminds us of Adorno's image
of the jitterbug, touched on in a previous chapter, the popular music
listener who, as automaton, is constrained to "work for their leisure" by dancing (jitterbugging) harder and harder, as if Andersen's
fable of the Red Shoes were given a thoroughly modern revision.

The melancholy subject of Marx's critique is real death, a large
part of it industrial death grim in a sense that not even Manson
could capture. The numbers cited by Marx are astonishing to our
Medicared sensibilities. The backdrop of death here, tied to actual
working conditions and painful reality, is not necessarily to be confused with the alienation that characterized late capitalist society in
Adorno's day (for in large parts of the world labour legislation had
restricted the severity of exploitation described here by Marx and
elsewhere by Engels[17]). But if the harshest aspects of capitalism were
relieved in certain parts of the world,[18] a static climate of alienation
was not. As we shall see shortly, certain Marxists, Adorno among
them, turned to metaphors of death when describing that alienation.
As we have seen, Manson turns to metaphors of death – wittingly
or not – in describing the compass of an alienated modern American
class consciousness.

Consider the textuality of Marx's writings in this regard. There
is a factuality that would obscure the melancholy nature of the figures. As noted, the images of death in Marx – the statistics of deaths
among workers in mid-nineteenth-century England, for example –
have a reality about them; people, many of them young, were killed
by real causes, and a real remedy was taken. On account of that
concrete framework of diagnosis and consequent action, the melancholia of Marx's textuality tends to recede into the background; we
are not distracted by how Marx phrases his text, or by the length
of *Capital* or the vivid nature of its examples. We are not interested
normally in Marx's poetics. Even when Marx transforms physical
death into the abstractions of labour time, the text of his work
retains a measured distance from the emotional nature of its subject
matter. Much of *Capital* is reportage, after all, and perhaps for this
reason it largely eludes examination as text. Marx's truths reside in
the diagnosis made by the text; the text in and of itself does not normally constitute a diagnosis. From time to time, however, the tone

of Marxism shifts, as in the following passage from Engels's supplement to volume 3 of *Capital*, where the reality of the growth of the accumulation of capital is looked upon with a bitter tone, part irony, part nostalgia for a time when the miseries of capitalism had established only a toehold in the life of the worker: "At that time, then [prior to the mid-nineteenth-century accumulation of capital], the stock exchange was still just a place where the capitalists plundered one another of their accumulated capitals, and it concerned the workers only as a new piece of evidence of the demoralizing general effect of the capitalist economy, confirming the Calvinist principle that divine election, alias accident, is already decisive in this life as far as bliss and damnation, wealth (pleasure and power) and poverty (renunciation and servitude) are concerned."[19] Here the bittersweet of gall comes to the fore to overwhelm the factual, however briefly. Yes there is a melancholy quality to Marx and Engels, not to be fully eclipsed by the apparent objectivity of their discourse.

With Manson, the factual recedes behind the gall. Whatsoever truths are to be discerned in his lyrics – the fraudulence of organized religion, for example – barely attract our attention as truths anymore for they are no more than commonplaces in a moderately liberal literature, as if they came out of *Harper's*. The factual in Manson, however, is a process carried out by his text. Repeated moderate "shock" elicits a maximum of tedium, ultimately the deadening of the soul. His audience stands slack jawed, zombie like, or vibrates in a virtual rage of inactivity. No doubt there are mating rituals enacted to Manson's work. But these would seem to take place in spite of the stasis of his text, as if the warm biological urge to mate rises up to spite Manson's mannered and precious sexuality. Fighting against such optimistic urges, Manson's work would fuse its audience into the voyeur class – the bourgeoisie writ small, staring in bewilderment at the size of its mortal destiny, at a *mortis* only moderately rigorous. Marilyn Manson, class hero in his hand.

Historical rigidness appears in Lukács's *History and Class Consciousness* as both nature and history: "The objects of history appear as the objects of immutable, eternal laws of nature. History becomes fossilised in a *formalism* incapable of comprehending that the real nature of socio-historical institutions is that they consist of *relations between men*."[20] He means by *fossilization* the "rigid, unhistorical, natural appearance of social institutions."[21] On this fossilized account (fostered in the interests of capitalism), nature, unlike history, is above human sway and thus eternal; like the fossil record, nature was determined long ago and by forces far beyond human volition. The category of "natural" is adapted from the nascent physical sciences[22] and then extended well beyond the fossil record so as to encompass unquestionable "social institutions," the most notable of which is capitalism, naturally.

After Lukács, the bourgeoisie bear responsibility for the eradication of history brought about through the fossilization of institutions into formalism. With the ashen death of history, humans are estranged from true understanding of their world by an "unbridgeable gulf" (the Styx leaps again to mind). Institutions that should be seen as living and thus mutable, susceptible to human influence, are represented as natural in the sense of the fossil record – as a nature long dead to human intercourse. But Lukács cites Marx: these natural institutions are no less a creation of humankind than are "flax, linen, etc."[23]

In his own way, Manson sets out a fossilized history. He reconfigures artifacts – the pseudo-Nazi trappings, for example – as real objects crossed over into the mythic. Transformed thus, these ersatz fascist symbols (alongside the blood-spattered invocations of the Archangel and the reconstituted monstrosities from Bosch triptychs) have none of the vitality of "relations between men." The link here – between Manson and Marx – is the melancholy gothic, readily apparent in Manson but present in Marx as noted above. Justifying the calculation of profit by appeal to "market forces" or the "invisible hand," capitalists give themselves free reign to drink from the blood of the working class. It seems more than coincidental that the works of the economist Ricardo, cited ubiquitously by Marx, date from around the time of Polidori's *The Vampyre*.

In Lukács's *The Theory of the Novel*, alienation surfaces midway through the chapter entitled "The Epic and the Novel," *in medias res*, halfway through a paragraph on madness and crime: a "fundamental dissonance of existence" prevents us from clinging to belief. We cling nonetheless; life goes on as if such beliefs were self-supporting entities, despite evidence that this is an absurdity.

Literature, however, recognizes what "life as a whole" will not, that absurdity is a "basic *a priori* constituent" of our lives:

Every form is the resolution of a fundamental dissonance of existence; every form restores the absurd to its proper place as the vehicle, the necessary condition of meaning. When the peak of absurdity, the futility of genuine and profound human aspirations, or the possibility of the ultimate nothingness of man has to be absorbed into literary form as a basic vehicular fact, and when what is in itself absurd has to be explained and analysed and, consequently, recognised as being irreducibly *there*, then, although some streams within such a form may flow into a sea of fulfilment, the absence of any manifest aim, the determining lack of direction of life as a whole, must be the basic *a priori* constituent, the fundamental structural element of the characters and the events within it.[24]

Lukács's dissonant existence denies recourse to superior things (God, ultimate good, inalienable right), or "supra-personal ideal necessities" as he calls them. Alienation, like a sieve, supports neither soul nor superior cause: "Where no aims are directly given, the structures [of] the soul ... lose their obvious roots in supra-personal ideal necessities; they are simply existent, perhaps powerful, perhaps frail, but they neither carry the consecration of the absolute within them nor are they the natural containers for the overflowing interiority of the soul."[25] Nor will rock music rise to the defence of superior things in Manson's hands for therein lies the emptiness of all things, superior (God) or base (speakable violence). As Lukács puts it, thinking poetics and textuality, this emptiness is "a basic vehicular fact."

Lukács's familiar notion of *second nature* acknowledges the melancholy absurdity of life. The forms of second nature are abstract and conventional, built up of dead meanings, "rigid and strange." The melancholy gothic arises again in the famous passage describing second nature as a "charnel house," a house where bodies or bones are deposited, as the remnants of "long-dead interiorities": "Second nature [*zweite Natur*] ... is a complex of senses – meanings – which has become rigid and strange, and which no longer wakens interiority; it is a charnel house of long-dead interiorities [*eine Schädelstätte vermoderter Innerlichkeiten*]."[26]

Implicit in second nature is a melancholy yearning for a "state of grace," a "first nature," a state of "pure cognition," meaning cognition unfettered by awareness of self and its ruptures. "When the structures made by man for man are really adequate to man, they are his necessary and native home; and he does not know the nostalgia that posits and experiences nature as the object of its own seeking and finding." First nature is nothing but a postulate, however, a spectre constructed out of shards of alienation: "The first nature, nature as a set of laws for pure cognition, nature as the bringer of comfort to pure feeling, is nothing other than the historico-philosophical objectivation of man's alienation from his own constructs."[27]

Both first and second nature make bourgeois illusions crystal clear. In the quotation above, Lukács describes first nature as objective, the "objectivation of man's alienation from his own constructs."[28] By this objectivity, nostalgia constitutes a longing produced by an alienated consciousness and then transformed into an objective symptom thereof.

Middle America, bastion of second nature, advances an absurd "first nature" as a necessary condition of meaning. The melancholy tenor of its class consciousness lies in Streisand singing "The way we were," in Bloom and the "letting go" of youthful liberties. To this dreary bourdon, Manson the Marginal constitutes a kind of first nature: he constitutes, after Lukács, "nothing other than the historico-philosophical objectification of man's alienation from his own constructs."[29] The redeeming element in Manson's oeuvre is the critique of Middle-American absurdities, a critique he can effect only as an outsider yearning – pining – for a first nature, for the restoration of vitality by means of a nostalgia for loathed things like swastikas and bishops' vestments. Beneath the staged persona, we detect that omnipresent yearning – "the nostalgia that posits and experiences nature as the object of its own seeking and finding"[30] – for a logical world, a "necessary and native home."

Manson's onstage world is peopled thus with artifacts pilfered from our collective history and brought back as if interlopers from some culture other than our own. There are two forms of artifactuation[31] at work in Manson: on the one hand, objects taken from a theatre supply house (or from antiquarians or flea markets) are treated theatrically as if vital; on the other hand, there is Manson himself as a vital commodity – the Manson of the concert stage and the DVD. If all of this produces the uncanny effect of being perfectly at home in someone else's house, such are the whiles of reification in the culture of Late Capitalism.

The vital spirit in the concept of reification is the Marxist notion that labour abstracted – as, for example, congealed labour time –

passes as if it were an inherent property of the thing produced: "the way a relation between men appears in the form of a natural property of a thing." The word *natural* can be taken in the two senses just touched on here after Lukács, the second and first natures. The two require, however, a historical sense originating in a third situation, as follows:

1. A point in time (a pre-capitalist Eden, a climate of use value) when relations between people appeared as truly natural, without recourse to exchange value and its abstractions
2. A point in time (pre-Marx) when such truly natural relations between people were obscured by the commodity exchange, a process by which the natural unity of the commodity made the exploitation of one person's labour by another seem to disappear. This disappearance is patently absurd but global in a climate of a second nature.
3. A point in time (post-Marx) when an ideal world can be postulated in the sense of recollected (as a nostalgia for situation 1) but only from a position – the proletariat in Late Capitalism – where return is impossible.

There is little trace of situation 1 to be found in Manson's work. But situation 2 is omnipresent: he does, after all, produce commodities – concerts and DVD's. I am concerned here, however, with situation 3. The world he both lives and portrays is an institutionalized absurdity – the institution of the church he mocks, but also the absurd institution of the rock concert itself. To this, the impossibility of return constitutes a melancholy fact.

Manson's audience understands the institutions of the past as grand commodities – the bishop's garb, the Nazi-like insignia – as weird things taken from a pawn shop. But they do not recognize Manson's own nature as a commodity. The nature of his work – his labour – is estranged from them by the force of his stage persona. In this sense there is an archaeological factor to Manson's work: he is the foreigner sifting through *our* ruins, finding *our* clay shards and *our* arrowheads with which to amuse *us*, but never confessing that he is one of us, never partaking of our joint lineage in justifying his presence. He is marginal in this sense too: like the *Man in the Glass Booth*, he is us representing himself as an outsider representing us to ourselves.

For Walter Benjamin, criticism was forensic, sorting through the charnel house, sifting the fossil records, reading the ciphers, deciphering the crime. What is it that drove the bourgeois to be just so? Everything (everything bourgeois), living and dead, transforms into a natural history to be read as allegory: "For radical natural-historical thought, however, everything existing transforms itself into ruins and fragments, into just such a charnel-house [using the term encountered in Lukács, *in eine solche Schädelstätte*'] where signification is discovered, in which nature and history interweave and the philosophy of history is assigned the task of their intentional interpretation."[32] Working on the charnel house floor of bourgeois sensibility, Benjamin sifts the archaic from the actual. He parses the residue, understands its allegories, glimpses its past, and thereby attempts the present. As Adorno puts it, "[Benjamin] is driven not merely to awaken congealed life in petrified objects – as in allegory – but also to scrutinize living things so that they present themselves as being ancient, 'ur-historical' and abruptly release their significance."[33]

Under these rubrics, the task of the critic becomes to read present-day bourgeois culture as if it were a ruin destroyed by capitalist ideology: "Exegetical power became the ability to see through the manifestations and utterances of bourgeois culture as hieroglyphs of its darkest secret – as ideologies."[34] Describing Benjamin's method, however, Adorno sets forth the central critical issues of his own method: examine bourgeois society, the "trance-like captivity of bourgeois immanence," in microscopic detail, eschew grand totalities, relate concrete details to material frameworks, avoid abstract and totalizing systematic constructions, and above all oppose any banal optimism appearing in the guise of positivity. The all too brief testament in Adorno's *Prisms* shows just how important Benjamin was to Adorno's critical formation: "He viewed the modern world as archaic not in order to conserve the traces of a purportedly eternal truth but rather to escape the trance-like captivity of bourgeois immanence. He sees his task not in reconstructing the totality of bourgeois society but rather in examining its blinded, nature-bound and diffuse elements under a microscope."[35]

When Adorno, in an essay on the two French writers Paul Valéry and Marcel Proust, chooses death in the guise of the museum as the term of comparison, the image recalls Lukács's "second nature" and the charnel house, alongside Benjamin's *nature morte* – still life as nature dead, the interpretation of the living as archaic: "The German word, '*museal*' ['*museumlike*'], has unpleasant overtones. It describes objects to which the observer no longer has a vital relationship and which are in the process of dying. They owe their preservation more to historical respect than to the needs of the present. Museum and mausoleum are connected by more than phonetic association."[36] And it brings to mind Manson's work, both subject matter and textuality, which preserves as if in museum and mausoleum the values of Middle America, locked in the glass case in the lobby.

Acknowledging another French poet, Paul Verlaine, in his first published work, *Poèmes saturniens* of 1866, Adorno invokes the death mask, the "saturnine gaze," a heavy, leaden, sluggish regard. For both Valéry and Proust, the museum is dead. For Valéry, the artwork housed in a museum is extracted from its vital circumstances – the life that produced it; cut off from its life blood, it dies. For Proust, the artwork is elevated above the quotidian to take on a second life; resurrected in the museum it becomes angelic in the gaze of the *amateur*. In neither instance does the artwork retain its original status as a use value. Rather, in both cases the work of art is turned into a commodity – an artifact – by the cold walls that encompass it, mausoleum-like. In similar fashion, following Adorno, Manson has extracted his subject matter from its vital circumstances; the death motif in his work is merely a trope of this fact. Resurrected in his guise, the past is made angelic, albeit the property of the dark angel. All of this is gathered tidily into the commodity of the concert and its DVD – now the stuff of fading youthful memories and remaindered DVD bins.

Adorno treats Valéry as a conservative, a reactionary, who, like Schoenberg, hits the nail on the head unwittingly. Lamenting the extraction of art from real life, Valéry stumbles upon the essence of capitalist economics, but without recognition. Adorno's Proust, on the other hand, is a devout liberal, drawn to the new lease on life given an artwork by extraction from real life. Resurrected, the artwork becomes an icon for adoration. As a thought experiment, consider the possibility that Adorno's Valéry would have been outraged at Manson's menageries of things torn from their moorings, but Adorno's Proust might well have been amazed by the transformation effected upon otherwise quotidian articles in Manson's hands, how in his hands a microphone becomes an instrument worthy of de Sade.

The removal of the artwork from its context creates the central problem of the museum, a problem with two faces. On the one hand, lying behind Adorno's Valéry is the thought that the artwork's removal renders it indecipherable, the way a commodity abstracts and thus obscures the labour exerted to create it. Museums on this account are vacuums, places where vital meaning has been extracted, much as in the shopping malls of Middle America where the meaning of labour has been extracted in service to the commodity fetish. For Adorno's Proust, on the other hand, removal of the artwork from its context imbues it with new meaning, as an artifact with a new purpose, albeit a purpose not entirely exhausted by fulfilling the commodity fetish. Either way the work ceases to exist in direct relation to its original purpose.

To what purpose Manson's music? By its spectacle, it would seem to fulfill the basic requisites of commodity by erasing work; this is not labour, these are not labourers on stage but angels halting briefly on the way to Hades. The sweat on stage is not produced by the quotidian rigours of playing instruments but is instead the product of dark and twisted liturgies. Forget the price of the ticket. This is magic theatre, miracles at the hands of Ticketmaster.

For Adorno's Valéry, a museum is most certainly not a means to resurrection. One cannot revive and sustain the life of a work of art by placing it into surgical cleanliness. Encapsulated in the vacuum of the museum, art dies, falling to the floor (after Joseph Wright's *An Experiment on a Bird in an Air Pump* of 1768): "For Valéry, art is lost when it has relinquished its place in the immediacy of life, in its functional context."[37] Strict application of Valéry's thought leads to an artistic notion comparable to *use value*. All artistic objects should remain in close proximity to their creator and thus remain linked directly to the original labour exerted to produce them. Vitality depends upon immediacy. The madding crowds captured in Manson's DVD, the burly and aggressive security guards, the cavernous halls – this is not the stuff of intimacy, let alone immediacy. The purpose of this observation, however, is diagnostic; Adorno is not taking Valéry's stance here but instead turning it to analysis: we cannot return to a pre-capital climate of immediacy. But having been turned out of paradise and in lieu of celebrating that fact, we can merely understand that the world is now "out of joint": "To renounce radically the possibility of experiencing the traditional would be to capitulate to barbarism out of devotion to culture. That the world is out of joint is shown everywhere in the fact that however a problem is solved, the solution is false."[38]

For Adorno's Proust, one must be a consumer, spellbound (and to a certain degree slack jawed), something like Adorno's entertainment listener, "inclined to that effusive and for artists highly suspect awe before works that characterizes only those separated from them as though by an abyss."[39] To understand an artwork, it has to be observed from afar, voyeuristically. From Proust's perspective, the *amateur* is situated in a historical landscape – a grand belvedere (again the Grand Hotel Abyss with its splendid balcony comes to mind) – of artworks. Valéry would say this is a dead and thus desolate landscape, and in that sense he confirms what Lukács offered Adorno as first and second natures. From Proust's perspective, however, artifacts must be elevated above quotidian life and into some kind of framing perspective. This perspective reflects as much about the *amateur* as it does about the artwork: "For [Proust] works of art are from the outset something more than their specific aesthetic qualities. They are part of the life of the person who observes them; they become an element of his consciousness ...Whereas Valéry's conservative belief in culture as a pure thing in itself affords incisive criticism of a culture which tends by its very historical nature to destroy everything self-subsistent, Proust's most characteristic mode of perception, his extraordinary sensitivity to changes in modes of experience, has as its paradoxical result the ability to perceive history as landscape."[40] Along the lines of Adorno's Proust, we are not repulsed by Manson writ large across the face of the world. The fact of his work's worldwide reproduction speaks to us about popular culture and its devotees in a way that a local performance could not.

The artwork in its museum becomes melancholy memory – the memory of everything that Valéry values so highly in its unmediated form and which has passed out of reach in a museum. For Proust the museum becomes the vehicle for an aesthetics of the second hand, of the decaying. The operant term in the following quotation is *second life*, after Lukács. If bourgeois life in general is a moribund *second life*, then the institutionalization of its works of art reflects this like a mirror. The connoisseur will come to appreciate, even to love, the process of decay encapsulated therein: "In the artifact's capacity for disintegration Proust sees its similarity to natural beauty. He recognizes the physiognomy of decomposing things as that of their second life. Because nothing has substance for him but what has already been mediated by memory, his love dwells on the second life, the one which is already over, rather than on the first."[41] On this account more credit, much more credit, should be accorded Manson's screaming fans, for on Proustian lines their hysteria may be at heart a truly sophisticated aesthetic of artistic decay, as if the lips on the mouth in Munch's *Cry* were about to crescent upward in appreciation of its painted self.

Adorno's Proust goes so far as to elevate the mediated – the old popular song that lives in associated memories – above the unmediated, the absolute of a self-sufficient work (middle-period Beethoven). Memory is saturnine – slow moving, death-like, leaden – and yet ever so powerful. It sees through absolute aesthetics to its decaying core: "In a famous passage he glorified inferior music for the sake of the listener's memories, which are preserved with far more fidelity and force in an old popular song than in the self-sufficiency of a work by Beethoven. The saturnine gaze of memory penetrates the veil of culture."[42]

Then Adorno turns adroitly to his point: not just artifacts are preserved in the museum but also subjectivities such as those encoded in memory, principally the subjectivity of the observer, be it Valéry, Proust, or some other observant standing beside the tomb of culture. Museums are as much about observer subjectivity – the act of production that changes the artwork into something other than real – as about actual objects. For a sociologist of the arts, this is a key assertion: the museum becomes a site of fieldwork on the psyche; a curator's duties are to look deeply into the self of the observer: "Proust's arguments in favor of museums also have as their point of reference not the thing itself but the observing subject. It is not coincidental that it is something subjective, the abrupt act of production in which the work becomes something different from reality, that Proust considers to be preserved in the work's afterlife in the museum."[43] This is our point about Manson: the work itself is overshadowed in critical interest by the subjectivities of its observers – the crowd in the pit (or in the parterre), be they expert or merely emotional.

Ultimately the audience's subjectivities – the gaze rather than the object gazed upon – become artifacts themselves, which Manson (after Zappa) acknowledges by abusing. The gaze of the viewer is itself turned into an artifact. The actual contents of the museum are only objects that elicit the gaze. Thus Adorno speaks

of a development that has "transformed works of art into the hieroglyphics of history and brought them a new content while the old
one shriveled up," a fact which no "conception of pure art"[44] can
deny. If one can decipher those hieroglyphics, through the Rosary
Stone of negative dialectics, one can read off the sociology of the
viewer. If one can decipher Manson clearly, it might just be possible
to conceive a sociology of Middle America in the 1980s and 1990s.

These are the values of Middle America for which Columbine is
but an index. Adorno's Valéry senses innately the stench of death:
"Dead visions are entombed here."[45] It is for him a shock, like that
of stumbling upon a corpse: "The shock of the museum brings
Valéry to historical-philosophical insight into the perishing of art
works; there, he says, we put the art of the past to death."[46] In Manson's video, we are shocked first at the portrait of death enshrined
in the tortured locks of hair, the black eye liner, and the leather and
then second at the impotency of the image. There is nothing to do
but gaze at Manson or yet again dance limply the *Totentanz*.

For Proust, on the other hand, whatever "seems eternal," as if it
were ready to live forever, contains the signs of eternity, thus contains within itself "the impulse of its own destruction."[47] Proust
takes a decisive stand against naturalism: nothing can be portrayed
as natural, for the act of portrayal destroys nature, rendering the
object portrayed in the form of a death mask to be preserved for
eternity. To cling to naturalism is barbaric, a life of sheer immediacy;
in attempting to capture and preserve the artwork, we give it the
life of a second nature. Thus Adorno quotes Proust: "In all areas
our age is obsessed with the desire to bring things before our eyes in
their natural surroundings and thus to suppress what is essential –
the mental event that raised them out of those surroundings."[48] And
thus Manson works to transmute chicken blood into vital plasma,
although we know fully it is a mere artifice, for we like our barbarism rare.

Comparing Valéry to Proust, then, Adorno sets forth two accounts
of museum culture, both assuming the death of the artwork. In the
first, the artwork dies by excision from vital circumstances in the
barren confines of the museum. In the second, the artwork is elevated to a second life infused solely by whatever vitality is to be
derived from memory. Following on Adorno's thought, excised or
resurrected, the original artwork is now as dead as the bourgeois
culture that spawned it.

The Manson DVD emerges out of the ubiquitous "FBI Warning: Federal law provides severe civil and criminal penalties for the unauthorized reproduction." The patriarchal finger-wagging of this blue-screen-of-authority in such close proximity to Manson's apparent deviance brings one up abruptly. (What would J. Edgar think?) Is this admonition here solely to ward off copyright infringement, or does the FBI's jurisdiction bleed in to cover Manson's dissolute spectacle itself? (And if so, should we close the curtains tight and check the telephone for tapping?)

How ironic the fact that this very commodity devoted blatantly to a flaunting of mores is wrapped in the protective caress of *the* federal agency that under its vaunted director, Mr Hoover, would have found the whole enterprise at a minimum unpatriotic (for the defamation of the flag alone) if not an outright pernicious influence on the nation's youth. Irony, however, has a way of emasculating if not outright eviscerating and then eating its object, and the presence of this almost biblical admonition not to go forth and multiply renders Manson's consequent antics slightly ridiculous.

The camera's opening pan moves across an undulating horde (briefly accompanied by the faint sound of insects) – audiences assembled at various locations on Manson's world tour. The stadia in which the concerts take place are themselves apocalyptic in the style of the Blake print: they call to mind the spaces of the final coming, towering and cavernous, filled with masses alternately fearful and yearning.

The effect, however, is all too reminiscent of Leni Riefenstahl, *Triumph des Willens*, and the surging Nazi salutes, arm straight and elevated. No doubt this is calculated, an evocation of guns and government. The requisite military trappings are provided by burly security guards, the storm troopers turned loose on the rock concert, forcing errant fans back violently, bodies hurling and being hurled back in return. Rushing the crowd, these hired thugs lack only for truncheons and police uniforms with pressed medal insignia. What is this place, London or Lagos?

The introduction is accompanied by a quiet drone, a distinct musical contrast to the tumult beneath the camera. Is this the mind of Manson, the psychopath dispassionately surveying the hypnotized crowd for a suitable victim? A tinkling piano melody cements this sense of detached gaze, truly scopic in its dispassionate authority over the object writhing before it.

The total effect is Romanesque in splendour. The massive auditoriums filled with frenzied bodies are visibly the world with all its newly discovered personae – Caucasian security guards with large industrial insignia in an Eastern European language (Prague or Warsaw?) emblazoned on industrial-sized jackets, a young oriental woman screaming unreservedly at the camera in a pleasure unrestrained by any shreds of conventional decorum (San Francisco or Tokyo?). These are the citizens of Caesar's new world.

Enter Caesar. Manson, borne on stage in a chariot by two nubile young women with equine headdress in imitation of some antiquity (Egyptian, Roman, Barnum and Bailey, Gilbert and Sullivan). Manson dressed in leather corset and elaborate head wear, the helmet with hair streaming. The tight corset in black is built of leather strips joined together by rivets, with trailing appendages of more black leather strips and thongs. He sports tall black boots with platform soles, crotch padding, lengthy evening gloves in black. This is not merely Marilyn Monroe but rather an apocalyptic Marlene Dietrich, the malevolent Blue Angel. Cool. The stage is covered in dry-ice fog and set in deep blue lighting. Manson salutes his audience and they wriggle like Beelzebub's minions. There is a sudden illumination of the stage: explosive red lights, puffs of smoke, a torn and otherwise abused American flag set as backdrop. The Devil arrives at work.

By its very excess, the scene gives itself away. A thin line of mock seriousness keeps it from gravitating into the sheer delightful idiocy of a Gilbert and Sullivan romp. The audience flirts with the margins of the allowable, but by its well regulated behaviour – screaming for the camera – it reduces transgression to mere titillation. Everything takes place safely within the confines of the museum; the cavernous auditorium – perhaps the gift of the Shriners – condones this flirtation with excess, as if it were as healthy as the track meet that will fill the bleachers next weekend, the same security guards in attendance. Manson attempts to breathe life into dead symbols, Marat, de Sade, the fascists, authoritarianism, and the military, but merely parades his impotence, made clearer by the vast hordes obedient to some other ethos. If this is revolution, why will all these people go back to their rabbit warrens after the concert? Take to the streets? Or take us to McDonalds?

Manson is a thing of great value. He has conceived the perfect entombment, the logical sequel to the life and death of Elvis. The performance is a thing of critical beauty, a museum piece, where *museum* equates with *mausoleum* in exactly the sense of Adorno's French writers. Along the lines of Valéry – by its very spectacle Manson removes his art from the vital context of life: no one in her right mind for a moment would confound his performance with politics any more than she would leap on stage to rescue Gretchen at her spinning wheel. But the audience would and does make the pleasant suspension of reality that drama requires, and believes in a mythical narrative, elevated above the existence of daily drudge or daily delight. This is Proust: Manson's audience are *amateurs* in a museum; they extract his dramatics from everyday life (from his real counterparts in the horrid jail cells of third-world dictatorships) and give them a transcendent, elevated quality, nailed to the cross. But in doing so, the members of his audience are no more than simple consumers, no more than tourists gawking at ruins of prison chambers in the Tower of London who will soon board tour buses returning them to their modern quarters leaving them devoid of anything but a modicum of very low back pain. This is not revolution; this is a wheel that, perennially, turns slowly over and over.

My Favourite Wagner. The "extras" in the *Ring* – the common people of the chorus – are in some ways more fascinating than the principals – the Gods and their offspring, licit and otherwise. For this reason, the third scene of the second act of *Götterdämmerung* is a favourite. The little people – like the prisoners in *Fidelio* – emerge from their warrens to sniff the air, as if instinctually (and not merely at Hagen's bellowing) before the conflagration.

This scene's structural role appears at first blush to be straightforward. It lies at the symmetrical heart of the opera – the third scene of five, in the second act of three (each flanking act comprising three scenes in its own right). In this sense the scene constitutes a dramatic pivot point around which swing the tensions sown in the first act and their tragic fruit borne out in the third. The fact that the principal characters, with the exception of Hagen the facilitator, are absent here merely underscores this pivotal role: the principal drama is unfolding elsewhere among much more important characters – offstage, between Siegfried, Gunther, and Brünnhilde – whose motivations we understand clearly. No doubt, then, the structural motivation of the scene was to give Hagen free reign by which to develop the dark side emerging in the first scene with Albericht.

In another sense, however, the scene lies at the asymmetrical heart of the *Ring* as a whole: things have been happening, and very slowly in Wagnerian fashion a momentum has been gathering. It is as if the chorus on stage has been watching matters for some time now (through sideways glances at the Gods, their masters), and while coming near to breaking out of the limits set by the proscenium, it rises up in unprecedented fashion and demands dramatic justice. It is after all the fourth night of four – like the start of the third period in hockey or the bottom of the seventh in baseball, with the home team down 3 to 1. Hagen is not alone in his thirst for revenge: chorus and audience too, having been roused from slumbers by Hagen's braying, is out for blood – the blood of Siegfried, Gunther, or even Hagen himself will do fine, thank you.

Both chorus and audience, in Pirandello fashion, are unleashed here from the normal closure necessitated by drama. One has the sense that Wagner let his guard slip briefly, albeit in a major way. As the opera proceeds, a symbolic content absorbs our interest by pitting the principal characters against each other in the dialectic bathos of Wagnerian "good versus evil" – Siegfried contra Hagen (with Gunther as middle term), Wotan and Brünnhilde (with Waltraute [Act 1, Scene 3] as middle factor). But here symbol gives way to allegory: just what have these conflicted characters achieved over some thirty hours of bad staging? And will enough blood be spilled to bring the whole thing off in dispensation for the earthly tedium? Will this prove dramatically just? In the latter case, even the chorus seems to have its suspicions, revealed by how they taunt Hagen in the scene.

The role given to the chorus – the little people (carrying machine rifles in the Chéreau *Ring*) – is one of negation. (And one wonders if this was a subconscious apparition on Wagner's part, emerging unannounced and unnoticed as he put together a little stuffing by which to link scenes 2 and 4.) The audience, like the chorus, being made to sense war, shifts Hagen in its sights. In his positive guise, Hagen is simply the protagonist of Siegfried's demise, thus bringing all the current principals (and the Gods above) together in a dramatic synthesis of their various tensions. His central moment lies in the forthcoming (again symmetrically positioned) second scene of the third act, bringing on the denouement of the whole *Ring* by restoring Siegfried's memory, goading on his recollections, and then slaying him. This synthetic role, however, really begins to take form in the third scene of the second act in Hagen's call to arms: "Arm yourselves well and do not rest!/Gunther comes to pay respects to you:/He has wooed a wife." But being naturally clumsy, Hagen over-does the matter, calling them too vigorously to arms, as if war were at hand: "Hoi-ho! Hoi-ho!/Gibich men, rise up!/Alarm! Weapons!" And thus they respond, excessively so: "Hagen! Hagen!/Who calls us to arms!/We come with our weapons ... /What need is there?/ What foe is at hand?/Who brings us strife?" The passage containing the chorus's response – delivered in a call-and-answer texture, with overlapping cries – is one of the longest and most vigorous of the act, some seventy measures during which the chorus spills out at first gradually then rapidly on stage, quietly at first, then coming together on a fortissimo and sustained "Ho! Hagen!"

The chorus initially does not understand Hagen's call, the fact that it is merely a wedding at hand, not full-scale war. The effect is one of spilling over, a too-abundant alarm on the chorus's part. Even the announcement of Gunther's impending arrival with a new wife is misunderstood in the alarm. Huh? What's that? Why the swords, Hagen? "Her kinsmen and vassals follow in anger?" And we envision the chorus stamping around clanging swords, spears, and shields – hot breath and cheeks.

No doubt the excess has a properly symbolic function within Wag-ner's narrative. Perhaps Hagen wants *all* the Gibichungs onstage to witness Brünnhilde's arrival and betrothal. But more likely Wagner wanted merely to make good enthusiastic use of his chorus – filling the stage and thus conceiving a spectacle of sufficient weight for the arrival of Brünnhilde with her shame. (He was paying them, after all.) As I suggest, however, the real effect is allegorical. Since this is not the most important moment for the chorus (which is in fact spread over the second and final scenes of the third act, as witness of Siegfried's demise, wherein the chorus is quite properly domesti-cated), we and they are left asking "What's all the fuss about Hagen/ Wagner? Where's the action? What's happening?" To which Hagen replies, in offhand fashion, "Slaughter sturdy steers and let their blood flow on Wotan's alter." And as if they hadn't heard right, the chorus, with swords and spears in hand, demands again, "What? Why are you calling us, then? Huh?" Hagen again, still in offhand manner, "Kill a boar for Froh and a goat in its prime for Donner, and sheep for Fricka, so she gives a good blessing." And yet again, the chorus demands, "Ok, we slaughter the animals, yes, then what?"

as if hopes were aroused earlier and slaying shouldn't be limited to things on four feet.

Finally it becomes clear to them that a celebration – with alcohol involved – is about to take place. Then and only then do they come around, but not without a parting shot at our indelicate protagonist: "Great fortune and health on the Rhine,/if Hagen the Grim makes so merry!" What a day,/if he can crack a smile!

The allegory here lies in the excess: for a moment our attention is drawn away from the dramatic end so as to rest on the opera itself as a vehicle for producing meaning. Here is mediation brought about immanently: by the clumsiness of his gestures, Hagen (fully in keeping with his character) draws us into a broader awareness – dramatic justice being our concern. "Why the fuss Hagen (and Wagner)? Is it all necessary?" Indeed, Wagner courts a great danger here: "Why the fuss – why *four nights* of it? – Wagner?"

Fitting, then, that this mediating gesture should have been contrived (or perhaps arose only instinctually) on Wagner's part for the little people – the extras, the nonentities – and that they in turn raise a collective middle finger in the air at Hagen and vicariously at Wagner. It seems uncanny: these are the people seldom if ever served by Wagnerian dramatic justice – as Adorno describes the normal state of affairs in regard to the *Ring*: "All that is intended is a dispensation from middle-class obligations. The insignificant are punished, while the prominent go scot-free. This at any rate is what happens in the *Ring*."[49]

Here, unwittingly on Wagner's part, it seems as if the little people – the lower spectrum of the middle classes, the vassals – get their dramatic justice. And their justice is allegorical, its discursive subject being excess in opera, Wagnerian opera in particular, and thus opera in general.

Sensing this, Hagen, standing in for Wagner, moves to suppress the excess. The seventy measures of chorus abandon – the unregulated call-and-answer – is brought up short by Hagen (at "*Starke Stiere*") with a sudden diminuendo to piano over ten measures. The excess spills over again in the chorus, rising back to forte (seven measures), but is suppressed again by Hagen ("*Einen Eber*") with a forte-piano return to quiet (eighteen measures). The pattern is established: again the chorus with its rebellious self-consciousness rears up and again Hagen reels them in ("*Das Trinkhorn*"). So it continues – rebellion and suppression – until the consciousness of the chorus is brought back to its properly domesticated dramatic role. The suppression is brought home in that parting shot to Hagen ("*Grosse Glück und Heil*"), rebellious but harnessed to a four-part chorale style some forty measures in length. The peasant rebellion – symbolic and allegorical – is dead. Played out over the length of the scene – symmetrically and asymmetrically centred – the chorus rises up in self-awareness, dragging its audience with it, only to fall back again. The materialist meaning of the opera, if not Wagner's operatic work as a whole, is contained herein: opera as a commodity is about control and no rebellion will be brooked herein.

Ultimately (and quite apart from the restoration of the gold), *Götterdämerung* is about dawning intelligence – about Siegfried, and then Guthrune, and then Brünnhilde, coming into awareness, in Siegfried's case via the restoration of memory through drugs, in Guthrune and Brünnhilde's cases via the revelation of treachery in the person of Siegfried's corpse. But these are merely the symbolic revelations of dramatic secrets locked well within the operatic narrative.

My favourite scene, however, carries as well a quite separate dawning intelligence – that dramatic justice is a matter of control on Wagner's part, control that he will let slip only briefly. It is as if the Gibichung people (a nascent operatic proletariat groomed by a weakling king and his corrupt agent) will sense its allegorical power – to question dramatic authority – for one radical moment, only to lose it again, in Wagnerian fashion, to wine (and mead), women (Brünnhilde and Guthrune), and song (opera as conventional singing). This is dramatic justice remaindered negatively.

8

Moses und Adorno

As the leading exponent of negative dialectics, Adorno can hardly fail to
understand that his own critical method, as applied to music since the
Enlightenment, comes dangerously close to self-negation.

Rose Rosengard Subotnik, *Developing Variations*

The consistency with which Adorno's critical voice engages its object
across the great breadth of his writing is nothing short of remarkable.[1] The perennial element in his work lies in his capacity to attack
new conundrums with a voice freshly supplied by dialectics, as if
the latter were elixir. The acerbic wit seems to pour forth, a veritable flood of negation goaded on by the waxing and waning tides of
reason and commodification.

The critical voice, however, is made all the more remarkable by the
extent to which a necessarily uncritical Adorno is hidden behind it,
the negative remainder left over after the union of voice and object
in Adorno's prose.[2] Our attention is seized and then exhausted by
the prickly dissonant brilliance – the wit, the verbal play, the meanings freshly juxtaposed. We are obligated nonetheless, if only by
the method itself, to work so as to see a conundrum here too: after
Adorno, the problem of identity must be applied to Adorno's own
identity. As Rose Rosengard Subotnik, cited in the epigraph, suggests, ultimately negative dialectics must turn its lens on Adorno
himself, on the excess of style and the excision of the personal.[3]

There is good reason for Adorno's erasure. The act of introducing
oneself, the practice of writing about oneself, tempt the very solipsism Adorno sets out to examine in the bourgeois consciousness. To
rely on the self without critical correction would be the height of
identity thinking: here I am, this is my opinion, take it or leave it.
Self without correction – such is the heart of smug bourgeois indif-
ference, the sublime confidence of the jackass who pronounces a

logical conundrum in appreciation of Schoenberg's music: "I know what I like, and I don't like that." Do you know what you don't like?

Such a logical fall from a state of critical grace is to be avoided at all cost for a critic of Adorno's stripe. The act of self-erasure discloses in physiognomic fashion an indisputable fact about the man: he is reluctant to be seen in anything but his critical clothes. But in writing himself out of the picture thus, Adorno reveals his very self as a remainder. In other words, when the object of his work (dialectics in the culture of Late Capitalism) is brought together with his hardened critical voice – grown steely and brittle over time, not merely impersonal but *impersonable* – the unity is not entirely seamless. A discrepant presence –Adorno's non-authorial persona – detaches itself from the union of object and voice and assumes a tangible quality, as a thing of substance. Object and voice negate dialectically; Adorno's method, to return to Rosengard Subotnik, produces self-negation.

We read this absence autobiographically when we match his gregarious critical voice with his otherwise reticent person and recognize a discrepancy.[4] Discerning intent here, we can say that Adorno sets up just such a discrepancy between his authorial voice and his person as a means of speaking in lieu of the first person. We sense the virtuosity in his prose and thereby sense a virtuoso, but only sense, never see. The prose is like a performance conducted behind a curtain. Adorno could not reveal himself otherwise, certainly not in a direct fashion. For Adorno the critic to make self-assertions in any other manner would be the methodological equivalent of solipsism clothed as vanity.[5]

The late essay "Sacred Fragment: Schoenberg's *Moses und Aron*"[6] takes a daunting topic – Schoenberg's sacred opera in light of the genre of sacred music.[7] In "Sacred Fragment," however, Adorno reveals himself in an unprecedented way, the nature of which stems from the subject matter, the object of the critique itself.

The sacred can be glimpsed only negatively. Adorno announces this clearly at the beginning of his essay: "Thus God, the Absolute, eludes finite beings ... The insoluble contradiction which Schoenberg has taken as his project and which is attested by the entire tradition of tragedy, is also the contradiction of the actual work."[8] Moses in Schoenberg's opera announces the problem to Aron in the first act, second scene: "No picture can give you a picture of the unrepresentable. [*Kein Bild kann dir ein Bild geben vom Unvorstell-baren.*]" And as Aron commands in the fourth scene, "Close your eyes; plug your ears. Only thus can you see and hear him! No living soul sees and hears him otherwise! [*Schließet die Augen, verstopfet die Ohren! So nur könnt ihr ihn sehn und hören! Kein Lebender sieht und hört ihn anders!*]" Sacred experience is not subject to a positive appreciation but knowable only as that which exceeds the positive, as left over once the organs of the positive – eyes and ears – are stopped up. Seeing is not believing.

The sacred negation implicit in his subject matter renders Adorno's own negative dialectics redundant. Consider the following, taken from *Negative Dialectics*. Adorno suggests that philosophy depends on the texts it criticizes; however, a critical "exegesis [*Deutung*] elevates neither interpretation nor the symbolic into an absolute but instead seeks after truth where the idea [*Gedanke*] secularizes the irretrievable essence [*Urbild*] of sacred texts."[9] Criticism (exegesis) is like the secularization of a sacred text (and thus not merely an interpretation or a symbolic rendering). To interpret (through criticism or through textual exegesis) is to recuperate that which cannot otherwise be recuperated in daily life – a reified bourgeois life in particular. One criticizes music in much the same way that one secularizes a religious text (a thing otherwise beyond exegesis on account of being religious). In other words, Adorno criticizes music in a manner comparable to the way the libretto and score of *Moses und Aron* criticize the biblical text: both secularize their texts.

Therein lies something of the resilience in Adorno's customary critical voice: its ability to treat the bourgeois secular as if it were a sacred enigma, something to be revealed only sideways, through the allegory of dialectic negation, never directly. This implicit perspective lends a consistent tone to the voice, as if it were constantly testifying.

But with *Moses und Aron*, Adorno's subject *is* a sacred text. The sacred element in the opera makes his secular negative dialectics redundant; the subject matter – the stuff of religion – is already negating. Implicitly, by addressing a religious text, Adorno is already testifying, by the very nature of the subject matter. Thus there is no need to secularize through the virtuoso critical voice of acerbic wit.

In other words, the sacred text in a "sacred" opera is both the starting point and the end of Adorno's exegesis. The sacred text denies him his customary critical voice and its customary negating task. To deprive Adorno of his voice and modus operandi (aimed normally at secularizing the bourgeoisie), however, is to deprive him of a shield behind which to hide. When writing about *Moses und Aron* without his customary negative dialectic armour, Adorno reveals himself.

Denied his customary voice to hide behind, Adorno does not, however, lapse into the first person. Instead he reveals himself *vicariously* through the characters in the essay – Moses and Schoenberg. They become the dramatis personae of an autobiography.

Moses und Aron is particularly apt for this process of autobiographical revelation. The opera, in its unfinished state, is the perfect embodiment of a subject matter that negates completion, for the opera presents itself as a sacred work not despite but on account of being physically incomplete. All sacred experience is incomplete (but not defective) on account of being impossible to experience entirely. Alexander Ringer expressed this insight succinctly in comparing the final measures of *Die Jakobsleiter, Moses und Aron,* and *A Modern Psalm,* all three left as torsos: their "extraordinary last measures are permeated by a palpable sense of metaphysical reality precluding any further act of 'completion,' if truth was to be served."[10]

The sacred Absolute, in other words, exceeds our complete comprehension. And we can comprehend this fact only negatively, as the remainder left over when we try to comprehend the sacred and, failing to do so, reflect on our failure, our inability to comprehend our world as a unity. Negation as a failure of unity is implicit in Adorno's critique. Negation as a reflection on failure, however, is already built into Schoenberg's sacred torsos.

Adorno addresses this self-negating form of sacred awareness at the very beginning of "Sacred Fragment," where he cites a line from the first of Schoenberg's choral Four Pieces, op. 27, entitled "*Unentrinnbar* [Inescapable]," a conundrum that speaks of men doing brave deeds of which their courage cannot conceive: "Brave men are those who accomplish deeds which their courage does not encompass."[11] How can bravery exceed courage? The two are synonymous.

This again is negative dialectics. We think we know courage: it is shown to us in the measure of our brave acts. Courage, brave acts – synthetic unity. But what if the act should exceed the capacity of the mind (as brave acts often do, where they put one's life in peril, for example)? Beyond the capacity of the mind lies the vehicle of its own negation: humans are brave beyond their own capacity to measure.

Old Testament theology is rife with riddles of this negative-dialectic sort. As a textual precedent, however, Old Testament theology makes Adorno's hardened dialectic voice redundant, his customary negative stance superfluous. His subject matter beats him to his method and his voice becomes like a shell broken open – shattered into its own sacred fragments, thus revealing its author.

Schoenberg beat Adorno to the topic of Moses, and thus Adorno was forced to refrain from addressing at length the biblical character who best embodied Adorno's own modern condition.[12] As I have said elsewhere, Moses is an exemplar of persecuted modernity:

> *Exodus* reads like a parable of Schoenbergian modernity ...
> Moses, faced with the general intransigence of the Israelites, that
> "stiff-necked people" (Acts 7:51) given to alternating excesses of
> lethargy and running amok, like Schoenberg's Viennese neigh-
> bors; Moses in the Sinai, a prototype of Schoenberg's twentieth-
> century wasteland; Moses the Schoenbergian contradiction –
> part shepherd, shy and retiring, part outspoken, short-tempered,
> tablet-smashing prophet to his people. What is one to do, hav-
> ing been chosen reluctant leader to a most fractious people? ...
> Moses's condition, like Schoenberg's, is the modern condition –
> reluctant, misunderstood, surrounded by hostility, given to faith
> laced heavily with suspicion. That the figure of Moses does not
> people Adorno's landscape is explained only because Schoenberg,
> in *Moses und Aron*, took up the Moses subject first and in a way
> that Adorno could never have equalled.[13]

There I noted that Schoenberg himself was Moses-like, straddling a modernist precipice.[14] "On the solipsistic, visionary side of Adorno's precipice lies Schoenberg's infallible self-assurance in inspiration, plagued, however, by a suspicion of the adequacy of one's craft, of the means of conveying the inspiration ... On the collective, work-aday-*Kapellmeister* side of Adorno's precipice lies the banal converse, the infallible craftsman suspicious of unruly and ungovern-able inspiration ... Prophet and *Kapellmeister* – the two positions are antagonistic, constantly in conflict in a sense strongly remin-

iscent of the Old Testament."[15] But I failed to see to what extent
Adorno himself was like Moses. Adorno's "people," the bourgeois
who populate his critiques, are equally intransigent, hence the stri-
dent tone of his critiques. By way of negation, Adorno smashes the
tablets handed down to him from Hegel. His wasteland is post-Wei-
mar Central Europe and his Sinai the exile in the Nazi years. He
is retiring – driven into modesty by the excesses of tyranny – but
equally vain, outspoken, and short-tempered. He is a walking contradiction transplanted directly from the Old Testament.

And moreover, I did not see to what extent Adorno himself was
like Schoenberg. Schoenberg's prophetic status made him aloof, but
Adorno's critical status made him aloof, too. For both Schoenberg
and Adorno, the critical self could easily become ideological at the
hands of both detractors and adherents. The case is clearer in the
instance of Schoenberg: he stands aloof, watching his very sense of
self becoming ideological at the hands of his tireless detractors: "In
the army, a superior officer once said to me: 'So you are this notori-
ous Schoenberg, then.' 'Beg to report, sir, yes,' I replied. 'Nobody
wanted to be, someone had to be, so I let it be me.'"[16] He watches
his craft run amok at the hands of his adherents: "Although I had
warned my friends and pupils to consider [the twelve-tone method]
as a change in compositional regards, and although I gave them the
advice to consider it only as a means to fortify the logic, they started
counting the tones and finding out the methods with which I used
the rows."[17]

Adorno had no disciples of the kind Schoenberg cultivated. But
as Adorno's critical project waxed, it too ran the risks of tyranny
and solipsism that Adorno saw in Schoenberg's modernist project.
The negative dialectic and its prose style might have veered dangerously in its own right toward a method like Schoenberg's twelve-
tone technique.

Much as we can see Moses as Schoenberg's autobiographical
Geist in the opera, so too we can see Schoenberg as Adorno's *Geist*
in "Sacred Fragment." Adorno did not set his sights low. The opera
is surely Schoenberg's greatest work. Its subject – Exodus – one
might argue is the greatest biblical subject matter short of Genesis.
It recounts not only the delivery of a people, but also the delivery of
knowledge, a special knowledge, a bitter self-knowledge, by a most
reluctant prophet. What could be on the one hand more sacred and
on the other a more accurate secular portrait of Adorno?

A sacred musical work necessitates a negative action, the removal of subjectivity. By the term *subjective*, Adorno means the weak traces of individuality, which are external to and thus "inappropriate for a sacred work."[18] The following passage merits repeated study: sacred music negates the sphere – the awareness – of the subjective: "How is cultic music possible without a cult? Its method is one of determinate negation: negation of the subjective aspect ...The purity of the procedure aims to eliminate whatever the individual has added to it externally. As the action of a cult obeys a law in accordance with the idea of something revealing itself in a genuine way (and not merely postulated), which completes itself above and beyond the awareness of those who take part in it, so shall the musical construct ... transcend the sphere of the subject."[19] Accordingly a sacred work cannot be made by a subjectivity, not through will, yearning, or even need: "Cultic music cannot simply be willed ... Yearning, need itself, does not suffice: a secular world scarcely tolerates sacred art."[20]

A sacred work such as *Moses und Aron* can be created, however, through the most intense rigour in its composition, a rigour that aims to give the work a totality.[21] Each total work – integrated, self-contained, and thus independent – is like an absolute and consequently has a "theological dimension [*theologische Moment*]."[22] "The demand for an immanent consistency in each work itself (beyond anything [achieved] to that point in time [or] that was sought before), the ideal of integral composition, was that of music as a totality. Self-contained and free-floating, in shape it tended toward the Absolute, like the philosophical systems of time past ... Every music concerned with totality, as a simile of the Absolute, has its theological aspect ... even if it is unaware of this, and even if it, through presenting itself as a creation, becomes anti-theological."[23] In its intense totality, Schoenberg's opera comes to resemble the Absolute, even though this is theologically impossible and even anti-theological. Adorno asserts this as follows: "Its absolute determination resembles the appearance of the Absolute, whether it will or will not be so, even when (as with Schoenberg's theological reflections but contrary to the great philosophical tradition) it denies that this essence can become apparent."[24] The appearance of Absolute is attained, then, as a kind of remainder: that which should not be attainable but is by dint of the hardest work. It is not intention that produces Absolutes but work – work exceeds intentions, as bravery exceeds courage. Unwittingly, the composer produces an image of the Absolute – "an image of the image-less [*Bild des Bilderlosen*]"[25] – and in doing so he negates any subjective intention on his part, succeeding only through dint of labour.

The essay "Sacred Fragment" is divided almost exactly in two. Devoted to an analysis of Schoenberg's opera and peppered with Adorno's witticisms, the voice in the latter half is that of Adorno's customary critiques. The voice of the first half, however, is markedly different for the reasons noted above. The style of the self – Adorno, the paratactic critic – is negated by its subject.

In order to glimpse this, I follow four sacred topoi that interlace through the first half of Adorno's text: the spectre of the Absolute; the act of "Naming," of describing that Absolute; the sacred musical work as the material form of an insoluble contradiction (the attempt to name the Absolute in a musical work); and the possibility of a self-knowledge that acknowledges the Absolute.

The central subject invoked in the essay is the biblical Absolute, the God of the Old Testament, a negative deity – noumenal, elusive, reclusive, and reluctant: "The Absolute ... eludes finite beings."[26] A dialectic gulf separates Absolute from concrete artwork: the Absolute is necessarily transcendent, bound to the eternal words of the sacred text, while the art work is aesthetic and thus free of external constraint: "The trans-subjective, transcendent obligation that binds itself to the Torah and the free aesthetic determination of the work stare at each other as if across a gulf."[27] For Adorno, however, certain musical genres can bridge this gulf; sacred (and even secular) musical works close the distance between the transcendent and the aesthetic. Even individual works of music can bridge this gulf by virtue of their subject matter – a sacred text or subject that permits transcendence. And other works of music, sacred or secular in content, bridge this gulf by becoming a totality in imitation of the totality of the Absolute. In imitation they take on a theological aspect: "Every music concerned with totality, as a simile of the Absolute, has its theological aspect."[28]

Works such as *Moses und Aron* and Mahler's Ninth Symphony take on absolute status without the contrivance of their composer. Like courage exceeding bravery, the sacred creative capacity transcends conscious creation.[29] Moved perhaps by some absolute force, the work must present its own self as sacred. Like a work of sacred music, these secular works transcend the subjective awareness of their participants by means of a cult ritual the outcome of which is no one person's responsibility, certainly not their composer's (think Schoenberg the naive).

I now turn to Adorno's prose style. The sentence following is representative: "As the action of a cult obeys a law in accordance with the idea of something revealing itself in a genuine way (and not merely postulated), which completes itself above and beyond the awareness of those who take part in it, so shall the musical construct ... transcend the sphere of the subject."[30] Despite its length, the basic sentence structure is remarkably simple, the whole presented as a simple comparison: as religious celebration acknowledges a revelation that points beyond awareness, so too shall music – certainly religious music – point beyond awareness (presumably to that which is negated by awareness, although this is not stated). Gone is the head-cracking syntax, the structure that seems to role along in fragments. Gone are the witticisms, the fraught juxtapositions; the sentence is straightforward, encompassing nothing more than it suggests. Gone and not necessarily missed. But the absence of the customary acidic voice is most striking: the relation of author to audience is that of equals. There is no invocation to think twice, no teasing; nothing usurps the audience as a collaborator in an exchange perpetrated behind the backs of the bourgeoisie. In truth, it is hard to distinguish this, and the whole first half of the essay, as Adorno's work. As suggested above, it is as if his work had been accomplished in a negated fashion already by the text and the operatic torso, and he was constrained to do something stylistically different. Speak directly, for a change.

As if to demonstrate this fact, Adorno adopts a reflexive syntax. A truly sacred work transcends its creators, and in doing so it presents itself [in reflexive verbs such as *behaupten von sich*], sets itself up [*sich aufwerfen*], not as a mere creation [*Schopfung*] but instead as a something obligating or binding [*verpflichtung*] that would transcend personal emotions such as yearning and their merely subjective expression.

To reiterate, sacred music works by negation: "Its procedure is one of determinate negation: negation of the subjective aspect."[31] It reveals itself in the gap between the Absolute and "the mental capacity" of those who take part in the production of the art work. The difference between the sacred Absolute and human comprehension is thus made concrete – revealed negatively – in sacred music. Thereby, everything Adorno normally sets out to do has been done for him.

"Naming" is the act of designating that which is otherwise unnameable.[32] Adorno establishes its historic and theological context as the "Jewish prohibition of making images"[*Das Bildverbot*]. Here again the prose is transparent: filled with juxtapositions, none of these mediate through negation: "Jewish religion allows no word that would alleviate the despair of all that is mortal. It associates hope only with the prohibition against calling on what is false as God, against invoking the finite as the infinite, lies as truth. The guarantee of salvation lies in the rejection of any belief that would replace it: it is knowledge obtained in the denunciation of illusion."[33] Irreconcilable states are juxtaposed here. Take blasphemy, for example. To Name is to blaspheme, since no mere name can do justice to the Absolute. But Name we must, for to remain silent is a sin of omission: "To be the mouth of the Absolute is for mortals blasphemy ... The Absolute eludes finite beings. Where they would name him, because they must, they betray him. [Should] they keep silent about this, however, they weaken themselves by their own impotence and sin against the other commandment, no less binding upon them, to name."[34] Naming, then, is an act of negative dialectics: Naming the Absolute, we fall short of its realization, and in falling short we confirm as a negative remainder the sacred distance between the Absolute and humankind. Naming is expressed in the form of a contradiction: one must neither Name nor refrain from Naming, neither break the code of silence nor remain silent.[35]

Moses und Aron is an act of Naming.[36] It aims to describe a sacred subject but, never completed, it falls short of its goal,[37] and in doing so (according to Ringer cited above) it succeeds perfectly in describing that which is indescribable – as Nameless: "Thus *Moses und Aron* is truly a fragment, and it would hardly be extravagant, were one to explain its incomplete state, to assert why it could not be completed."[38]

So too, Adorno's critical work is a form of Naming. His life's work is an attempt to Name the real and proper state of things – truths – as viewed through the lens of the negative dialectic. Knowing full well the impossibility of doing so, and yet constrained by the need to Name, Adorno is the acme of the reluctant intelligence that both sacred and profoundly critical subjects demand.

Having seen contradiction at work elsewhere in Adorno's critiques, we are well accustomed to its expression in compact parables and fables by now.[39] But the insoluble contradictions of the Absolute touched on in "Sacred Fragment" are of a higher order and are cast upon the waters by a much greater author. In both their size and topic, they are not merely reflections on the dialectics of bourgeois existence. They are Absolutes, Absolutely "insoluble" and "impossible." Consider the following two quotations: "The insoluble contradiction which Schoenberg has taken as his objective and which is drawn from the entire tradition of tragedy is equally that of the actual work."[40] And "The idea of tragic, the insoluble conflict between finite and infinite that Schoenberg took up as his subject ... The impossibility is historical, that of sacred art today, apparently that of the binding, all-inclusive work that Schoenberg aspired to."[41] Elsewhere in Adorno's prose, the contradictions are rhetorical – Kernsprüche in form and intent – aimed at dislocating the customary thought process. But the contradictions isolated in "Sacred Fragment" are profound and solemn, aimed not merely at dislocation but at revelation. Adorno's customary enterprise is to reveal familiar things around us as if seeing them in a new light. The aim of "Sacred Fragment" is to reveal that things are beyond sight.

Self-knowledge is described at the onset of "Sacred Fragment" by reference to the line of verse from the first of the choral Four Pieces, op. 27 quoted above. Adorno's full passage is as follows. Although in its conundrum the lyric quoted is equivalent in style to Adorno's customary voice, the continuation is uncomplicated: "'Brave men are those who accomplish deeds which their courage does not encompass.' The beginning of Schoenberg's choral pieces op. 27 – the title of which brings back to mind that everything is in fragments, like the tablets Moses shattered – proclaims not only the basic sense of Schoenberg's life but also one of the basic experiences that give his large incomplete Biblical opera a soul."[42] A basic knowledge of one's life is not merely an awareness of who one is – one's preferences and tastes, the facts of one's history, one's potential. It is more the knowledge of one's limitations and a negative self-knowledge of things that surpass one's limits (like being brave beyond the limits of one's courage).

Moses's self-knowledge is Adorno's: the knowledge that all understanding is given in pieces and thus as broken, the modesty of extreme asceticism as portrayed in *Minima Moralia*, of a slim hope for survival tied to an Exodus by exile to America. America becomes in turn a paradise to which Adorno was denied – not physically, but critically. Having led his people through the wasteland of European Late Capitalism, Adorno could not enter peacefully into American capitalism, no matter what its blandishments. Adorno was, in a figurative sense, condemned to wander the desert by his critical awareness.

Schoenberg poured his very being into *Moses und Aron*, and in doing so, Adorno says, he attained the "threshold of self-knowledge." Adorno speaks of Schoenberg on the verge of understanding that an aesthetic impossibility can become possible through metaphysical content: "[As] Schoenberg clearly felt himself to be like a courageous man, and thus as he invested much of himself in Moses, so he advanced to the threshold of self-knowledge about his undertaking – the impossibility of the aesthetic whole, but that it becomes [possible] through its absolute metaphysical content."[43] Self-knowledge, in this sense, is not merely a knowledge of the features of the self but knowledge of the possibilities lying beyond, a knowledge of deeds to be accomplished that, dauntingly, surpass one's courage. In Schoenberg, this self-knowledge produced a kind of heightened awareness or subjectivity – a "powerful, dominant self": "That which would overcome every form of subjectivity must draw forth a dominating, strong 'I' amidst all the subject weaknesses."[44]

Self-knowledge is the basic sense of a life as this goes beyond the normal sense of self. It is produced by a powerful self-examination, extracted from weak subjectivity. It is produced negatively, drawn from the fragmentary and contradictory. And all this is implicit in *Moses und Aron*, with nothing left for Adorno to do.

The four interlaced sacred topoi – the spectre of the Absolute, the act of "Naming," the sacred musical work as insoluble contradiction (the attempt to name the Absolute), and the possibility of a self-knowledge – apply, then, to Schoenberg's opera as a sacred work. But all four apply in comparable ways to Adorno's customary critical prose style. If they are absent from the first part of "Sacred Fragment," they will reappear and, in this sense, they can be reviewed here before considering once more their absence.

Adorno's prose in and of itself is absolute. Driven by a dialectic necessity, Adorno's thoughts do not come of their own volition. Late

Capitalism produces – *deus ex machina* – the conditions and the concrete instances, the reified material, the subject matter of criticism. Adorno only reflects on what is delivered into his critical hands as if by the higher force of the capitalist, his "Supreme Commander."

His prose Names. Adorno's prose does not work directly, in standard prose style, to describe its object. For Adorno, critical objects cannot be named directly – by "identity thinking." Instead, he works by means of contradiction – through negative dialectics – to Name that which otherwise could not be. This act of Naming does not refer back to its author, since negative dialectics and its style, as noted above, customarily erase the authorial voice and its intent.

And finally, his prose leads to an absolute form of self-knowledge. Adorno's prose is set forth as a contradictory set of fragments incapable of producing an aesthetic whole. In this fragmentary state, the actual state of his prose appears far above any intention or program. The constellation of knowledge it produces is thus accidental, above its author's direct intention, and thus immanently an absolute form of self-knowledge.

In these four senses, then, Adorno's customary prose is not unlike Schoenberg's opera. Both verge on the absolute and in doing so they approximate the sacred. Staring at Schoenberg's score, Adorno must have felt as if he were staring in a mirror.

Adorno dressed in Schoenberg's clothing stares out at us from the typescript of "Sacred Fragment." Equating himself with Schoenberg is an activity Adorno readily sought to avoid not the least by discerning naïveté in the composer, as discussed in an earlier chapter. The equation, however, would have demanded confrontation sooner or later, and thus "Sacred Fragment." In opera and in essay, both composer and critic occupy a position entirely in keeping with Adorno's modern human, pinned uncomfortably to the wall by the need to Name.

The only escape from the equation Adorno-equals-Schoenberg was to ratchet the authorial voice elsewhere so tightly that it assumed a veneer behind which Adorno-the-man could hide and in doing so preclude comparison with Schoenberg.[45] Elsewhere in Adorno's work this self-erasure is accomplished by a litany of acidic *Kernsprüche* built of counterpointed contradictions. But one cannot outdo the supreme Absolutes of the sacred, no matter how tightly wound one's voice or how witty one's contradictions. In the first half of "Sacred Fragment" Adorno doesn't try to hide behind voice or method. Instead he writes about Schoenberg's sacred opera and in doing so reveals himself without self-erasure, opening himself thus to comparison and self-revelation.

Given its nature as self-reflexive, "Sacred Fragment" is one of the most important works Adorno wrote on music. It guides us to Adorno, although indirectly, as if the man were himself immanent in the prose – the remainder left over when we subtract his over-wrought persona from its object. For Adorno to write critically about himself would have been solipsism. But to deflect autobiography onto the criticism of an opera such as *Moses und Aron* and its composer is a kind of allegory, one that just might grant self-knowledge an objectivity.

Conclusion

I set forth in the introductory chapters a critical method based on negative dialectics after Adorno, a method applied in the remainder of this book. The central core of this method is a musical subjectivity given objective form in the shape of an unexpected remainder – a discrepancy produced when bringing together two apparently congruent ideas. I hold this objective result to be the equivalent of the results produced by positivist music criticism, not least because both are forms of musical labour.

I began the introduction by rehearsing several meanings of a term taken from my title – *after*, as in *after Adorno*. I shall conclude by rehearsing several meanings of the infinitive *to follow*, bearing in mind Adorno and praxis, and Stanley Aronowitz's definition of the latter – the "Greek term for a reflective political practice."[1] I have sought here to follow Adorno, *follow* in the sense of an action undertaken regularly by a follower – a practice or praxis, in other words – even if *to follow* means simply *to understand*.

The two terms *after* and *follow* overlap. In particular, one of the several meanings of *after* rehearsed above connotes *to follow* in a strictly temporal sense – to come after, to live and produce at a time after Adorno's death. But this is a passive sense of the term *follow*, and surely passivity is not what we mean by *praxis*; rather, the passive sense is instead the very essence of the accusation sometimes levelled against Adorno that he is all theory and no praxis, lazing on the balcony of the Grand Hotel Abyss. In this sense, unfortunately, some criticism conceived after Adorno has been dismissed: it is passé, without potential for praxis, and thus fruitless. The subjectivities implied in such a dismissal are too voluminous to catalogue and then refute in the space of a conclusion.

Pursuing *to follow* as it implies mimesis is much more fruitful
– one might follow Adorno by mimicking – mimesis being central
to his thought. Let me stress, however, that these essays are funda-
mentally of my own contrivance. I might try to essay like Adorno,
especially in the small essays written "along the lines of" the *Minima
Moralia*, but I am avowedly incapable of adopting his style, following its virtuosic twists and turns, let alone its technique. If my limitations in the field of late-nineteenth and early-twentieth-century
Central European philosophy are not patent yet to the reader, they
would soon become so were I to attempt to mime Adorno's critical
technique. Adorno's ability – like that of a good composer – grows
out of a knowledge of its time and its time's own knowledge (ultimately philosophical) of its constraints. A century later, it would be
futile to try to emulate these, were I fully capable of following the
philosophical space implicit in Adorno's thought. Imitation on my
part is faint indeed, restricted perhaps to brevity and the occasional
arcane usage, and moderated I hope by a particularly North American sense of humour.

I have, however, aimed to follow Adorno in the sense of *to cleave*
or *to adhere*. I firmly believe in Adorno as a thinker about music
and thus I am a follower of the man in the sense of his amateur and
advocate. It is probably better to modify this, however, to conceive
of *follow* in the sense of *to follow along with* Adorno for a while.
Now we can begin to speak of praxis, that is to say the practice of
bending or inclining the mind toward Adorno and then with Adorno's aid toward a musical subject matter.

The strongest sense of praxis, however, is that of an effect produced as a logical consequence – given certain established truths, "it
follows that." From a basis of Adorno's work, I am led to conceive
of music in a different way. This I take to be Adorno's praxis, to lead
us so as to conceive of music in unanticipated ways and doing so in
a demonstrably logical way, despite circuitous prose.

In this peaceable era (and bearing in mind the intellectually radical era of my youth), is this sense of praxis comparable to a stone
thrown through a window or a police car set on fire, to revolution, a dictatorship overthrown, or corruption revealed? Is my work
an activist's political praxis? No. No such violent object steers the
course of this book. For me, music's purposefulness without purpose
will not lend it the kind of reason that produces or even condones
political revolution, violent or otherwise. Such matters are best left

out of the hands of musicians and their distracted audiences, and especially out of the hands of music critics.

Enabling us to conceive of music in unanticipated ways is political, however, a form of political praxis. On account of a sense of purpose robbed of itself – purpose without purpose – music is a congenial guide to the antinomies. As much as the industry of spin would seek to smooth over the inscribed contradictions of our existence, by our unquestioning adulation of music we reinscribe those selfsame contradictions. Music criticism after Adorno merely addresses that fact, hoping to make clear its politics.

This is the political praxis I derive from Adorno as his follower and with which I close this book. In our commodity era, music is our congenial friend, our servant ready and willing to do our bidding, principally to sooth and distract. Such needs for distraction, however, are nowhere a necessity of our existence. They are luxuries all too capable of commodification and thereby distortion. Although it appears to us that we must have music, we are quite capable of doing without. And yet we will have music. Thus our servant muse has cemented within us a false need and thereby transformed us into its false master. Let me conclude with the following, cast in terms of praxis after Adorno: while liking, indeed loving this servant muse, we ought never to trust music for a moment.

Orpheus in the Underworld

I had to work my way across the Styx. After Orpheus, too many guitarists had forced their way across Charon's stream with God-knows-what two-chord strumming and bleating. When Charon spied my accordion, his face grew long: he knew exactly my business, what I was about to effect. His eyes narrowed, then a little smile of derision grew across his lips. But he fought, oh how he fought, through "Cielito Lindo," "Somewhere My Love," "Hotel California," "The Wiffenpoof Song," and finally "Norwegian Wood," the latter with the drone in the left hand. Eventually – finally – he nodded, rolled up in his greatcoat (for it was damp and cold down there), and passed out in the bow. It took me twenty minutes to cross the river.

When I found the building, the elderly man sitting just inside the door strained to hear me, but in fact he was quite deaf, so I had to write on the edge of his newspaper, "Beethoven." Following him down the corridor, I caught a whiff of cooking. The building was like a suites hotel – broad corridors, heavy-grade carpeting. We found him in his rooms off an alcove in which a dieffenbachia withered against a window.

Half out of deference, mostly out of fear of losing him – my Euridice – I could not look him in the face but stared at the carpet or the walls. He was much taken by the accordion and insisted on a demonstration, after which he put the thing on himself. The right hand he found easy, of course, but the buttons of the left hand completely eluded him.

Frankly, it didn't take much to persuade him to return. A little flattery, sweeping gestures with the hands, leaflets from the Beethoven *Haus* in Bonn. He was aware that over time there had been innovations and these would take some acclimatization. Women on the street in pants – he couldn't quite countenance that idea.

Gazing over his head out the window, I proposed that he accompany me that very hour. I am certain that he sat there looking at me. Although there was a mirror in the room in which I could have verified the fact, I did not dare look in it for fear of meeting his eyes. A minute went by. Then there were conditions, really quite absurd given his stature, his worldly stature; he must have an annual salary in perpetuity, total artistic control over all his music, etc. Apparently he understood little or nothing of the renown his music, indeed his very being, had attained in the years since his death. It seemed absurd, comic: Beethoven, worried about his existence in a world that would hang upon his every breath.

The departure was in fact abrupt; nothing packed (but then one carries little on the journey across the Styx). He rose and spoke briefly to someone in an adjacent room. Taking his coat and hat, he accompanied me into the street. At the water's edge, it was drizzling and grey. "I don't have to stay in Bonn, then," he asked. "No Maestro, of course not, just visit now and then."

For the return trip, I had a tiny transistor radio, producing (with a horrid tinny sound) a gospel hour from a city in the southwest. Charon was fascinated. We settled ourselves in the hold. "Are you certain that *all* my works are still being performed?" "Why yes, Maestro, of course. I am quite certain no work of yours is so diminutive that it hasn't been catalogued. Scholars pour over your work; it is performed all over the world. It commands both the highest

respect and considerable material reward, all of which you will par-
take in." "All my work?" "Why yes, not a jot doesn't elicit at least
some interest." He grew silent for a moment.

"But you know there are some works of mine that needn't be
done often. Perhaps some might be retired for a while. I do have reservations about the *Tripelkonzert*. Really the thing should have been
pulled, that and some *Lieder*. Could I do this? Have them taken out,
for a while?" I was completely taken aback. "Why yes, of course.
Every such thing as you wish will be accorded its due merit in good
time. The musical world, really, is at your beck and call." Charon, at
the helm, was looking at me, arms folded across his chest, the tiller
under his armpit. I could feel Beethoven's eyes on me too.

"Do I really have the capacity to do such a thing? In this new
musical world you speak of?"

"Why yes, of course, Maestro." Again, I was taken aback. "But
you must understand that such a gift as yours has produced its
own momentum. In all honesty, it will take some time to realize
such a wish – the extraction of the Triple Concerto, or let us say its
modification."

"I *will* have complete and utter artistic control. I am Beethoven,
after all."

"Yes, master, yes. Please, be still. Look, the shore."

"This is a contract between us – me and you, he who brings me
back. We have a contract, an oath."

"Yes, of course. Here is my hand. And my word: complete and
utter control."

"I don't believe you."

"Maestro!"

"I don't believe that in your world you can produce such a thing
as complete artistic control. In your world it seems (and we are not
so devoid of news across the Styx) that an artist has little or no control there, even less than in my day."

"But Maestro! Be still, please."

"Look me in the eye, will you! I will not contract with a man who
cannot look me in the eye! I will not!"

From shore I watched him depart. He is a small man, slightly off
his mark visually, a little run down. His hat and coat were quite
wet by that time, and a lock of hair had pasted itself to a collar. He
looked at me, then down at the hull, and to the distant shore, and
then sat down and nodded to Charon.

of:

As the boat slipped away, he turned to me. The look in his eyes was of disbelief. His hands worked themselves as he leaned over his knees and wept.

Notes

1 Bearing in mind Henry Pickford, *Critical Models*, 260. "Models thus are
the instruments for producing 'critical social consciousness.'" And these
models are not necessarily explanatory but instead mimetic in function.
See Subotnik, "Adorno's 'French' Model," in *Developing Variations*, 212–
13: "Adorno's critical pieces often seem to work less well as explanations
of particular effects than as verbal equivalents, homologues, or even models of those effects"; but see ibid., 213: "He tries ... to prevent having his
ideas tied up into a neat bundle." See as well Pickford, preface to Adorno,
Critical Models. Models are, in this sense, not strictly methodological. See
the caveats on method expressed in the editor's introduction to Adorno,
Lectures on Negative Dialectics, xii: "Adorno repeatedly emphasized that
his material works could not be subsumed under a fixed 'method,' that
they could not be separated from their objects, and that their contents
could not simply be transferred to other topics."

The principal characteristic of Adorno's models, as I understand them
here, is immanence. See Adorno, *Lectures in Negative Dialectics*, 8–9:
"The essence of this model of an antagonistic society is that it is not a
society *with* contradictions or *despite* its contradictions, but *by virtue of*
its contradictions," this in the sense of *immanent*.

2 And in this sense the endnotes will attempt to convey something of the
context of any given thought, thus leaving the body of the text to the task
of essaying.

3 I shall keep in mind Adorno's own conception of the term as set forth in
"The Essay as Form," in Adorno, *Notes to Literature* 1: 3–23.

4 Mendel, "Evidence and Explanation."

5 See Paddison, *Adorno's Aesthetics*, 57.

6 Andrew Bowie's essay in the *Cambridge Companion*, which I have drawn on in later chapters, gives a sense of the controversy.

7 I am bearing in mind readings of *dialectic* as set forth by Eike Gebhardt in Arato and Gebhardt, *The Essential Frankfurt*, 396–404.

8 Thus it builds on thoughts expressed in my review of Spitzer in *Music Theory Spectrum*.

CHAPTER ONE

1 Melancholy in the sense of the "message in a bottle," the lonely despair of the emigrant, as noted in Claussen, *One Last Genius*, 161, 236. And see Adorno, *Minima Moralia*, 209: "Even at that time the hope of leaving behind messages in bottles on the flood of barbarism bursting on Europe was an amiable illusion." Compare Geuss, *Outside Ethics*, 117.

2 There are many definitions of this term, some of which will be addressed in chapter 2; in this regard, the following works are particularly note-worthy: Buck-Morss, *Origin of Negative Dialectics*, see chaps 3, 4, and 12; Rose, *Melancholy Science*, chaps 3 and 4; Jameson, *Marxism and Form*, 55–9; Paddison, *Adorno's Aesthetics*, 103–5, 112; Hullot-Kentor, *Things Beyond Resemblance*, 225, 229–30.

3 But compare Jennifer Rycenga, "Queerly Amiss," in Gibson and Rubin, *Adorno: A Critical Reader*, and Zuidervaart, *Social Philosophy*, 133–7. See as well three essays by Hull, Mullin, and Schlipphacke, collected as "The Feminist Response," in Delanty, *Adorno*, 4: 343–409.

4 The gay interpretation is in fact already embedded – immanent – in the straight. See Adorno, *Lectures on Negative Dialectics*, 7: "The contradic-tion in things themselves, contradiction *in* the concept, not contradiction *between* concepts."

5 See O'Connor, *Adorno's Negative Dialectic*, a most comprehensive treat-ment of negation and dialectics. See the qualification of Adorno's Kant: "From Adorno's perspective, the valuable side of Kant's philosophy provides the ingredients which are necessary for overcoming subjective idealism; that is, it contains arguments that support a form of critical materialism" (20). The syntheses I shall speak of do not necessarily make explicit such a critical materialism and thus cannot be qualified as "dia-lectic" (which is not to suggest they are "merely" idealist, but simply not fully developed). It might be, however, that such a synthesis fulfills one of the dialectical criteria O'Connor derives for Adorno from Hegel: "What is important in Hegel's idea of dialectic, in Adorno's view, is that it names

that critical moment of thought that deepens our experience of the object"
(34).

6 "The True is the whole. But the whole is nothing other than the essence
consummating itself through its development. Of the Absolute it must be
said that it is essentially a *result*, that only in the *end* is it what it truly
is; and that precisely in this consists its nature, viz. to be actual, subject,
the spontaneous becoming of itself." Hegel, *Phenomenology of Spirit*, 11.
And see O'Connor, *Adorno's Negative Dialectic*, 33, speaking of Hegel:
"Unsatisfactory judgements are overcome until finally concept and object
agree."

7 I am indebted to an anonymous reader of this manuscript who encapsulated this proposition in terms even more succinct than I give now.

8 Adorno, *Negative Dialectics*, 5.

9 Ibid., 14.

10 Buck-Morss, *Origins of Negative Dialectic*, 109. Adorno's writings on
Western European classical music were considered irretrievably difficult by North American musicologists in the decades after his death.
See Subotnik, *Developing Variations,* especially chapter 1. The attention
accorded Adorno by classical music scholars is sometimes as unsympa-
thetic as that elicited from popular music scholars. See Deathridge, review
of *In Search of Wagner*, 83, and review of *Sound Figures*, 305.

11 See Bernstein *Adorno*, 345, the passage that begins, "Dialectic operates
through contradiction."

12 Adorno, "On the Fetish Character in Music," in *Essays*, 295.

13 Gracyk, "Adorno, Jazz and the Aesthetics of Popular Music," 531; Schönherr, "Adorno and Jazz," 95–6.

14 Some of Adorno's strongest advocates occasionally miss this element
too. See Jay, *Adorno*, 120. See, however, Buhler, "Frankfurt," and Powell,
"Theory of Radio," who take this fact to heart. But see Born, "Against
Negation," on the limitations to Adorno's critique.

15 A succinct appraisal of Adorno's jazz critics is found in Harding, *Writing
of the Ruins*, 103 and 112. The chapter containing these appraisals is a
comprehensive assessment of Adorno's jazz criticism. See as well Cooper,
"Adorno with the Grain," 102–4: Adorno's "own crystallized categories
determine his experience of music in advance."

16 Adorno, "Perennial Fashion – Jazz," in *Prisms*, 129.

17 Adorno drew a distinction in formal terms between classical music (certainly with Beethoven symphonies as a locus) and jazz and popular music,
but in this book the formalist division is less relevant, if not a distraction.

For a concise summary of the formalist position, see Thomson, *Adorno: A Guide for the Perplexed*, chapter 2, the distinction between standardization and non-standardization in particular. In terms of critique, however, Thomson holds, as I do, that the two are in important terms equals: "Adorno undercuts any attempt to establish an automatic hierarchy amongst the different types of music: neither standardized nor non-standardized music has a privileged relationship to critique"(50).

18 See Hullot-Kentor, "Right Listening," 181, 196, and the notion of "*the* artwork," the primacy of the object, which presumes no distinction between classical and popular. Compare Goehr, "Dissonant Works," 225.

19 Adorno, "Arnold Schoenberg," in *Prisms*, 149.

20 Ibid., 149–50. "Je mehr sie den Hörern schenkt, desto weniger bietet sie ihnen zugleich. Sie verlangt, dass der Hörer ihre innere Bewegung spontan mitkomponiert, und mutet ihm anstelle blosser kontemplation gleichsam Praxis zu." Adorno, "Arnold Schönberg 1874–1951," in *Prismen*, 153.

21 Compare Alan Durant, *Conditions of Music*, 80–2, on dissonance.

22 Compare Max Paddison, *Adorno, Modernism and Mass Culture*, 84: "The progression is always tripartite: (i) the dilemma is uncompromisingly stated (Sentence I); (ii) the tension between the poles ... leads to what could almost be seen as a kind of synthesis, in the best Hegelian manner (although Adorno would regard it more as an 'illumination' of the implications of the initial statement) (Sentence II); (iii) finally comes the reformulation of the initial dilemma, now inverted, and even more uncompromisingly stated than ever (Sentence III). Although revealed, the terms of the contradiction remain unreconciled."

23 A notion of *work* transmuted as alienated *guilt* – "individuals ... made to assume guilt" – is suggested in Goehr, "Dissonant Works," 224.

24 We shall return to this discrepancy throughout our text. Compare Bernstein's introduction to Adorno, *Culture Industry*, 8, citing Adorno's *Aesthetic Theory* in a translation from 1984, 139: "Adorno stresses the ersatz character of the pleasure the culture industry offers the consumer. Real pleasure is not even on offer; the promissory note, which is the plot and staging of the work, is in reality all that is on offer, thus making the original promise illusory: 'all it actually confirms is that real point will never be reached, that the diner must be satisfied with the menu.'"

25 Adorno, "Arnold Schoenberg," in *Prisms*, 150–1.

26 See Dahlhaus, *Schoenberg and the New Music*, 16–19, for a succinct appreciation of the complex issue of naïveté.

27 See Schoenberg, *Style and Idea*, 80; and J. Peter Burkholder, "Schoenberg the Reactionary."

28 Schoenberg, *Style and Idea*, 173.

29 As "l'art pour l'art." See Schoenberg, *Style and Idea*, 121–3.

30 Schoenberg, *Style and Idea*, 86.

31 Schönherr, "Adorno and Jazz," 95–6.

32 See McDonald, "Training the Nineties."

33 Adorno, *Negative Dialectics*, 5; *Negative Dialektik*, 16–17.

34 See Adorno, *Lectures on Negative Dialectics*, 7–8, the distinction in quantity between a concept and its subsumed elements.

35 Compare J.M. Bernstein's notion of moral remainder in *Adorno*, 331.

36 Subotnik, "Adorno's 'French' Model," 207.

37 Adorno, *Negative Dialectics*, see 149–51.

38 In *Melancholy Science*, Rose provides an excellent treatment of identity thinking. The notion is linked with a critique of rationality, put succinctly by J.M. Bernstein in the introduction to Adorno, *Culture Industry*, 4: "Subsumptive or instrumental rationality disregards the intrinsic properties of things, those properties that give each thing its sensuous, social and historical particularity, for the sake of the goals and purposes of the subject ... Such a rationality must treat unlike (unequal) things as like (equal), and subsume objects under (the unreflective drives of) subjects."

39 Adorno, *Negative Dialectics*, 5; *Negative Dialektik*, 17.

40 Wiggershaus, *Frankfurt School*, 602, refers to an Other, comparable to my sense of remainder as a thing referred to by negative dialectics: "negative dialectics meant: be mindful of the Other."

41 Compare Bowie's "inverted history of *Geist*," in "Meaning of Music," 271.

42 Adorno, "Subject and Object," in Adorno, *Adorno Reader*, 141.

43 Jarvis, "Adorno, Marx, Materialism," 97, emphasis is this author's.

44 See Adorno, "Subject and Object," in Adorno, *Adorno Reader*, 139.

45 Adorno, *Negative Dialectics*, 5; *Negative Dialektik*, 17. I revise Ashton's translation thus: "Thinking is identifying. Conceptual order supplies contentedly [freely, without reservation] that which thinking would [want to] understand. Its appearance and its truth entwine."

46 Aspects of Adorno's divergence from Hegel are expressed well by Bowie in "Meaning of Music": "In Hegel ... the philosophical system can only claim to be complete by repressing the 'non-identical', the resistance of the real to definitive subsumption under concepts."(269) And "Adorno often seems to think this repression is the same repression as that occasioned by the commodity structure and instrumental reason." Bowie's critique of the latter position is invaluably controversial.

47 The principle that a thing must constitute one of two possibilities: "Either it will rain today or it will not rain today." Either *p* or its negation, *not-p*, must be true, for there can be no middle term between them.

48 Adorno, *Negative Dialectics*, 5; *Negative Dialektik*, 17.

49 A more literal translation devolves into the incomprehensible: "[The total-
ity] is not open to comprehending the [fixed] appearance of the conceptual. [Totality is not like] immanence [which is able] to break through
the appearance of total identity, in its own way [to its own degree]. Since,
however, totality is structured according to logic, whose core represents
the principle of the excluded middle, everything – whatever will not fit in
[to a totality] – all qualitative distinctions acquire the mark of a contradiction. Contradiction is the non-identical [subsumed] under the aspect
of identity. To unified thought, the primacy of the contradiction principle in dialectic [dispenses with] heterogeneity. Where it collides with
its limits, [thought] exceeds itself. Dialectics is the consequent sense of
nonidentity."

50 Adorno, *Negative Dialectics*, 5; Adorno, *Negative Dialektik*, 17. Here
again a more literal translation tempts the strictures of English usage and
grammar but puts emphasis on the effect of a consciousness striving for
unity: any attempt at unity will produce differentiation, dissonance, and
negation of that selfsame unity. "The differentiated appears divergent,
dissonant, negative so long as the consciousness must push forth [*nach-
drangen*] its own formation from unity."

51 See Geuss, *Outside Ethics*. Reworking Hegel, Adorno arrives at a two-
stage process for self-knowledge, positive and negative; the second of the
two involves "a long sequence of increasingly complex and convoluted
negations, refutations of various incorrect (and usually reductive) theories that have been propounded about spirit: spirit is *not* this, *not* that, *not*
some third thing. Overall the procedure will look very much as if it vio-
lates another tacit assumption of traditional procedures of definition, in
that one will seem not so much to be saying what the *definiendum* is, but
merely (at excessive length) what it is *not*. In the realm of spirit, though,
the approach through a negative dialectic is the only one appropriate"
(117).

52 Adorno, *Negative Dialectics*, 145.

53 Ibid., 5.

54 Ibid.

55 Ibid., 6.

56 One of these falsehoods is the immutability of reason, which occupied
Adorno. As Simon Jarvis puts it, reason is susceptible to revision under
dialectics: "Reason cannot avoid being aesthetic, in the minimal sense
that its concepts are all entangled with experience, rather than being rigid
atoms of designation." *Adorno: A Critical Introduction*, 178.

57 Buck-Morss, *Origin of Negative Dialectics*, 58.
58 Ibid., 58–9.
59 Ibid., 63.
60 Adorno, "Arnold Schoenberg," in *Prisms*, 149–50.
61 Adorno, "Die Actualität der Philosophie," translated in Buck-Morss,
   Origin of Negative Dialectics, 77.
62 Buck-Morss, *Origin of Negative Dialectics*, 80.
63 Marx, *Grundrisse*, 450–2.
64 Ibid., 452.
65 Buck-Morss, *Origin of Negative Dialectics*, 99.
66 Ibid., 100.
67 Lukács, *History and Class Consciousness*, 87.
68 Rose, *Melancholy Science*, 47.
69 For Rose, something is not reified if conception represents it adequately:
   "In Adorno's terms, something is non-reified when the concept is identical
   with its object." *Melancholy Science*, 47.
70 Ibid., 46, citing Adorno, *Negative Dialectic*, 146, translation amended by
   Rose.
71 Ibid., 31.
72 As Rose notes, ibid., 40–1, Adorno falls out with Lukács, whose reconciliation of subject and object "relapses into idealism" and thus is insufficient
   to a description of the material circumstances – the fractured state – of
   capitalism.
73 Ibid., 43. The linkage of thought and materialism is aimed at dispelling
   the notion that the reified "nature" of modernism is merely psychological:
   "Adorno's theory of reification was based on commodity fetishism in
   a way which depended ... on Marx's theory of value, especially on the
   distinction between use-value and exchange-value. He was particularly
   concerned that reification should not be conceptualised as a 'fact of consciousness', a subjective or socio-psychological category."
      This truth about commodities extends to cover philosophical thought.
   Jarvis makes it the developing object of Adorno's materialism. In citing
   the following quotation, I equate original labour (doing philosophy, for
   example) with "historical experience." Just as Coltrane's putative mysticism breaks down to reveal musical labour, so too philosophical texts
   break down to reveal their making in terms of materialism: Adorno
   developed "the idea of materialism as a kind of *interpretation*. No analysis
   which simply subordinated philosophical questions to a prior set of dog-
   matically assumed sociological or historical theses could carry philosophical conviction. Instead of being subjected to an external set of standards,

philosophical texts were to be made to speak, as it were, from the inside
out. The key concepts of philosophical texts, even, and indeed especially,
the most apparently abstract concepts, carried historical experience sedi-
mented inside them. The contradictions, fractures, or slips in those texts
could be used to make those texts themselves speak of the suppressed historical experience which had made them possible." Jarvis, "Adorno, Marx,
Materialism," 85–6.

74 Rose, *Melancholy Science*, 45.

75 Ibid., 48. "To say that consciousness of society is completely reified
implies that no critical consciousness or theory is possible. It is to say that
the underlying processes of society are completely hidden and that the
utopian possibilities within it are inconceivable."

76 Ibid.

77 Leppert's commentary in Adorno, *Essays*, 35–6, citing Adorno, "Cultural Criticism and Society," in *Prisms*, 32. Hegel is redeemed by Brian
O'Connor thus: "Adorno does not accept that dialectic has [an] ineluct-
able progressive characteristic. He agrees that dialectic represents a
moment of complication in thought, one that may be informative. But we
cannot conclude, he thinks, that each complication is necessarily productive. To be obliged, as Adorno sees it, to proceed forward – toward
the absolute – is identity thinking: it is motivated by the belief that the
nonidentity of subject and object – the point at which concept and object
do not coincide – can eventually be overcome. However, what is important
in Hegel's idea of dialectic, in Adorno's view, is that it names that critical
moment of thought that deepens our experience of the object." O'Connor,
Adorno's Negative Dialectic, 34.

78 O'Connor, *Adorno's Negative Dialectic*, 34.

79 Ibid. And see Sziborsky, *Rettung*, 24, and chap. 2.

80 Ritsert, *Vermittlung*.

81 This is presumably Hegel's conception of the middle term. See Marcuse,
Reason and Revolution, 38, 49, and 77. And see Adorno, *Negative Dialectics*, 16n.

82 "Between the 'incomprehensibility' of the serious products and the 'inesca-
pability' of easy listening there is in the end for Adorno no 'third thing'
any more. The mediating middle-term [*die vermittelnde Mitte*], the *tertium
conparationis*, is lacking whereby the extremes can be 'reconciled' or the
opposites can be 'neutralized'. 'The situation has polarized in the extremes.'"
Ritsert, *Vermittlung*, 4, cited in Paddison, *Adorno's Aesthetics*, 120.

83 Stephen Bronner, *Of Critical Theory*, 182–3.

84 Ibid., 183.

85 The temporal nature of synthesis and thereby the priority of object is addressed by Adorno in the passage "Mediating the First," in Adorno, *Against Epistemology*, 7–8.

86 O'Connor, *Adorno's Negative Dialectic*, 45–6.

87 See Bernstein, "Negative Dialectic as Fate," in Huhn, *Cambridge Companion*.

88 Ibid., 38.

89 Jameson, *Marxism and Form*, 54.

90 Ibid., 57.

CHAPTER TWO

1 Einarsson and Taylor, *Just for Nice*.

2 Ibid., 9.

3 Wimsatt and Beardsley, "The Affective Fallacy," 22.

4 Consider the term *empathy*, as set forth in a letter from Walter Benjamin to Adorno, in Adorno et al., *Aesthetics and Politics*, 140: "empathy with the commodity."

5 Wimsatt and Beardsley, "The Affective Fallacy," 21.

6 Adler, "Guido Adler's 'The Scope,'" 16. See Dineen, "Adorno, Jitterbug," and "Still Life with Insects."

7 And see recipes for soda-cracker pies in Mickler, *White Trash Cooking*, 106–7.

8 See Riethmüller, "Adorno musicus," on Adorno and musicology.

9 Hullot-Kentor, *Things beyond Resemblance*, 219.

10 Huyssens, *After the Great Divide*, 188.

11 Cusset, *French Theory*, xv.

12 Wellmer, *Persistence*, 71.

13 Born, "Against Negation," 241.

14 See Horkheimer and Adorno, *Dialectic*, 7.

15 Ibid., 7–8.

16 Gebhardt provides one indication of how important a just-for-nice consciousness might be for Adorno: "Mediated consciousness is not bad, unreal consciousness but the only consciousness available. The often indiscriminate rejection by the Left of 'bourgeois subjectivism' frequently fails to distinguish between abstracted, illusory, self-sufficient subjectivity, which is passive toward society, and a subjectivity which is an active form and function of determinate negation. Even a false consciousness may be a true consciousness in this sense and a harbinger of transcendence, a map of new territory." In Arato, *Frankfurt School*, 397.

17 See Adorno, "The Scientific Experiences of a European Scholar in America," *Critical Models*, 215–42; Claussen, *One Last Genius*, 205; Jenemann, *Adorno in America*: Jenemann goes so far as to suggest love: "What makes Adorno so threatening and difficult ... is that his criticisms of America are inseparable from his genuine *love* for it" (188). Nevertheless, the book's introduction is a more measured appraisal of the fascination America held for Adorno and its relationship to American studies: "If anything, Adorno's interest in and knowledge of America, by virtue of his hunger to understand all the intricate inner workings of the mass media, often outstripped those of the native 'experts' with whom he was unfavorably compared" (xviii–xix).

18 See Hanslick, *On the Musically Beautiful*, 58.

19 Ibid., 29.

20 See the category of emotional listener in Adorno, *Introduction to the Sociology of Music*, 8–10.

21 Adorno, *Essays*, 228.

22 Ibid., 297.

23 See Adorno, "Mammoth," in *Minima Moralia*, 115–16.

24 Ibid, various moralia, 102–13.

25 Adorno, "Perennial Fashion – Jazz," in *Prisms*, 128.

26 Ibid., 123.

27 Ibid., 128.

28 Ibid., 121.

29 Ibid., 123.

30 Ibid., 124.

31 Ibid.: "The paradoxical immortality of jazz has its roots in the economy."

32 Ibid.

33 Ibid.

34 Ibid., 130–1.

35 Schoenberg, *Style and Idea*, 51.

36 Adorno, "Perennial Fashion – Jazz," in *Prisms*, 132.

37 Ibid., 122.

38 Ibid., 127–9.

39 But as Bronner and Kellner point out, elitism enabled criticism: "Adorno's uncompromising critique raises the much-debated issue of the cultural elitism which allegedly informed the Institute's perceptions of mass culture. Indeed, there is no doubt that the 'inner circle' was composed of highly cultured European intellectuals and radicals who found life in the United States extremely distasteful. Clearly, they blamed mass culture for making the working classes blind to their own exploitation, and thus for creating

obstacles to radical social change. Despite their biases, however, it was nonetheless the critical theorists who provided the first set of sustained and systematic insights into the important new roles that mass communications and culture were playing in contemporary societies. It was precisely their status as European exiles which enabled them to gain insights into the ideological nature and social functions of mass culture." Bronner and Kellner, *Critical Theory and Society*, 14. And see Andrew Ross, "The New Sentence and the Commodity Form: Recent American Writing," 367–8.

40 Middleton, *Studying Popular Music*. See Griffiths, "The High," for a prospectus of popular music and analysis; on Middleton and Adorno, see p. 407. But compare the extended critique by Bowie, "Adorno, Heidegger, and the Meaning of Music."

41 Middleton, *Studying Popular Music*, 63.

42 Ibid., 45.

43 Thus it is not utopian in the formalist sense that Drew Milne attributes to it. See Milne, "Processual Performance," 352: "The political significance of art, for Adorno, lay in its ability to articulate a relative freedom from the ideology of capitalism, suggesting utopian dimensions and radical alternatives, while also bearing witness to truths of social experience otherwise obscured by the culture industry. Art, so to speak, refreshes the parts of culture that the culture industry does not reach."

44 Bowie, in "Adorno, Heidegger, and the Meaning of Music," levels a similar criticism, albeit with a greater force drawn from a perspective attuned to Heidegger.

45 Middleton, *Studying Popular Music*, 38.

46 Ibid., 39.

47 Ibid.

48 Ibid., 38. Middleton's thought is clearly indebted to Walter Benjamin. See Middleton, chap. 4. But see Adorno et al., *Aesthetics and Politics*, 102–3, on Adorno's critique of Benjamin's work.

49 Compare Zuidervaart, *Social Philosophy*, 137–90.

50 Middleton, *Studying Popular Music*, 38–9, citing Simon Frith, *Sound Effects*, 10. And see Moretti, "The Spell of Indecision," 339: "In the past two decades the dominant attitude toward modernism within Marxist criticism has completely changed ... Benjamin and Adorno associated 'fragmentary' texts with melancholy, pain, defenselessness, and loss of hope. Today, these same texts, along with the whole aesthetic field they evoke, would suggest the far more exhilarating concepts of semantic freedom, detotalization, and productive heterogeneity. In the deliberate obscurity

of modern literature, Benjamin and Adorno saw the sign of an impending threat; now this obscurity is taken rather as a promise of free interpretive play. For them, the key novelist of the modern world was, quite clearly, Franz Kafka; today, just as clearly, he has been replaced by James Joyce, whose work is just as great, but certainly less urgent and uncanny."

51 See Moore, *The Beatles*, 81–2, on the Beatles and Beethoven in terms of classicism.

52 Middleton, *Studying Popular Music*, 39. Citing John Stratton, "Capitalism and Romantic Ideology in the Record Business," *Popular Music* 3 (1983): 143–56.

53 Max Paddison, in "Authenticity and Failure," 199, sets forth two notions of authenticity in musical works, both of which "impinge" upon the idea of musical autonomy. The first concerns the individuality of the art work. The second, which goes straight to the core of this book's understanding, posits that autonomy is constrained by belief and material circumstance: "On the one hand, authenticity concerns the way a work appears to be what it is because it can be no other way, an idea which contains a range of related concepts, including those of self-contained structural consistency and of totality; on the other hand, pitted against this is the idea that the authentic modernist work is characterized by failure in these terms and that the social and historical impinge on the apparently autonomous world of the work of art, fracturing its integrity and making its consistency look suspect and ideological in the face of the horrors of the real world which culminate in Auschwitz."

54 Dineen, "Adorno, Jitterbug," 55–75.

55 Middleton, *Studying Popular Music*, 53.

56 Ibid., 51, cited in Dineen, "Adorno, Jitterbug," 71.

57 Adorno, "Motifs," in *Quasi una Fantasia*, 23.

58 Adorno, *Essays*, 128.

59 Ibid., 293–4.

60 Adorno, *Introduction to the Sociology of Music*, 15.

61 Ibid., 16–17.

62 Adorno, *Essays*, 295.

63 Ibid.

64 Ibid., 416.

65 Ibid., 417.

66 Ibid., 295–6.

67 Ibid., 296.

68 Ibid., 296–7.

69 Ibid., 298.

70 Ibid., 313.
71 Ibid., 293.
72 Kolisch, *Kolisch Papers.*
73 Adorno and Berg, *Correspondence*, 112.
74 Adorno and Benjamin, *Correspondence*, 342.

CHAPTER THREE

1 On mediation in music, see Paddison, *Adorno's Aesthetic*, 108–48, and "Die vermittelte Unmittelbarkeit." And see Ritsert, *Vermittlung*, 14–34, on two senses of *Vermittlung*, one derived from the Marxist notion of productivity or productive power [*Produktivkräfte*], the other as mediation without middle [*ohne Mitte*]. Compare Arato, *The Essential Frankfurt School Reader*, 199–200, where mediation is linked with a much larger consciousness, political in nature. See Arato's definition of *mediation* achieved by comparing Lukács and Adorno: "Mediation, then, in the form of 'transcendent critique,' is the totalization that locates works in a social totality, economically structured but without a future-oriented dynamic. This totality, the *Gesamttotalität*, is therefore false: 'the whole is untrue' ... Mediation, in the form of micrology, in the form of an 'immanent critique' that has not forgotten its interest in a future-oriented transformation of the false whole of society, is therefore the only possible avenue for a conceptual unfolding that involves a dynamic relation of subject-object in Lukács's sense ... Of course, Adorno's bleak picture of the *Gesamttotalität* presupposes one crucial anti-Lukácsian premise: the nonexistence of a social *Gesamtsubjekt* of action ... The Lukácsian project of a mediation or de-fetishization in which revolutionary theory is met half-way by the self-mediation *or* self-de-fetishization of reality in the emergence of class consciousness, collapses in Adorno's work." Citing Adorno's *Philosophy of New Music*, 26.
2 Inclining toward Hegel, if no further than the preliminaries of the *Phenomenology of Spirit*.
3 And this implies a transformation of the first through abstraction. See Adorno, *Essays*, 188: "The most powerful effects of Beethoven's form depend on the recurrence of something, which was once present simply as a theme, that reveals itself as a result and thus acquires a completely transformed sense. Often the meaning of the preceding passage is only fully established by this later recurrence."
4 Compare Zuidervaart, *Adorno's Aesthetic Theory*, 141–2: "Art reception itself must be a dialectical process between spontaneous reactions and

discursive judgments, a process involving both immanence and distance toward the artwork ... Recipients must take distance from their empirical selves and adopt a reflective attitude toward the work of art. Only if the recipient's most intense subjective reaction belongs to a penetrating and comprehensive experience can the possibility of truth be materialized. In this way, says Adorno, adequate aesthetic experience can be a moment of objective artistic truth ... Genuine aesthetic experience mediates discursive and nondiscursive logic in order to let the truth content of a piece emerge." And see Espiña, "Wahrheit als Zugang," 56: "Primat der Negation bedeutet aber Primat der Vermittlung, nicht ihre Aufhebung."

5 See Adorno, *Beethoven*, item 358, pp. 171–3. In one of his less transparent passages, Adorno suggests that attainment involves a two-fold mediation: "What is mediated is art, that through which the artwork becomes something other than its mere factuality, must be mediated a second time by reflection: through the medium of the concept," and see ibid., item 233.

6 Ibid., item 223, p. 98. Adorno, *Beethoven: Philosophie*, item 223: "Zum Es-dur-Trio op. 70: der erste Satz gibt großartige Beispiele von 'Vermittlung'*: Die Motiv[e] kommen erst sukzessiv in den beiden Streichern, dann im Klavier. Dessen mechanischer Charakter ist zur Darstellung des dialektischen Sinnes ausgenutzt. Der objective, gleichsam kleinere Klavierklang präsentiert hier die Themen jeweils als *Resultat*, als gewonnene." *In the margin, Adorno writes: "NB der 'Lauf' und die 'Melodie' des Hauptthemas identisch. Daher der Lauf 'vermittelt' = distantziert." [NB the run and the melody of the principal theme identical. Thus the run "mediates" = distances.]

7 Ibid.

8 See Sziborsky, "Die Dimension," 12; aesthetic *Erfahrung* [experience] as an act of consciousness, not of *Wahrnehmung* [perception].

9 Compare Jameson, *Marxism and Form*, 340: "Thus dialectical thought is in its very structure self-consciousness and may be described as the attempt to think about a given object on one level, and at the same time to observe our own thought processes as we do so ... For Hegel ... the thinker comes to understand the way in which his own determinate thought processes, and indeed the very forms of the problems from which he sets forth, limit the results of his thinking. For the Marxist dialectic ... the self-consciousness aimed at is the awareness of the thinker's position in society and in history itself, and of the limits imposed on this awareness by his class position – in short of the ideological and situational nature of all thought and of the initial invention of the problems themselves."

10 Compare ibid., 85: "From the physical intimidation of the Fascist state to the agonizing repetitions of neurosis, the idea of freedom takes the same temporal form: a sudden perception of an intolerable present which is at the same time, but implicitly and however dimly articulated, the glimpse of another state in the name of which the first is judged."

11 Adorno, *Beethoven*, item 365, p. 175.

12 Schubert as well. But see Burnham, "Landscape as Music," in a collection of essays on Adorno in *19th-Century Music*, where Schubert and repetition are discussed without reference to mediation.

13 Elucidation of this distinction is beyond the scope of this chapter. But see Adorno, *Beethoven*, items 216–23, pp. 89–98, and in particular the discussion of time.

14 Ibid., item 48, p. 21.

15 Weber Nicholsen, *Exact Imagination*, 8, reminds us that lateness is not only a property of style but of capitalism as well: "Adorno formulates the essential feature of late work as the disjunction of subjectivity and objectivity, so that as work becomes late it becomes increasingly inorganic. In this sense, late work characterizes the direction the arts take as modernism advances within the context of 'late capitalism,' a phrase that Adorno too uses." Citing Adorno "Spätkapitalismus oder Industriegesellschaft," *Gesammelte Schriften* 8 (1992): 354–70.

16 See Weber Nicholsen., *Exact Imagination*, 41–3.

17 Adorno, *Beethoven*, item 318, p. 159.

18 See Kerman, *The Beethoven Quartets*, chap. 9.

19 See Spitzer, *Music as Philosophy*, 7–8, on Stephen Rumph's discussion of counterpoint in late Beethoven, and 61, on strict Baroque idioms as antithetical.

20 Adorno, *Beethoven*, item 319, p. 159.

21 See Rosen, *The Classical Style*, 436–7.

22 Adorno, *Beethoven*, item 97, p. 39.

23 Spitzer, *Music as Philosophy*, 25, conceives of Beethoven's late style as an extension of Classical principles, "albeit raised now to a higher power. The plurality of Classical rules ... is heightened by Beethoven, making it harder to hear how they might be accommodated by any overarching principle or sensibility. In other words, stylistic heterogeneity is relegated from a surface phenomenon to a governing principle. Regarding the individual manner of the style ... there is a corresponding sense that Beethoven loses himself in this wealth of material, rather than blending the conventions into a unified voice. Instead of speaking *through* these conventions,

Beethoven lets them stand freely and discovers expression *within* them.
Finally, while Beethoven reduces musical material to its archetypal shapes
and contours ... he does so in order to compose *against the grain* of its
natural properties ... This, then, is a model of the late style." And see
Spitzer, 41, on Adorno's "paradox."

24 Adorno, *Beethoven*, item 321, p. 160.

25 Ibid., item 266, p. 128.

26 Compare Rosen, *The Classical Style*, 444.

27 Adorno, *Beethoven*, item 267, p. 129.

28 See Spitzer, *Music as Philosophy*, 44, on Adorno's notion of an allegorical
late style, and 64–6 on the allegorical aspect as a challenge to Schenkerian
theory.

29 Adorno, *Beethoven*, item 44, p. 21.

30 Ibid., item 322, p. 160.

31 Ibid., 45. "The primary-musical form of his own views was inherently
mediated by the spirit of his social class in the period around 1800."

32 But compare Rosen, "Should We Adore," 7.

33 Subotnik, *Developing Variations*, 17. And see *Minima Moralia*, 36, and
J.M. Bernstein's discussion in *Adorno: Disenchantment*, 64–6.

34 Being purposeful without purpose, a *Zweckmässigkeit ohne Zweck*. See
Paddison, *Adorno's Aesthetics*, 57, his discussion of "spiritualization" in
particular.

35 And in this sense is comparable to the logic of positivism. See Bowie,
"Adorno, Heidegger, and the Meaning of Music," 257: "The resolution
of dissonances in tonal music is, to listeners used to the conventions of
Western music, like the conclusion of an argument from premises."

36 See Spitzer, *Music as Philosophy*, 4: "The formally abstract and self-
contained ('autonomous') Classical style of Haydn, Mozart, and Beethoven
is celebrated as the benchmark for rationality in music, as well as the ideal
balance of this rationality with the individual and societal dimensions of
human subjectivity. With Beethoven's late style, this utopian high-water
mark in Western music encounters its catastrophe: a repertory which
critically reflects upon the foundations of musical Classicism, while at the
same time reconstructing them from quite a different position. Beethoven's
object, therefore, is nothing less than the foundation and limit of human
reason itself. This, in a nutshell, is the gist of Theodor Adorno's reading of
the late style." See as well my review of Spitzer in *Music Theory Spectrum*.

37 Again compare Bowie, "Adorno, Heidegger and the Meaning of Music,"
272, on expression and convention, bearing in mind all the while Bowie's
caveats on Adorno and hermeneutics.

38 Adorno, *Essays*, 565.
39 Adorno, *Beethoven*, item 308, p. 155.
40 Ibid., item 309, p. 155.
41 Ibid., item 311, pp. 156–7.
42 Ibid., item 318, p. 159. And see Dineen, "Fugue, Space, Noise, and Form."
43 Subotnik, *Developing Variations*, 21–2.
44 Ibid., 22.
45 Adorno, *Beethoven*, item 200, p. 80.
46 Ibid.
47 See Paddison, "Authenticity and Failure."
48 Adorno, *Beethoven*, 151. "Der musikalischen Erfahrung des späten Beethoven muß die einheit von Subjektivität und Objektivität, das Runde des symphonischen Gelingens, die Totalität aus der Bewegung alles Einzelen, kurz eben das verdächtig geworden sein, was den Werken seiner mittleren Zeit ihr Authentisches verleiht." Adorno, *Beethoven: Philosophie*, 219.
49 Ibid., 151–2. "Er durchshaut die Klassik als Klassizismus. Er lehnt sich auf gegen das Affirmative, unkritisch das Sein Bejahende in der Idee der klassischen Symphonik ... Er muß das Unwahre im höchsten Anspruch der klassizistischen Musik gefühlt haben: daß der Inbegriff der gegensätzlichen Bewegung alles Einzelnen, das in jenem Inbegriff untergeht, Postivität selber sie." Adorno, *Beethoven: Philosophie*, 219.
50 Compare, however, Hermand, "Der vertonte Weltgeist."
51 See Goehr, *Imaginary Museum*.
52 For a recent review of thought on the ontology of performance, see Stecker, "Methodological Questions."
53 If only a fractured awareness, after – in the sense of departing from – Kant and Hegel.
54 That would be a false consciousness to be identified with the fetish, a fetishization of thought. See O'Connor's introduction to Adorno, *Adorno Reader*, 13: "In false consciousness the subject cannot accept arguments which point to autonomy as semblance." See Bowie, "Adorno, Heidegger and the Meaning of Music," 251–2, on illusion (*Schein*) in music, which "contributes to existing injustices by reconciling likeness to reality as it already is." See Buck-Morss, *Origin*, 112, her four categories of bourgeois philosophy expressed as symptoms of commodification.
55 According to Carl Dahlhaus, "Zu Adornos," 174, the criteria of musical accomplishment shift from "greater [größere]" to "most accurate [wahrere]."
56 See Wind, *Endkrise*.

57 See Klumpenhouwer, "Commentary," and "Late Capitalism," on the ramifications this holds for music analysis.

58 Implicit in this kind of work is what Stanley Aronowitz calls an "*obligation* of speculative – i.e. critical – reason," Aronowitz, *The Crisis in Historical Materialism*, 47. See Petersen-Mikkelsen, "Zur Aktualität," on musical commodity, work, and Adorno. And see Uehlein, "Beethovens Musik," 227, the passage around the sentence "In der Musik kommt der substantielle Inhalt selber zur Darstellung [In music, substantial content itself achieves representation]."

59 The number in parenthesis indicates the number of measures before or after the bar line to which the rehearsal number is attached. 72(+1) indicates the first measure after that bar line (thus the first measure); 72(-1) indicates the first measure prior to the bar line.

CHAPTER FOUR

1 Schoenberg, *Fundamentals of Musical Composition*, 21.

2 Ibid., chaps 5 and 8. For the purposes of contrast, any two or more harmonies will suffice, although he retained the terms tonic form and dominant form even where other harmonies – subdominant or mediant, for example – serve in lieu.

3 Ibid., 30, 59n1. And see Dineen, "Schoenberg's Logic and Motor."

4 Caplin, *Classical Form*, chap. 1, refers to these as "formal functions."

5 Schoenberg, *Fundamentals of Musical Composition*, 8.

6 See Adorno, *Lectures on Negative Dialectics*, 198: "Music theory really teaches only how a movement begins and ends, nothing about the movement itself or its development." And see Adorno, *Philosophy of New Music*, 78–9: "To date, official music theory has made no effort to clarify precisely the concept of 'continuation' as a category of form, even though without the contrast between 'event' and continuation, the major forms of traditional music – including Schoenberg's – cannot be understood."

7 See Rosen, *Classical Style*, chap. 2, "Theories of Form," on the limitations to the sonata form as a descriptive device: "The most dangerous aspect of the traditional theory of 'sonata form' is the normative one"(32).

8 By such nineteenth-century theorists as A.B. Marx, for example.

9 In this instances, however, the harmonic contrast occurs within the first measure, in the tonic form itself, between a quite traditional tonic chord and a quite untraditional chord. The contrast is sufficient to set a precedent for harmonic development through the remainder of the song. As I have proposed elsewhere, the piece would seem to hang together on the

association of these two chords. See Dineen, "Schoenberg's Logic and Motor." The association of these two chords is based, like the sentence form, on an extant schema – the relation of the tonic chord to the augmented sixth chord, the latter's ability at tonal synthesis having occupied Schoenberg at length in his *Harmonielehre*. And see Dineen, "Tonal Problem, Carpenter Narrative" and Dineen, "The Tonal Problem as a Method" on the chord of the augmented sixth as vehicle of musical form.

10 Adorno, "Arnold Schoenberg," in *Prisms*, 161; and see Adorno, *Essays*, 150.

11 Adorno, *Essays*, 638.

12 See Spinner, *A Short Introduction*, for analyses of Schoenberg in the terms of the *Formenlehre*.

13 J.M. Bernstein refers to fragmentary writing. See Adorno, *The Culture Industry*, 7: "Fragmentary writing is premised upon the refusal of the operations that establish 'rational' connections between statements in theoretical discourse (inference, entailment, deduction) and their linguistic representatives ('therefore,' 'because,' etc.). For Adorno, these operations are the markers for domination in the conceptual realm." And see Held, *Introduction*, 211; Hoffman, *Figuren des scheins*; and Hohendahl, *Prismatic Thought*.

14 Compare Weber Nicholsen, *Exact Imagination*, 61: "Adorno's conception of a more authentic use of language tends to manifest itself in *Notes to Literature* as an inconspicuous background murmuring or rustling – as *Rauschen*, in fact. In the constellation of ideas and images that make up his implicit conception of language, then, *Rauschen* is a key word. It indicates both the substance of the conception and its enigmatic manifestation in Adorno's work." And see her definition of "configurational language," 61–2.

15 Adorno, *Minima Moralia*, 42.

16 See the editor's introduction to Adorno and Berg, *Correspondence*, viii. And see the translators' introduction to Adorno, *Alban Berg*, x–xi.

17 Adorno and Berg, *Correspondence*, 28.

18 See Paddison, "The Language-Character of Music."

19 Schoenberg, *Style and Idea*, 414.

20 Ibid., 411.

21 In this regard, the demonstration that follows takes up precedents set by Weber Nicholsen, *Exact Imagination*, 79–84, and especially 113–24, and Schnebel, "Komposition von Sprache," 129–45. See, however, Weber Nicholsen, *Exact Imagination*, 102, on the limitations of the relationship between music and prose in Adorno's work.

22 Adorno, "Bach Defended," in *Prisms*.

23 Ibid., 135.

24 Ibid.

25 Ibid.

26 The connection of harmonies by common tones was one of the essential guidelines taught by Schoenberg. See Schoenberg, *Theory of Harmony*, 39. Adorno would have known this feature of Schoenberg's theoretical thought either from the *Harmonielehre* (which Schoenberg in turn got as *echte Wiener Harmonielehre* from Bruckner and Simon Sechter), or from his lessons with Berg. The smoothest harmonic progressions are created according to what the Viennese call the "law of the shortest way" and in particular by keeping the common tone in the same part, while observing the ban on perfect parallel intervals in succession.

27 Schoenberg, *Fundamentals of Musical Composition*, 27.

28 Adorno, "Bach Defended," in *Prisms*, 135.

29 Adorno, "Bach gegen seine Liebhaber verteidigt," in *Prismen*, 138.

30 But see Zehentreiter, "Adornos materiale."

31 Adorno, "Schoenberg and Progress," in *Philosophy*, 27–102.

32 But compare Alastair Williams, *New Music*.

33 Adorno, "Arnold Schoenberg," in *Prisms*, 150.

34 Schoenberg, "Composition with Twelve Tones (I)," in *Style and Idea*, 222.

35 I have taken up Adorno's appraisal elsewhere with reference to naïveté. See Dineen, "Adorno and Schoenberg's Unanswered Question." See as well, Schoenberg, "Letter to Kurt List, Dec. 10, 1949," in Auner, ed., *A Schoenberg Reader*, 335–9. Adorno, as Thomas Mann's expert witness in the writing of *Doktor Faust*, was suspect in Schoenberg's eyes. See Stückenschmidt, *Schoenberg*, 495–6. For the Adorno-Schoenberg pas de deux, see Goehr, "Totentanz der Prinzipien."

36 Quotation from G.W.F. Hegel, *The Phenomenology of Mind*, trans. J.B. Baillie (New York: Dover, 1964), 561.Cited in Adorno, *Philosophy*, 29.

37 Adorno, *Philosophy*, 29.

38 The only logically pure community was Eden, and only because its inhabitants (with the exception, perhaps, of the snake), not knowing themselves, could not conceive of any other community.

39 Schoenberg, *Style and Idea*, 124.

40 Adorno, *Philosophy*, 31.

41 See Schoenberg, *Theory of Harmony*, 309–30.

42 Ibid., 346.

43 Webern, *The Path*.

44 Adorno, *Philosophy*, 31.

45 Schoenberg, *Theory of Harmony*, 258.
46 Adorno, *Philosophy*, 32.
47 See Dineen, "Schoenberg's Modulatory Calculations."
48 Adorno, *Philosophy*, 32.
49 Ibid., 32.
50 Ibid., 33.
51 Ibid.
52 Ibid., 33–4.
53 Ibid., 34.
54 This is, of course, not true of the works designed to fulfill a particular social function – dance music or music for religious celebration, for example.
55 See Carpenter, "The Janus-Aspect of Fugue."
56 Adorno, *Philosophy*, 96.
57 Ibid., 46.
58 Ibid., 47.
59 Ibid.
60 Ibid., 48.
61 Ibid., 49.
62 Ibid., 61.
63 Ibid., 77.
64 Ibid., 50.
65 Adorno, *Essays*, 184–5.
66 See Hullot-Kentor, *Things beyond Resemblance*, the chapter "Popular Music and the 'Aging of the New Music,'" 170–9 in particular.
67 Adorno, *Philosophy*, 50.
68 Ibid., 50. And compare Adorno, "The Aging of the New Music," in *Essays*, 186, on tonality and the First Chamber Symphony and the Fourth String Quartet.
69 From this perspective, it would be an error to represent Schoenberg as a winner (and Stravinsky as a loser). See Chua, "Drifting," 3.
70 Adorno, *Philosophy*, 52–3.
71 Ibid., 54–5.
72 See Sziborsky, *Adornos Musikphilosophie*, 190–5.
73 Adorno, *Philosophy*, 87–8.
74 Ibid., 88.
75 This would go against the grain of some recent work on modernism. See John Roberts' appraisal: The "current Weberian version [of] philosophical aesthetics has little to do with the spirit of Adorno's negative dialectics, and more to do with a melancholic attachment to a lost modernist art object and to cultural mourning." Roberts, "Marxism and Art Theory," 24.

76 Adorno, "Arnold Schoenberg," in *Prisms*, 151.
77 Ibid., 160–1.
78 Ibid., 164.
79 Ibid., 165.

CHAPTER FIVE

1 On the import Adorno's Wagner bears for musicology, see Baragwanath, "Musicology." Compare Huyssens, *After the Great Divide*, the chapter "Adorno in Reverse," which presents an intricate analysis of Adorno's approach to culture with close reference to Wagner.
2 The result may be the kind of "radical evil" that concerns philosophers of ethics. See MacLennan, review of Peter Dews, *The Idea of Evil*, 151–2, which considers an ethical Adorno as rooted in a period preceding the historicism of Hegel and Marx.
3 See Held, *Introduction to Critical Theory*, 35.
4 See Baragwanath, "Musicology," 53n7.
5 In Arato, *The Essential Frankfurt School Reader*, 118–37.
6 Baragwanath, "Musicology," 53, and see Horkheimer, "Egoism and the Freedom Movement."
7 Adorno, *Authoritarian Personality*. See Jenemann, *Adorno in America*, chapter 1.
8 Adorno, *In Search of Wagner*, 12.
9 Ibid., 15.
10 Ibid., 14.
11 A term applied, of course, to his Mahler monograph.
12 See Gray, *About Face*, a most comprehensive treatment of physiognomy in a broad Central-European context, beginning with reference to Lavater, *Essays*.
13 Adorno, *In Search of Wagner*, 117.
14 Klumpenhouwer, "Late Capitalism," 384. See Horkheimer, "Egoism and the Freedom Movement," 16: "What is expressed in philosophy as the contempt for instinctual desires turns out in real life to be the practice of their repression." See Cook, *The Culture Industry*, 7–8, who points out how "Nazi leaders and the culture industry" play upon repressed "impulses and drives."
15 See Klumpenhouwer, "Late Capitalism," 384. Note the caveats placed by Horkheimer on Freud's "biological metaphysics," in Horkheimer, "Egoism and the Freedom Movement," 55–60. Cook refers in this regard to "extra-psychic factors" – this to forestall gravitating toward treating Freud's

analyses as purely psychological events – "internalizations." See *The Culture Industry*, pp. 4–9. See the discussion of narcissism on pp. 9–10, 13–16.

16 Cook, *The Culture Industry*, 4.

17 See Adorno, *Dream Notes*, 2–3, the Brünnhilde dream from 1937.

18 Adorno, *In Search of Wagner*, 123.

19 Ibid.

20 So as to avoid the pitfalls of biography as it is normally conducted. See Claussen, *One Last Genius*. Claussen's preface, "How to Read This Book," and the longer first chapter, "Instead of an Overture: *No Heirs*," raise the issue of biography, principally how Adorno envisioned the genre and how a biographer *after Adorno* should tailor the biographical pursuit to honour Adorno's vision. The locus is a quotation where Adorno describes "the Goethe cult": "This suits crude bourgeois consciousness as much because it implies a work ethic that glorifies pure human creativity regardless of its aim as because the viewer is relieved of taking any trouble with the object itself. The viewer is supposed to be satisfied with the personality of the artist – essentially a kitsch biography. Those who produce important works of art are not demigods but fallible, often neurotic and damaged, individuals." (2–3, citing Adorno, *Aesthetic Theory*, 171.) The question of biography is raised briefly in a review devoted in part to Claussen's book: see John Abromeit, "Remembering Adorno," 28.

21 Adorno uses the term *physiognomic* [*physiognomik*] extensively in "Spengler after the Decline," in *Prisms*. And see Gray, *About Face*, 190–1.

22 Adorno, *Essays*, 586.

23 The passage is taken from page 335 in the old translation. See Adorno, *Aesthetic Theory*, Hullot-Kentor translation, 236.

24 Zuidervaart, *Adorno's Aesthetic Theory*, 219.

25 Adorno, "Arnold Schoenberg," *Prisms*, 151. This notion of an "undeveloped nature" becoming evident is surely one aspect of the term *physiognomy*.

26 Sample, "Adorno on the Musical Language of Beethoven," 384. Compare Adorno, *Philosophy*, 31, as discussed in the previous chapter. And see Kager, "Einheit in der Zersplitterung," 94–7, on the subjective and objective nature of musical materials.

27 Adorno, *In Search of Wagner*, 11.

28 Ibid., 14, translation adjusted by the author.

29 Adorno, *Essays*, 375.

30 Adorno, *In Search of Wagner*, 14.

31 Ibid., 15.

32 Ibid., 14–15.

33 Ibid., 15.

34 Ibid.

35 Ibid., 16.

36 Ibid., 17.

37 See Mahnkopf, "Adorno und die musikalische Analytik," 240–4, the notion of analysis as work and its five conditions; De la Motte, "Adornos musikalische Analysen," on Adorno's sometimes puzzling analyses; Jarvis, *Adorno: A Critical Introduction*, 132; Johnson, "Analysis." Compare Agawu, "What Adorno Makes Possible." Ayrey, "Universe of Particulars," 356, holds that for the "self-consciously subjective musician," Adorno's *Aesthetic Theory* is "insufficiently 'musical,'" a criticism that belies Adorno's neglect at the hands of most North American music theorists.

38 Adorno, *Essays*, 375.

39 Adorno, *In Search of Wagner*, 31.

40 See Jameson, *Marxism and Form*, 16: "As in parliamentary demagoguery, the listening masses submit to the conductor with a kind of hypnotized fascination," and the discussion of the leitmotiv thereafter.

41 Adorno, *In Search of Wagner*, 32.

42 Ibid., 34.

43 See Jameson, *Late Marxism*, 220–2.

44 Adorno, *In Search of Wagner*, 42.

45 Ibid.

46 Ibid.

47 Adorno, *Essays*, 597–8.

48 Compare Williams, "Technology of the Archaic." Although his intention is not to undermine Adorno's materialist aesthetics, the appeals to Derrida and Benjamin seem to do that.

49 See Seubold, "Die Errinerung," 144–51, on Adorno and Mahler's use of "traditional materials."

50 See Subotnik, "Adorno's 'French Model,'" 218–19.

51 Adorno, *Mahler*, 32.

52 Ibid., 125.

53 In the essay "National Socialism and the Arts," Adorno tells of a course he offered once on Hanslick: "In the winter term of 1932–33, immediately before Hitler took over, I had to conduct at Frankfurt University a seminar on Hanslick's treatise *On the Musically Beautiful* – which is essentially a defense of musical formalism against the doctrine of Wagner and the programmatic school. Although the seminar was focused on philosophical

issues, the participants, about thirty, were mostly musicologists." Adorno, *Essays*, 376.

54 Hanslick, *On the Musically Beautiful*, xxiii.

55 Ibid., 58.

56 Ibid., 29.

57 Consider the notion of a "judgmental synthesis." See Bowie, "The Meaning of Music," 259.

58 See Bowie, "The Meaning of Music," 256–64, on the dual meaning of *Weise* as *manner* and *melody*, with reference to Heidegger and to the musicologist Heinrich Besseler. And see p. 253: "The 'material' [of musical creation] itself is sedimented spirit, something social, which has been preformed by the consciousness of people," quoting Adorno's *Philosophy of Music*. Again take note of Bowie's Adorno critique.

59 To distinguish between Adorno and Hanslick on lines of Adorno's engagement with Kant, Hanslick's famous locution can be subsumed under a notion of the appearance of purposefulness without purpose [*Zweckmässigkeit ohne Zweck*]. But to put the common distinction between Kant and Adorno crudely, nothing forbids the division of the listening subject from musical object (the "tonally moving forms") in Hanslick, whereas the two are linked in Adorno's thought. Following Adorno's "Copernican turn" (discussed in chapter 1 above), such forms are constituted by identity thinking and thus the hitherto-purely-formal musical object becomes an active constituent of meaning impressed upon the listening subject: "turned into the *prius* of what according to its concept would have it be the *posterius*." Adorno, "Subject and Object," in *The Adorno Reader*, 143. See Paddison, "Authenticity and Failure," 208–10.

60 Hanslick, *On the Musically Beautiful*, 58.

61 Ibid.

62 Adorno, *In Search of Wagner*, 32.

63 Hanslick, *On the Musically Beautiful*, 58–9.

64 Ibid., 59.

65 Adorno, *Introduction to the Sociology of Music*, 4.

CHAPTER SIX

1 Adorno, *Introduction to the Sociology of Music*, 4–5.

2 Ibid., 19.

3 Ruhlmann, "Frank Zappa," 9.

4 Gray, *Mother!*, 33.

5 Courrier, *Dangerous Kitchen*, 55.

6 James, *Necessity Is*, 31.

7 Ibid., 32.

8 Webern, *The Path*.

9 James, *Necessity Is*, 31–4.

10 Zappa, "All About Music."

11 Adorno, *Minima Moralia*, 173. Adorno makes explicit the master-slave dialectic by reference to Hegel in one of the omitted passages. See Bernstein, *Adorno*, 52–3, on this passage.

12 Adorno, "Die Aktualität der Philosophie," "The Actuality of Philosophy." See as well the writings on language discussed in Weber Nicholsen, *Exact Imagination*, 62–3, for example "Theses on the Language of the Philosopher," "The Essay as Form," "On Lyric Poetry," and "Skoteinos." On parataxis, see Adorno, "Parataxis on Holderlin's Late Poetry," *Notes to Literature*, 2: 109–49.

13 Adorno, "The Actuality of Philosophy," 127.

14 Ibid., 129.

15 Ibid., 127–8.

16 See Benjamin, *The Origin of German Tragic Drama*, 34–5.

17 Adorno, "*The Actuality of Philosophy*," 127.

18 Shierry Weber Nicholsen, *Exact Imagination*, 60, refers to the concept of constellation with the two terms *configuration* and *parataxis*. Given the decay of language, she says, citing Adorno, a philosopher is constrained to "'place words around the new truth in such a way that their configuration yields the new truth'... Such a use of language alters the words in turn, creating 'a unity of concept and thing that is dialectically intertwined and cannot be disentangled through explication'" (citing Adorno, "Thesen über die Sprache des Philosophen," *Gesammelte Schriften* 1: 369). On her account, this is a negating procedure: "It is the negation of continuity that marks the edges of the parts, rendering them discrete" (84). For her, in parataxis, particles of prose thought lose their function and "serial transition replaces logical connection"; "logical coherence" is abandoned "in favor of what Adorno calls 'aconceptual synthesis.'" She relates parataxis to configuration thus: "Parataxis ... is the basis of configuration; the unity of the whole is composed of the dissociations between the discrete parts as well as of their associations" (83–4). The third and much of the fourth chapters of her book are devoted to elucidating these ideas.

19 Adorno, "The Actuality of Philosophy," 127.

20 Compare J.M. Bernstein on Adorno's description of Berg's musical form, in *Adorno*, 286–7.

21 Climbing to second rank on the "Top Classical Crossover" chart in 1993. http://en.wikipedia.org/wiki/The_Yellow_Shark. Accessed 5 April 2010.

22 From about 1911, the time of the first *Harmonielehre* edition onward. But see Dineen, "Schoenberg and the Radical Economies."

23 Schoenberg, *Style and Idea*, 222.

CHAPTER SEVEN

1 Hunter, "Buuuuummmmd," 66.

2 I shall not address here Manson's most recent work, sometimes appraised as a "glam" reversal of former values.

3 Bloom, *The Closing of the American Mind*, 336.

4 Lukács, *The Theory of the Novel*, 38.

5 Alternatively, mahogany or polished steel, neither of which lack for associations with caskets.

6 To which *The Dead Kennedy's* seems crude by comparison.

7 Manson, "Columbine," 23.

8 Manson, *The Long Hard Road*, 249.

9 Manson to Avi Lewis, cited in Wright, "I'd Sell You Suicide," 375.

10 Klosterman, *Fargo City Rock*, 138.

11 Wright, "I'd Sell You Suicide," 377.

12 Manson, *The Long Hard Road*, 261.

13 See ibid., 246–67.

14 Manson, "Columbine," 25.

15 Marx, *Capital*, 1: 795. Marx concludes that "the well-to-do classes had a lease of life which was more than double the value of that which fell to the lot of the less favoured citizens."

16 Mandeville, *Fable*, 212–13, 328, cited in Marx, *Capital*, 1: 765.

17 Engels, *The Condition of the Working Class*.

18 If only to be foisted on other, less legislatively advantaged workers in other parts of the world.

19 Marx, *Capital*, 3: 1046.

20 Lukács, *History and Class Consciousness*, 48.

21 Ibid., 47.

22 And their adaptation in the comparative method of investigation in the social sciences, such as Franz Bopp's investigation of language dissemination.

23 Lukács, *History and Class Consciousness*, 48.

24 Lukács, *The Theory of the Novel*, 62.

25 Ibid.

26 Ibid., 64.
27 Ibid.
28 Ibid.
29 Ibid.
30 Ibid.
31 The neologism is intended to mean the creation of artifacts.
32 Adorno, "The Idea," in Hullot-Kentor, *Things beyond Resemblance*, 265.
33 Adorno, "A Portrait of Walter Benjamin," in *Prisms*, 233.
34 Ibid., 235.
35 Ibid., 236.
36 Adorno, "Valéry Proust Museum," in *Prisms*, 175.
37 Ibid., 180.
38 Ibid., 176.
39 Ibid., 180.
40 Ibid., 181.
41 Ibid., 182.
42 Ibid., 182.
43 Ibid., 183.
44 Ibid., 185.
45 Ibid., 176–8.
46 Ibid., 177.
47 Ibid., 178.
48 Ibid., 178–9.
49 Adorno, *Wagner*, 15.

CHAPTER EIGHT

1 See Rose, *Melancholy Science*, chapter 2, especially the discussion of stylistic "strategies," 12–13, and the distinction between "subjective" and "objective"; Paddison, *Adorno's Aesthetics of Music*, 13–20 on the writing style; Goehr, "Reviewing Adorno," in Adorno, *Critical Models*, xiii, on the motivation for the style.
2 Compare Henry Pickford, the preface to Adorno, *Critical Models*, viii: "The Adorno emerging here is far from the stereotypical mandarin aesthete." I am speaking here of his written prose style, not necessarily the voice of his lecture style or of his radio interviews. Compare, for example, *Negative Dialectics* to *Lectures on Negative Dialectics*.
3 Subotnik, *Developing Variations*, 213.
4 By *reticence*, I mean the sense of writing critically about himself. I do not mean a reticent person. In the sense of the person described by Soma

Morgenstern, as cited in Jäger, *Adorno*, 35–7, he was anything but. Instead we mean *reticent* in a monadic sense, as if Adorno the critical writer were "windowless."

5 His biographies attest to the fact that vanity was, however, an aspect of his person. See, for example, Müller-Doohm, chapter 6, especially pp. 82–3, and 93.

6 Adorno, "Sacred Fragment," and "Sakrales Fragment."

7 See Kerling, "Moses und Aron."

8 Adorno, "Sacred Fragment," 226.

9 Adorno, *Negative Dialektik*, 64; compare *Negative Dialectics*, 55. And see Michael Rosen, *Hegel's Dialectic*, 166.

10 Ringer, "Faith and Symbol," 82.

11 Adorno, "Sacred Fragment," 225. "Tapfere sind solche, die Taten voll-bringen, an die ihr Mut nicht heranreicht," Adorno, "Sakrales Fragment," 306. In this and subsequent translations, the translation used is this author's unless otherwise indicated. Subsequent page references to the published translation by Rodney Livingstone are included in brackets to enable comparison. Compare: "the power behind the human mind, which produces miracles for which we do not deserve credit," Schoenberg, *Style and Idea*, 85, and "A creator has a vision of something that has not existed before this vision," ibid., 215.

12 Compare: "Had the ghost of Adorno been present, he might have asked that the figure of Moses also be introduced into the funeral oration, espe-cially the figure as given shape by Schoenberg in his unfinished opera." Lydia Goehr, "Reviewing Adorno," in Adorno, *Critical Models*, liv.

13 Dineen, "Modernism and Words," 355.

14 See Ringer, "Arnold Schoenberg and the Politics of Jewish Survival," 24; Ringer, *Arnold Schönberg: Das Leben*, 253, on Schoenberg's modern position. Edward Said refers to an "exile's contrapuntal awareness," surely held by both Moses (figuratively) and Schoenberg (in both the figurative and literal senses). Cited in Goehr, "Music and Musicians in Exile," 86.

15 Dineen, "Modernism and Words," 359–60.

16 Schoenberg, *Style and Idea*, 104.

17 Ibid., 214.

18 Adorno, *Quasi una Fantasia*, 314 [231].

19 Ibid., 311 [229].

20 Ibid., 310 [228].

21 Ibid., and see 233.

22 Ibid., 317 [234].

23 Ibid., 317 [233–4].

24 Ibid., 318 [234].

25 Ibid., 312 [229].

26 Ibid., 307 [226].

27 Ibid., 308 [227].

28 Ibid., 309 [228].

29 "Enlightenment has always taken the basic principle of myth to be anthropomorphism, the projection onto nature of the subjective." Horkheimer and Adorno, *Dialectic*, 6. Compare Bernstein, *Adorno*, 92, on anthropomorphism and objectivity; and see Buck-Morss, *The Origin of Negative Dialectics*, 78.

30 Adorno, *Quasi una Fantasia*, 311 [229]. And see Düttman, *Gift of Language*, chapter 1 (on Heidegger and Franz Rosenzweig), and chapter 4.

31 Adorno, *Quasi una Fantasia*, 229.

32 See Weber Nicholsen, *Exact Imagination*, 69: "Adorno refers ... to 'the abyss into which language plunges when it tries to become name and image.' Insofar as names stand for this impossible ideal, they cannot be thought of as individual words, which, as concepts, will also be divided from the things they refer to ... Literary language may be most authentic when it tries to capture namelessness." Compare Bernstein, *Adorno*, 277: Adorno identifies the impulse to orient ourselves toward the object in this way as the impulse "to *name* the object, *as if* naming were not labeling (or pointing or referring) but an always complex perfected expression of the thing itself." And see Buck-Morss, *The Origin of Negative Dialectics*, 88–90, on "Name" in the work of Benjamin and Adorno; see Grenz, *Adornos Philosophie*, 211–21.

33 Horkheimer and Adorno, *Dialectic*, 23.

34 Adorno, *Quasi una Fantasia*, 306–7 [225–6].

35 Horkheimer and Adorno, *Dialectic*, 23. And see Krankenhagen, *Auschwitz darstellen*, 79, on "Darstellungverbot" and Auschwitz.

36 See Adorno, *Quasi una Fantasia*, 312 [230]: "The Jewish ban on image, around which the text is centered, determines at the same time the musical approach [*Ansatz*]."

37 "[*Moses und Aron*] belongs to that group of works produced in the twentieth century, and crucial to our present aesthetics, which have their own possibility as essential theme ... It asks of itself ... whether the thing can be done at all, whether there are modes of communication adequate." Steiner, *Language and Silence*, 131.

38 Adorno, *Quasi una Fantasia*, 307–8 [226].

39 See Buck-Morss, *The Origin of Negative Dialectics*, 100–1.

40 Adorno, *Quasi una Fantasia*, 307 [226].

41 Ibid., 308 [226–7].
42 Ibid., 306 [225].
43 Ibid., 307 [226].
44 Ibid., 308 [227].
45 "Adorno's work is on the same horizon even more recondite than Schoenberg's, and as a person he was ultimately more self-protective and austere." Hullot-Kentor, "The Philosophy of Dissonance," 312.

CONCLUSION

1 Aronowitz, *The Last Good Job*, 192.

Works Cited

Aronowitz, Stanley. *The Crisis in Historical Materialism: Class, Politics, and Culture in Marxist Theory*. Minneapolis: University of Minnesota Press 1981
– *The Last Good Job in America: Work and Education in the New Global Technoculture*. Lanham, MD: Rowman and Littlefield 2001
Abromeit, John. "Remembering Adorno." *Radical Philosophy* 124 (March/April 2004): 27–38
Adler, Guido. "Guido Adler's 'The Scope, Method, and Aim of Musicology' (1885): An English Translation with an Historico- Analytical Commentary." Translated and with commentary by Erica Muggleston. *Yearbook for Traditional Music* 13 (1981): 1–21
Adorno, Theodor. "The Actuality of Philosophy." No translator given. *Telos* 31 (1977): 120–33
– *The Adorno Reader*. Edited by Brian O'Connor. Oxford: Blackwell 2000
– *Aesthetic Theory*. Edited by G. Adorno and R. Tiedemann. Translated by R. Hullot-Kentor. Minneapolis: University of Minnesota Press 1997
– *Against Epistemology: A Metacritique. Studies in Husserl and the Phenomenological Antinomies*. Translated by Willis Domingo. Cambridge: MIT Press 1982
– "Die Aktualität der Philosophie." In *Philosophische Frühschriften*. Edited by R. Tiedemann. Vol. 1 of *Gesammelte Schriften*. Frankfurt am Main: Suhrkamp 1996: 325–44
– *Alban Berg: Master of the Smallest Link*. Translated by Juliane Brand and Christopher Hailey. Cambridge: Cambridge University Press 1991
– "Arnold Schoenberg, 1874–1951." In Adorno, *Prisms*, 147–72
– *Ästhetische Theorie*. Edited by G. Adorno and R. Tiedemann. Frankfurt am Main: Suhrkamp 1970

- *Beethoven: Philosophie der Musik; Fragmente und Texte*. Edited by R. Tiedemann. Vol. 1, *Fragment gebliebene Schriften*, of *Nachgelassene Schriften, Abteilung 1*. Frankfurt am Main: Suhrkamp 1994
- *Beethoven: The Philosophy of Music*. Translated by E. Jephcott. Cambridge: Polity 1998
- *Critical Models: Interventions and Catchwords*. Translated by Henry W. Pickford. Introduction by Lydia Goehr. New York: Columbia University Press 1998
- *The Culture Industry: Selected Essays on Mass Culture*. Edited by J.M. Bernstein. Various translators. London: Routledge 1991
- *Dream Notes*. Translated by Rodney Livingstone. Edited by Christoph Gödde and Henri Lonitz. Cambridge: Polity 2007
- *Essays on Music*. Edited by Richard Leppert. Translated by Susan H. Gillespie et al. Berkeley: University of California Press 2002
- "The Idea of Natural History." Translated by R. Hullot-Kentor. *Telos* 60 (1984): 111–24. Reprinted in Hullot-Kentor, *Things beyond Resemblance*, 252–69
- *In Search of Wagner*. Translated by R. Livingstone. London: Verso 1981
- *Introduction to the Sociology of Music*. Translated by E.B. Ashton. New York: Continuum 1989
- *Lectures on Negative Dialectics*. Edited by R. Tiedemann. Translated by R. Livingstone. Cambridge: Polity 2008
- *Mahler: A Musical Physiognomy*. Translated by E. Jephcott. Chicago: University of Chicago Press 1992
- *Minima Moralia*. Edited by R. Tiedemann. Vol. 4 of *Gesammelte Schriften*. Frankfurt am Main: Suhrkamp 1996
- *Minima Moralia: Reflections from Damaged Life*. Translated by E. Jephcott. London: Verso 1974
- *Negative Dialectics*. Translated by E.B. Ashton. New York: Continuum 1973
- *Negative Dialektik*. Frankfurt am Main: Suhrkamp Verlag 1975
- *Notes to Literature*. 2 vols. Translated by Shierry Weber Nicholsen. New York: Columbia University Press 1991
- *Philosophische Frühschriften*. Edited by R. Tiedemann. Vol.1 of *Gesammelte Schriften*. Frankfurt am Main: Suhrkamp 1996
- *Philosophy of New Music*. Translated by Robert Hullot-Kentor. Minneapolis: University of Minnesota Press 2006
- *Prismen: Kulturkritik und Gesellschaft*. In vol. 10.1, *Kulturkritik und Gesellschaft I* of *Gesammelte Schriften*. Edited by R. Tiedemann. Frankfurt am Main: Suhrkamp Verlag 1955

- *Prisms*. Translated by Samuel and Shierry Weber. Cambridge: MIT Press 1967
- *Quasi una Fantasia: Musikalische Schriften II*. Frankfurt am Main: S. Fischer 1963
- *Quasi una Fantasia: Essays on Modern Music*. Translated by R. Livingstone. London: Verso 1998
- "Sacred Fragment." In *Quasi una Fantasia: Essays*, 225–480
- "Sakrales Fragment." In *Quasi una Fantasia: Musikalische*, 306–31
- "Spätkapitalismus oder Industriegesellschaft," *Gesammelte Schriften* 8 (1992): 354–70
- *Versuch über Wagner*. In *Die musikalischen Monographien*. Edited by G. Adorno and R. Tiedemann. Frankfurt am Main: Suhrkamp 1971
- *Vorlesung über Negative Dialektik. Fragmente zur Vorlesung 1965–66*. Edited by R. Tiedemann. Frankfurt am Main: Suhrkamp 2003
Adorno, Theodor and Walter Benjamin. *The Complete Correspondence 1928–1940*. Edited by Henri Lonitz. Translated by Nicholas Walker. Cambridge: Harvard University Press 1999
Adorno, Theodor, Walter Benjamin, Ernst Bloch, Bertolt Brecht, and Georg Lukács. Translation editor, R. Taylor. *Aesthetics and Politics*. London: Verso Press 1977
Adorno, Theodor and Alban Berg. *Correspondence 1925–1935*. Edited by Henri Lonitz. Translated by Wieland Hoban. Cambridge: Polity 2005
Adorno, Theodor, et al. *The Authoritarian Personality*. Abridged edition. New York: W.W. Norton and Company 1982
Agawu, Kofi. "What Adorno Makes Possible for Music Analysis." *19th-Century Music*, 29, no. 1 (Summer, 2005): 49–55
Arato, Andrew and Eike Gebhardt. *The Essential Frankfurt School Reader*. New York: Continuum 1982
Auner, Joseph, ed. *A Schoenberg Reader: Documents of a Life*. New Haven: Yale University Press 2003
Ayrey, Craig. "Universe of Particulars: Subotnik, Deconstruction, and Chopin." *Music Analysis* 17, no. 3 (1998): 339–81
Baragwanath, Nicholas. "Musicology and Critical Theory: The Case of Wagner, Adorno, and Horkheimer." *Music and Letters*, 87, no. 1 (2006): 52–71
Beaumont, Matthew, Andrew Hemingway, Esther Leslie, and John Roberts, eds. *As Radical as Reality Itself: Essays on Marxism and Art for the 21st Century*. New York: Peter Lang 2007
Benjamin, Walter. *The Origin of German Tragic Drama*. Translated by J. Osborne. London: Verso 1998

- *Ursprung des deutschen Trauerspiels*. Frankfurt am Main: Suhrkamp 1969

Benjamin, Walter and Gretel Adorno. *Correspondence 1930–1940*. Edited by Henri Lonitz and Christophe Gödde. Translated by Wieland Hoban. Cambridge: Polity 2008

Bernstein, J.M. *Adorno: Disenchantment and Ethics*. Cambridge: Cambridge University Press 2001

- "Negative Dialectic as Fate: Adorno and Hegel." In Huhn, *Cambridge Companion to Adorno*, 19–50

- "Why Rescue Semblance?" In Huhn and Zuidervaart, *Semblance of Subjectivity*, 177–212

Bloom, Allan. *The Closing of the American Mind*. New York: Simon and Schuster 1987

Born, Georgina. "Against Negation, for a Politics of Cultural Production: Adorno, Aesthetics, and the Social." *Screen* 34, no. 3 (Autumn 1993): 223–42

Bowie, Andrew. "Adorno, Heidegger, and the Meaning of Music." In Huhn, *Cambridge Companion to Adorno*, 248–78

Brinkmann, Reinhold and Christoph Wolff, eds. *Driven into Paradise: The Musical Migration from Nazi Germany to the United States*. Berkeley: University of California Press 1999

Bronner, Stephen. *Of Critical Theory and Its Theorists*. Oxford: Blackwell 1994

Bronner, Stephen and Douglas Kellner, eds. *Critical Theory and Society: A Reader*. Toronto: Routledge 1989

Buck-Morss, Susan. *The Origin of Negative Dialectics: Theodor W. Adorno, Walter Benjamin, and the Frankfurt Insitute*. New York: Free Press 1977

Buhler, James. "Frankfurt School Blues: Rethinking Adorno's Critique of Jazz." In Hoeckner, *Apparitions*, 103–30

Burkholder, J. Peter. "Schoenberg the Reactionary." In Walter Frisch, editor, *Schoenberg and His World*. Princeton: Princeton University Press 1999: 162–91

Burnham, Scott. "Landscape as Music, Landscape as Truth: Schubert and the Burden of Repetition." *19th-Century Music* 29, no. 1 (Summer 2005): 31–41

Caplin, William. *Classical Form : A Theory of Formal Functions for the Instrumental Music of Haydn, Mozart, and Beethoven*. New York: Oxford University Press 1998

Carpenter, Patricia. "The Janus-Aspect of Fugue: An Essay in the Phenom-
enology of Musical Form." PhD diss., Columbia University, 1971
Chua, Daniel K.L. "Drifting: The Dialectics of Adorno's Philosophy of
New Music." In Hoeckner, *Apparitions*, 1–17
Claussen, Detlev. *Theodor Adorno: One Last Genius*. Translated by Rod-
ney Livingstone. Cambridge, MA: Belknap Press 2008
Cook, Deborah. *The Culture Industry Revisited: Theodor W. Adorno on
Mass Culture*. Lanham, MD: Rowman and Littlefield 1996
Cooper, Harry. "On 'Über Jazz': Replaying Adorno with the Grain." *Octo-
ber* 75 (Winter 1996): 99–133
Courrier, Kevin. *Dangerous Kitchen: The Subversive World of Frank
Zappa*. Toronto: ECW Press 2002
Cusset, François. *French Theory: How Foucault, Derrida, Deleuze, and
Co. Transformed the Intellectual Life of the United States*. Translated by
Jeff Fort. Minneapolis: University of Minnesota Press 2008
Dahlhaus, Carl. *Schoenberg and the New Music*. Translated by D. Puffett
and A. Clayton. Cambridge: Cambridge University Press 1987
– ed. *Musikalische Hermeneutik*. Regensburg: Gustav Bosse Verlag 1975
– "Zu Adornos Beethoven-Kritik." In Kolleritsch ed., *Adorno und die
Musik*, 170–79
Deathridge, J. Review of *In Search of Wagner*, by Theodor Adorno.
19th-Century Music 7 (1993): 81–5
– Review of *Sound Figures* by Theodor W. Adorno. *Journal of the Royal
Musical Association* 126 (2001): 304–10
Decker, Peter. *Die methodologie kritscher sinnsuche: Systembildende
konzeptionen Adornos im lichte der philosophischen tradition*. Verlag
Palm & Enke Erlangen 1982
De la Motte, Dieter. "Adornos musikalische Analysen." In Kolleritsch, ed.
Adorno und die Musik, 52–63
Delanty, Gerard, ed. *Theodor W. Adorno*. 4 vols. London: Sage 2004
Dineen, Murray. "Adorno and Schoenberg's Unanswered Question."
Musical Quarterly 77, no. 3 (1993): 415–27
– "Still Life with Insects: Adorno Defended against His Devotees."
Criticus Musicus 1, no. 1 (1993): 25–35
– "Adorno, Jitterbug, and Adequate Listener." *repercussions* 7–8
(1999–2000): 55–75
– "Modernism and Words: Schoenberg, Moses, and Adorno." In *Schoen-
berg and Words*, edited by R. Berman and C. Cross. New York: Garland
2000

- "Fugue, Space, Noise, and Form." *International Studies in Philosophy*
  36, part 1 (2004): 39–60
- "Schoenberg's Logic and Motor: Harmony and Motive in the Capric-
  cio No. 1 of the Fantasien Op. 116 by Johannes Brahms." *Gamut* 10
  (2001): 3–28
- "The Tonal Problem as a Method of Analysis." *Theory and Practice* 30
  (2005): 69–96
- "Tonal Problem, Carpenter Narrative, and Carpenter Motive in Schubert's Impromptu, Op. 90, No. 3." *Theory and Practice* 30 (2005):
  97–120
- "Schoenberg's Modulatory Calculations: *Wn* Fonds 21 Berg 6/III/66
  and Tonality." *Music Theory Spectrum* 27, no. 1 (April 2005):
  97–112
- "Schoenberg and the Radical Economies of *Harmonielehre*." *Culture Unbound* 1 (2009):http://www.cultureunbound.ep.liu.se/v1/a08/
  (accessed 16 March 2010)
- Review of Michael Spitzer, *Music and Philosophy: Adorno and Beethov-
  en's Late Style*, in *Music Theory Spectrum* 31, no. 2 (Fall 2009): 368–72
Durant, Alan. *Conditions of Music*. Albany: State University of New York
  Press 1984
Düttman, Alexander Garcia. *The Gift of Language: Memory and Promise
  in Adorno, Benjamin, Heidegger, and Rosenzweig*. Translated by Arline
  Lyons. Syracuse: Syracuse University Press 2000
Einarsson, Magnús and Helga Benndorf Taylor. *Just for Nice: German-
  Canadian Folk Art*. Hull, QC: Canadian Museum of Civilization 1993
Engels, Friedrich. *The Condition of the Working Class in England in 1844*.
  London: Penguin 1987
Espiña, Yolanda. "Wahrheit als Zugang zur Wahrheit. Die Bedeutung der
  immanenten Kritik in der Musikphilosophie Adornos." In Klein and
  Mahnkopf, eds., *Mit den Ohren*, 52–70
Frith, Simon. *Sound Effects: Youth, Leisure and the Politics of Rock 'n'
  Roll*. London: Pantheon 1983
Geuss, Raymond. *Outside Ethics*. Princeton: Princeton University Press
  2005
Gibson, Nigel, and Andrew Rubin, eds. *Adorno: A Critical Reader*.
  Oxford: Blackwell 2002
Goehr, Lydia. "Music and Musicians in Exile: The Romantic Legacy of a
  Double Life." In Brinkmann and Wolff, *Driven into Paradise*, 66–91
- *The Imaginary Museum of Musical Works: An Essay in the Philosophy
  of Music*. New York: Oxford 1992

- "Dissonant Works and the Listening Public." In Huhn, *Cambridge Companion to Adorno*, 222–47
- "Adorno, Schoenberg and the *Totentanz der Prinzipien* – in Thirteen Steps." *Journal of the American Musicological Society* 56 (2003): 595–636
Gracyk, T.A. "Adorno, Jazz and the Aesthetics of Popular Music." *Musical Quarterly* 76 (1992): 526–42
Gray, Michael. *Mother! The Frank Zappa Story*. London: Plexus 1993
Gray, Richard T. *About Face: German Physiognomic Thought from Lavater to Auschwitz*. Detroit: Wayne State Press 2004
Grenz, Friedemann. *Adornos Philosophie in Grundbegriffen. Auflösung einer Deutungsprobleme*. Frankfurt: Suhrkamp 1974
Griffiths, Dai. "The High Analysis of Low Music." *Music Analysis* 18, no. 3 (October 1999): 389–453
Hanslick, Eduard. *On the Musically Beautiful: A Contribution towards the Revision of the Aesthetics of Music*. Translated and edited by G. Payzant. Indiana: Hackett 1986
Harding, James Martin. *Adorno and "A Writing of the Ruins": Essays on Modern Aesthetics and Anglo-American Literature and Culture*. Albany: State University of New York Press 1997
Hegel, G.W.F. *Phenomenology of Spirit*. Translated by A.V. Miller. Oxford: Oxford University Press 1977
Held, D. *Introduction to Critical Theory: Horkheimer to Habermas*. Berkeley: University of California Press 1980
Hermand, Jost. "Der vertonte Weltgeist. Theodor W. Adornos Beethoven-Fragmente." In Bernard Müßgens, Oliver Kautny, Martin Gieseking, eds. *Musik in Spektrum von Kultur und Gesellschaft. Festschrift für Brunhilde Sonntag*. Osnabrück: Epos Music, 2001, 151–65
Hoeckner, Berthold, ed. *Apparitions: New Perspectives on Adorno and Twentieth-Century Music*. New York: Routledge 2006
Hoffman, Rainer. *Figuren des scheins: Studien zum sprachbild und zur denkform Theodor W. Adornos*. Bonn: Bouvier Verlag Herbert Grundmann 1984
Hohendahl, Peter. *Prismatic Thought*. Lincoln: University of Nebraska Press 1995
Horkheimer, Max. "Egoism and the Freedom Movement: On the Anthropology of the Bourgeois Era." Translated by David J. Parent. *Telos* 54 (1982–83): 10–60
Horkheimer, Max and Theodor Adorno. *Dialectic of Enlightenment*. Translated by J. Cumming. New York: Continuum 1991

– *Dialektik der Aufklärung: Philosophische fragmente.* Frankfurt: S. Fischer Verlag 1969

Huhn, Tom, ed. *The Cambridge Companion to Adorno.* Cambridge: Cambridge University Press 2004

Huhn, Tom, and Lambert Zuidervaart, eds. *The Semblance of Subjectivity: Essays in Adorno's Aesthetic Theory.* Cambridge: MIT Press 1997

Hull, Carrie L. "The Need in Thinking: Materiality in Theodor W. Adorno and Judith Butler." In Delanty, *Adorno*, 4: 343–68

Hullot-Kentor, Robert. "The Philosophy of Dissonance: Adorno and Schoenberg." In Huhn and Zuidervaart, *Semblance of Subjectivity*, 309–19

– "Right Listening and a New Type of Human Being." In Huhn, *Cambridge Companion to Adorno*, 181–97

– *Things beyond Resemblance: Collected Essays on Theodor W. Adorno.* New York: Columbia University Press 2006

Hunter, James. "Buuuuuummmmmd." *Village Voice* 41, no. 50 (10 Dec. 1996): 66–70

Huyssens, Andreas. *After the Great Divide: Modernism, Mass Culture, Postmodernism.* Bloomington: Indiana University Press 1986

Jäger, Lorenz. *Adorno: A Political Biography.* Translated by Stewart Spencer. New Haven: Yale University Press 2004

James, Billy. *Necessity Is ... The Early Years of Frank Zappa and the Mothers of Invention.* London: SAF Publishing 2000

Jameson, Fredric. *Marxism and Form: Twentieth-Century Dialectical Theories of Literature.* Princeton: Princeton University Press 1971

–– *Late Marxism: Adorno, or the Persistence of the Dialectic.* New York: Verso 1990

Jarvis, Simon. *Adorno: A Critical Introduction.* New York: Routledge Press 1998

– "Adorno, Marx, Materialism." In Huhn, *Cambridge Companion to Adorno*, 79–100

Jay, Martin. *The Dialectical Imagination: A History of the Frankfurt School and the Institute of Social Research 1923–1950.* Boston: Little, Brown and Co. 1973

– *Adorno.* Cambridge: Harvard University Press 1984

Jenemann, David. *Adorno in America.* Minneapolis: University of Minnesota Press 2007

Johnson, Julian. "Analysis in Adorno's Aesthetics of Music." *Music Analysis* 14, nos 2–3 (1995): 295–313

Kager, Reinhard. "Einheit in der Zersplitterung. Überglegungen zu Adornos Begriff des 'musikalischen Materials.'" In Klein and Mahnkopf, eds, *Mit den Ohren*, 92–114

Kerling, Marc. "Moses und Aron." In Gerold W. Gruber, ed., *Arnold Schönberg: Interpretationen seiner Werke*. Germany: Laaber 2002

Kerman, Joseph. *The Beethoven Quartets*. New York: Norton 1966

– *Contemplating Music: Challenges to Musicology*. Cambridge: Harvard University Press 1985

Klein, Richard and Claus-Steffen Mahnkopf, eds. *Mit den Ohren denken: Adornos Philosophie der Musik*. Frankfurt: Suhrkamp 1998

Klosterman, Chuck. *Fargo Rock City: A Heavy Metal Odyssey in Rural Nörth Daköta*. New York: Scribner 2001

Klumpenhouwer, Henry. "Commentary: Poststructuralism and Issues of Music Theory." In Krims, *Music/Ideology*, 289–310

– "Late Capitalism, Late Marxism and the Study of Music." *Music Analysis* 20, no. 3 (2001): 367–405

Kolisch, Rudolf. *Kolisch Papers*. Houghton Library, Harvard University Library. MS Music 195, Series: I. Correspondence A. Letters to Rudolf Kolisch. Item 7, Adorno, Theodor W., 1903–1969. Letters, postcards, telegram to Rudolf Kolisch, 1947–1969. 6 folders.

Kolleritsch, Otto, ed. *Adorno und die Musik*. Graz: Universal Edition 1979

Krankenhagen, Stephan. *Auschwitz darstellen: Ästhetische positionen zwischen Adorno, Spielberg und Walser*. Weimar: Böhlau Verlag 2001

Krims, Adam, ed. *Music/Ideology: Resisting the Aesthetic*. Amsterdam: Gordon and Breach 1998

Lavater, Johann Caspar. *Essays on Physiognomy, Designed to Promote the Knowledge and the Love of Mankind*. Translated from the French by Henry Hunter. John Murray: London 1789

Lukács, Georg. *History and Class Consciousness: Studies in Marxist Dialectics*. Translated by R. Livingstone. Cambridge: MIT 1971

------*The Theory of the Novel: A Historico-Philosophical Essay on the Forms of Great Epic Literature*. Translated by A. Bostock. Cambridge: MIT Press 1971

MacLennan, Gregor. Review of Peter Dews, *The Idea of Evil* (Oxford: Blackwell, 2008). In *New Left Review* 60 (Nov/Dec 2009): 147–56

Mahnkopf, Claus-Steffen. "Adorno und die musikalische Analytik." In Klein and Mahnkopf, eds, *Mit den Ohren*, 240–7

Mandeville, Bernard de. *The Fable of the Bees*. 5th ed., London 1728

Mann, Thomas. *Doctor Faust: The Life of the German Composer Adrian Leverkühn as Told by a Friend*. Translated by H.T. Lowe-Porter. New York: Knopf 1948

Manson, Marilyn. "Columbine: Whose Fault Is It?" *Rolling Stone*, 24 June 1999, 23–5

– *Guns, God and Government Tour*. Eaglevision DVD 300149, 2002

– *The Long Hard Road Out of Hell*. With Neil Strauss. New York: Harper Collins 1998

Marcuse, Herbert. *Reason and Revolution: Hegel and the Rise of Social Theory*. 2nd ed. New York: Humanities Press 1954

Marx, Karl. *Capital: A Critique of Political Economy*. 3 vols. Translated by Ben Fowkes and David Fernbach. New York: Penguin Books and The New Left Review 1976

– *Grundrisse: Introduction to the Critique of Political Economy*. Translated by Martin Nicolaus. New York: Penguin Books and the New Left Review 1973

McDonald, M.B. "Training the Nineties, Or the Present Relevance of John Coltrane's Music of Theophany and Negation." *African American Review* 29 (1995): 275–82

Mendel, Arthur. "Evidence and Explanation." Conference Proceedings, *International Musicological Society*, viii, *New York 1961*. Kasel: 1982, ii, 2–18

Mickler, Ernest. *White Trash Cooking*. Berkeley: Ten Speed Press 1986

Middleton, Richard. *Studying Popular Music*. Buckingham: Open University Press 1990

Milne, Drew. "Processual Performance: Critical Notes on Adorno's Autonomous Artwork." In Matthew Beaumont, Andrew Hemingway, Esther Leslie, and John Roberts, eds, *As Radical as Reality Itself: Essays on Marxism and Art for the 21st Century*. Bern: Peter Lang 2007, 347–66

Moore, Alan. *The Beatles: Sgt. Pepper's Lonely Hearts Club Band*. Cambridge: Cambridge University Press 1997

Moretti, Franco. "The Spell of Indecision." In Nelson and Grossberg, *Marxism and the Interpretation of Culture*, 339–46

Müller-Doohm, Stephan. *Adorno. Eine Biographie*. Frankfurt: Suhrkamp 2003

– *Adorno: A Biography*. Translated by R. Livingstone. Cambridge: Polity 2005

Mullin, Amy. "Adorno, Art Theory, and Feminist Practice." In Delanty, *Adorno*, 4: 369–90

Nelson, Cary and Lawrence Grossberg, eds. *Marxism and the Interpreta-tion of Culture*. Urbana: University of Illinois Press 1988
O'Connor, Brian. *Adorno's Negative Dialectic: Philosophy and the Possi-bility of Critical Rationality*. Cambridge: MIT Press 2004
O'Neill, John, ed. *On Critical Theory*. London: Seabury Press 1976
Paddison, Max. *Adorno's Aesthetics of Music*. Cambridge: Cambridge University Press 1993
– *Adorno, Modernism and Mass Culture: Essays on Critical Theory and Music*. London: Kahn & Averill 1996
– "Authenticity and Failure in Adorno's Aesthetics of Music." In Huhn, *Cambridge Companion to Adorno*, 198–221
– "The Language-Character of Music: Some Motifs in Adorno." In Klein, *Mit den Ohren*, 71–91. [Reprint of an article in the *Journal of the Royal Musicological Association*, 116, no. 2 (1991): 267–79]
– "Die vermittlete Unmittelbarkeit der Musik. Zum Vermittlungsbegriff in der Adornoschen Musikästhetik." In *Musikalischer Sinn: Beiträge zu einer Philosophie der Musik*. Edited by A. Becker and M. Vogel. Frank-furt: Suhrkamp 2007, 175–236
Petersen-Mikkelsen, Birger. "Zur Aktualität der Ästhetischen Theorie Theodor W. Adornos und iherer Vorbereitung in der 'Philosophie der neuen Musik.'" In Wolfgang Martin Stroh and Gunter Mayer, eds. *Musikwissenschaftlicher Paradigmenwechsel? Zum Stellenwert marx-istischer Ansätze in der Musikforschung*. Oldenburg: Bibliotheks- und Informationssystem der Universität Oldenburg 2000
Pickford, H.W. "Critical Models: Adorno's Theory and Practice of Cul-tural Criticism." *Yale Journal of Criticism* 10, no. 2 (1987): 247–70
Powell, Larson. "'Die Zerstörung der Symphonie': Adorno and the Theory of Radio." In Hoeckner, *Apparitions*, 131–50
Riethmüller, Albrecht. "Adorno musicus." *Archiv für Musikwissenschaft* 47, no. 1 (1990): 1–26
Ringer, Alexander L. "Arnold Schoenberg and the Politics of Jewish Sur-vival." *Journal of the Arnold Schoenberg Institute* 3, no. 1 (March 1979): 11–48
– *Arnold Schönberg: Das Leben im Werk*. Weimar: Verlag J.B. Metzler 2002
– "Faith and Symbol – On Arnold Schoenberg's Last Musical Utterance." *Journal of the Arnold Schoenberg Institute* 6, no. 1 (June 1982): 80–95
Ritsert, Jürgen. *Vermittlung der Gegensätze in sich. Dialectische Themen und Variationen in der Musiksoziologie Adornos*. Frankfurt: Studi-entexte zur Sozialwissenschaft 1988

Roberts, John. "Marxism and Art Theory: A Short Conspectus." In Beaumont et al., eds., *As Radical as Reality Itself*, 21–8

Rose, Gillian. *The Melancholy Science: An Introduction to the Thought of Theodor W. Adorno*. New York: Columbia University Press 1978

Rosen, Charles. *The Classical Style: Haydn, Mozart, Beethoven*. New York: Norton 1972

– "Should We Adore Adorno?" Review of Theodor Adorno, *Philosophy of Modern Music*, translated by Anne G. Mitchell and Wesley V. Blomster; *Essays on Music*, selected by Richard Leppert; *Beethoven: The Philosophy of Music*, edited by Rolf Tiedemann, translated by Edmond Jephcott. *New York Review of Books*, 24 October 2002: 59–66

Rosen, Michael. *Hegel's Dialectic and Its Criticism*. Cambridge: Cambridge University Press 1982

Ross, Andrew. "The New Sentence and the Commodity Form: Recent American Writing." In Nelson and Grossberg, *Marxism and the Interpretation of Culture*, 361–80

Ruhlmann, William. "Frank Zappa: The Present Day Composer." In Richard Kostelanetz, ed. *The Frank Zappa Companion: Four Decades of Commentary*. New York: Schirmer 1979

Rycenga, Jennifer. "Queerly Amiss: Sexuality and the Logic of Adorno's Dialectics." In Gibson and Rubin, *Adorno*, 361–78

Sample, Colin. "Adorno on the Musical Language of Beethoven." Review of Theodor Adorno, *Beethoven, Philosophie der Musik* (Frankfurt: Suhrkamp, 1993). In *Musical Quarterly* 78, no. 2 (1994): 378–94

Schlipphacke, Heidi M. "A Hidden Agenda: Gender in Selected Writings by Theodor Adorno and Max Horkheimer." In Delanty, *Adorno*, 391–409

Schnebel, Dieter. "Komposition von Sprache – sprachliche Gestaltung von Musik in Adornos Werk." In Schweppenhauser, *Theodor W. Adorno*, 129–45

Schoenberg, Arnold. *Fundamentals of Musical Composition*. Edited by G. Strang with L. Stein. London: Faber and Faber 1967

– *Style and Idea: Selected Writings of Arnold Schoenberg*. Translated by Leo Black. Berkeley: University of California Press 1975

– *Theory of Harmony*. Translated by R. Carter. Berkeley: University of California Press 1978

– *Stil und Gedanke*. Frankfurt: Fischer Taschenbuch Verlag 1992

Schönherr, U. "Adorno and Jazz: Reflections of a Failed Encounter." *Telos* 87 (1991): 85–96

Schweppenhäuser, Hermann, ed. *Theodor W. Adorno zum Gedächtnis.* Frankfurt am Main: Suhrkamp 1971

Seubold, Günter. "Die Erinnerung retten und dem Kitsch die Zunge lösen. Adornos Mahler- und Berg-Interpretation gehört als Kritik des (Post-) Modernismus." In Klein and Mahnkopf, eds., *Mit den Ohren,* 134–66

Spinner, Leopold. *A Short Introduction to the Technique of Twelve-Tone Composition.* London: Boosey and Hawkes 1960

Spitzer, Michael. *Music as Philosophy: Adorno and Beethoven's Late Style.* Bloomington: Indiana University Press 2006

Stecker, Robert. "Methodological Questions about the Ontology of Music." *Journal of Aesthetics and Art Criticism* 67, no. 4 (Fall 2009): 375–86

Steiner, George. *Language and Silence: Essays on Language, Literature, and the Inhuman.* New York: Atheneum 1977

Stratton, John. "Capitalism and Romantic Ideology in the Record Business." *Popular Music* (3), 1983: 143–56

Stuckenschmidt, H.H. *Schoenberg: His Life, Work, and World.* Translated by H. Searle. New York: Schirmer 1977

Subotnik, Rose Rosengard. *Developing Variations: Style and Ideology in Western Music.* Minneapolis: University of Minnesota Press 1991

– "Adorno and the New Musicology." In Gibson and Rubin, *Adorno: A Critical Reader,* 234–254

– "The Historical Structure: Adorno's 'French' Model for the Criticism of Nineteenth-Century Music," *19th-Century Music,* 2, no. 1 (1978): 36–60; reprinted in *Developing Variations,* 206–38

Sziborsky, Lucia. *Adornos Musikphilosophie. Genese – Konstitution – Pädagogische Perspectiven.* München: Wilhelm Fink 1979

– "Die Dimension der ästhetischen Erfahrung." In *Adorno in Seinen muskalischen Schriften.* Regensburg: Gustav Bosse 1987, 7–20

– *Rettung des Hoffnungslosen. Untersuchungen zur Ästhetik und Musikphilosophie Theodor W. Adornos.* Würzburg: Königshausen und Neumann 1994

Thomson, Alex. *Adorno: A Guide for the Perplexed.* New York: Continuum 2006

Uehlein, Friedrich A. "Beethovens Musik ist die Hegelsche Philosophie: sie ist aber zugleich wahrer." In Klein and Mahnkopf, eds, *Mit den Ohren,* 206–28

Wagner, Richard. *Das Rheingold.* Part 1 of *Der Ring des Nibelungen.* Directed by Patrice Chéreau. Phillips DVD 070 402–9, 1988

Weber, Shierry. "Aesthetic Experience and Self-Reflection as Emancipatory
Processes: Two Complementary Aspects of Critical Theory." In O'Neill,
On Critical Theory, 78–103

Weber Nicholsen, Shierry. *Exact Imagination, Late Work: On Adorno's
Aesthetics*. Cambridge: MIT Press 1997

Webern, Anton. *The Path to the New Music*. Edited by W. Reich. Translated by L. Black. Bryn Mawr, PA: Theodore Presser 1963

Wellmer, Albrecht. *The Persistence of Modernity: Essays on Aesthetics,
Ethics, and Postmodernism*. Translated by David Midgley. Cambridge:
MIT Press 1991

Wiggershaus, Rolf. *The Frankfurt School: Its History, Theories and Political Significance*. Translated by M. Robertson. Cambridge: Polity 1994

– *Wittgenstein und Adorno: Zwei Spielarten modernen Philosophierens*.
Wallstein Verlag 2000

Williams, Alastair. *New Music and the Claims of Modernity*. Aldershot:
Ashgate 1997

– "Technology of the Archaic: Wish Images and Phantasmagoria in
Wagner." *Cambridge Opera Journal* 9, no. 1 (March 1997): 73–87

Wimsatt, W.K. and Monroe Beardsley. "The Affective Fallacy." In *The
Verbal Icon: Studies in the Meaning of Poetry*. Lexington: University of
Kentucky Press 1954

Wind, Hans [Kurt Blaukopf]. *Die Endkrise der bürgerlichen Musik und
die Rolle Arnold Schönbergs*. Vienna: Krystall-Verlag 1935

Wright, Richard. "'I'd Sell You Suicide': Pop Music and Moral Panic in the
Age of Marilyn Manson." *Popular Music* 19, no. 3 (2009): 365–85

Zappa, Frank. "All About Music." In *The Real Frank Zappa Book*. With P.
Occhiogrosso. New York: Poseidon 1989

– "Freak Out." LP. Verve Records 1966

Zehentreiter, Ferdinand. "Adornos materiale Formenlehre im Kontext der
Methodologie der strukturalen Hermeneutik – am Beispiel einer Fall-
skizze zur Entwicklung des frühen Schönberg." In Giselher Schubert,
ed., *Biographische Konstellation und künstlerisches Handeln*. Mainz:
Schott 1997

Zuidervaart, Lambert. *Adorno's Aesthetic Theory: The Redemption of
Illusion*. Cambridge: MIT Press 1991

– *Social Philosophy after Adorno*. Cambridge: Cambridge University
Press 2007

Index

negative synthesis, 7; and nice,
31, 34; optimism, 27–8; versus positive dialectics, 17; and
reification, 22; and remainder,
13–14, 34, 131, 197n40; sacred,
174, 176; and Schoenberg, 50;
and society, 42; as transformed
negation, 5; and truth, 14, 19,
198n51; Zappa, 131
negative synthesis, 5–6, 8, 10, 24,
31, 34

O'Connor, Brian, 24, 26, 194–5n5,
195n6, 200n77, 209n54
Orpheus, 188

Paddison, Max, 196n22, 204n52,
208n34
Parks, Van Dyke, 135
perennial (perennial fashion),
40–1, 51, 66, 151; and Adorno's
voice, 172; jazz, 13; Mahler, 72;
Manson, 147–8, 167; "Perennial
Fashion" (essay), 7, 36–8; Zappa,
127, 135
physiognomy (physiognomic), 118,
162, 214n12, 215n21; Manson,
150; Wagner, 103, 106–7,
110–12; Zappa and Schoenberg,
134, 137
Pirandello, Luigi, 168
positivism, 17, 25, 33, 208n35
praxis, 9, 19–20, 28, 186–8
Presley, Elvis, 166
Preston, Don, 123
Proust, Marcel, 145, 159–64, 167

Rand, Ayn, 143
reason, 198n56, 210n58; bourgeois, 98; Enlightenment, 33;

instrumental, 197n46; musical, 64, 187, 208n36. *See also*
Adorno (therein identity),
bourgeois, negation, negative
dialectics
reify (reified, reification), 22–3,
113, 157, 174, 184, 199nn69,
73, 200n75; classical music, 50,
52–5; mainstream sociology,
25–6
remainder, chapter 1, 10, 137–8,
197nn35, 40; Adorno, 172–3,
185; Coltrane, 20–1; constellation, 21, 128; defined, 13–14,
186; dialectics, 18, 21, 23;
friendly, 28; gay, 4–5, 18, 20;
hating opera, 118; jackass, 9;
Mahler, 119; and Marxism, 20;
music, 27–8; negative, 17, 42;
nice, 34; reified, 22; sacred, 181;
Schoenberg, 11, 19, 84, 101;
Spice Girls, 56; synthesis, 24;
truth, 19; unity, 16, 24, 175, 178;
Wagner, 171; Zappa, 124, 127,
131
Rice, Anne, 140
Riefenstahl, Leni, *Triumph des
Willens*, 165
Rolling Stones, The, 56, 142

sacred (sacred absolute), 77, 151,
173–85
Sade, Marquis de, 144; and Jean-
Paul Marat, 160, 166
Sanders, Pharoah, 134
saturnine, 139, 146, 160, 163
Schenker, Heinrich, 111, 208n28
Schoenberg, Arnold, 23; absolute
music, 132; and Adorno, 177,
184–5, 223n45; Adorno on, 8,